CYBERCRIME AND SOCIETY

CYBERCRIME AND SOCIETY

MAJID YAR

Los Angeles | London | New Delhi
Singapore | Washington DC

First published 2006

Reprinted 2009

SAGE Publications Ltd
1 Oliver's Yard
55 City Road
London EC1Y 1SP

SAGE Publications Inc.
2455 Teller Road
Thousand Oaks, California 91320

SAGE Publications India Pvt Ltd
B-1/I 1 Mohan Cooperative Industrial Area
Mathura Road
New Delhi 110 044

SAGE Publications Asia-Pacific Pte Ltd
33 Pekin Street #02-01
Far East Square
Singapore 048763

British Library Cataloguing in Publication data

A catalogue record for this book is available
from the British Library

ISBN 978-1-4129-0753-8
ISBN 978-1-4129-0754-5

Library of Congress control number: 2005934725

Typeset by C&M Digitals (P) Ltd, Chennai, India
Printed on paper from sustainable resources
Printed in Great Britain by TJI Digital, Padstow, Cornwall

For Rodanthi

Contents

Preface

Academic criminology is a peculiar beast, not least because its subject matter, unlike that of many other sciences, is not an objective phenomenon (what the philosophers call a 'natural kind'). Rather, crime is a veritable moveable feast, defined only by social and cultural conventions. New crimes appear and old crimes disappear, and what counts as a crime will vary across societies and contexts. The creation of new crimes may be most evident in times of rapid social, political, economic, technological and cultural change, as heretofore unseen forms of human activity and interaction become possible, bringing with them (real or perceived) challenges and threats to order and well-being. The rapid development of the Internet stands as an exemplar of such change: just ten years ago it was in its infancy, yet it is now a fact of life for billions of people around the globe. It has brought in its wake significant changes in the ways we work, trade, study, learn, play, consume, communicate and interact. At the same time, a whole host of crime problems have emerged in tandem with life online. Politicians, police, businesspeople and citizens now have a new vocabulary with which to identify such dangers: hacking, spoofing, phishing, viruses, Trojans, malware, piracy, downloading, spyware, chat room grooming, and so on. However, as is often the case, academic criminology has been rather slow to reorient its gaze to include these shifts. The vast majority of university criminology and criminal justice degree programmes (of which there are a rapidly increasing number) have been content to retain their focus upon a familiar array of crime issues: violence, public disorder, drugs, burglary, street crime, and the like. I would not deny the ongoing importance of these issues for developing a critical understanding of crime and its consequences. However, criminology would be remiss not to extend its vision of the 'contemporary landscapes of crime' to include those developments arising in the cyberworlds we increasingly inhabit. The origins of this book lie in a determination to encourage just such a reorientation.

Despite the relative marginality of cybercrime within undergraduate and post-graduate criminology teaching to date, there have been in recent years a number of noteable scholarly efforts to chart and analyse Internet crime problems. Academics situated across a range of disciplines (sociology, law, psychology, computing, economics, politics, and media studies) have contributed to a growing literature on cybercrime. Previous work by the likes of Yaman Akdeniz, Dorothy Denning, Peter Grabosky, Yvonne Jewkes, Brian Loader, Paul Taylor, Sandor Vegh and David Wall (to name but a few) has informed and enriched my own understanding of cybercrime. However, the inspiration for the present book arose from a twofold realization. First, as valuable as the existing literature on cybercrime may be, I found little work that sought to draw *across* the kinds of disciplinary perspectives noted above in order to unite sociology, law, cultural studies, political science, and political economy viewpoints on cybercrime. Second, I found myself equally stretched to find within the pages of a single-volume work a clear yet critical overview of the wide range of cybercrime issues: hacking, terrorism, piracy, hate speech, fraud, child pornography, surveillance, privacy, and so on. Hence the primary aims of the present volume: to introduce students and scholars to the widest possible range of cybercrime debates; to bring the richness of inter-disciplinary analysis to bear on these problems; and to do so in a way that is critical with respect to the claims often made about the dangers of online crime. I have attempted to assist readers, who may well be charting for first time some unfamiliar waters, by providing a glossary of keywords (that contains all of the key terms listed at the beginning of each chapter), some questions to reflect upon and (hopefully) discuss with others in the course of their studies and research, and recommendations for further reading drawn from the work of the growing number of colleagues who share my fascination with cybercrime. While the book is intended, at one level, to serve as an introduction to this area of study, I would hope that academics already familiar with the subject matter will also find value in *Cybercrime and Society*; by looking at some familiar issues in perhaps unfamiliar ways, I would like to think that I have helped to broaden and deepen our understanding of cybercrime in some fashion. If this book serves to inform, engage, and provoke readers to any significant degree, then I will be content to consider the writing of it to have been a worthwhile investment of time, effort and energy.

Acknowledgements

Books, even those bearing a single name under the title, are almost invariably the product of collective effort. I owe a debt of gratitude to the editorial staff at Sage, most especially Caroline Porter, who surely sets new standards for editorial efficiency, enthusiasm and support. Similarly, thanks are due to my former colleagues at Lancaster University, in particular, Ryan Conlon (who brought this project my way, and has been generous with his time and expertise), and Sue Penna and Martin O'Brien, whose sage advice and friendship are greatly appreciated. Colleagues at the University of Kent have also supported me during the critical phase during which the largest part of the book was written and refined – Derek Kirton was kind enough to read and comment on parts of the book, and Alan Story provided a wealth of expertise and information about intellectual property matters. A word of thanks also for Yvonne Jewkes and David Wall, whose comments on the manuscript proved both thoughtful and helpful. Last, but most definitely not least, I must thank Rodanthi Tzanelli, who generously gave her time and attention to draft versions of the book, and without whose support and encouragement the book would have been considerably more difficult to write.

ONE

Cybercrime and The Internet

An Introduction

Overview

Chapter 1 examines the following issues:

- how cybercrime is perceived and discussed in society, politics and the media;
- the kinds of questions that criminologists ask about cybercrime;
- the emergence and growth of the Internet, the role it plays in a wide range of everyday activities, and how this growth creates new opportunities for offending;
- how cybercrime can best be defined and classified;
- whether and to what extent cybercrime can be considered a 'new' or 'novel' form of criminal activity;
- the extent of cybercriminal activities, and the problems associated with accurately measuring them;
- the challenges that cybercrime presents for criminal justice systems and for criminological explanation.

key terms

Anonymity
Crime
Cybercrime
Cyberspace
Deviance
e-commerce
Globalization
Hacking
Hidden crime
Information society

Internet
Moral panic
Official statistics
Piracy
Policing
Pornography
Recording of crime
Reporting of crime
Representations of Crime

Social inclusion and Social exclusion
Stalking
Surveillance
Surveys of crime and victimization
Transnational crime and policing
Viruses

Perceptions of cybercrime

1.1 *March, 2000.* A joint operation by the FBI and the UK police leads to the arrest of a computer hacker who calls himself 'Curador'. He is charged, and subsequently convicted, of stealing details of 26,000 credit cards from e-commerce websites worldwide, which he proceeded to post elsewhere on the Internet. The cost of his activities is estimated at $3 million (£1.8 million). Curador's real name is Raphael Gray; he is 18 years old.

(Philippsohn, 2001: 55; Furnell, 2002: 36–7)

4 May 2000. A computer 'worm' called the 'Love Bug' rapidly infects computer worldwide. It uses infected machines to email itself to other users, corrupting files on computers as it goes. Within hours, millions of computers are affected, including those of UK and US government agencies. The damage caused by the 'Love Bug' is placed at between $7 billion and $10 billion. The prime suspect is Onel de Guzman, 24-year-old college dropout from the Philippines. In August 2000 all charges against de Guzman are dropped – the Philippines simply doesn't have laws that cover computer hacking under which he could be tried and convicted.

(Philippsohn, 2001: 61; Furnell, 2002: 159–61)

11 February 2003. FBI Director Robert Mueller tells the US Senate that 'cyberterrorism' is a growing threat to US national security. He claims that Al-Qaeda and other terrorist groups are 'increasingly computer savvy' and will, in future, have ever greater opportunities to strike by targeting critical computer systems using electronic tools.

(US Dept. of State, 2003)

4 February 2004. Graham Coutts, a 35-year-old musician from Hove, UK, is convicted of murdering Jane Longhurst, a 31-year-old school teacher. Coutts, who strangled his victim, is reported to have been 'obsessed' with images of violent sexual pornography, which he had viewed on the Internet just hours before the murder. In the wake of the trial, UK and US government officials announce that they will investigate ways of eradicating such 'evil' sites from the Internet.

(BBC News, 9 March 2004)

The above are just a few instances of what appears to be an explosion of crime and criminality related to the growth of new forms of electronic communication. Since the mid-1990s, the Internet has grown to become a fact of life for people worldwide, especially those living in the Western industrialized world. Its relentless expansion, it is claimed, is in the process of transforming the spheres of business, work, consumption, leisure, and politics (Castells, 2002). The Internet is seen as part of the globalization process that is supposedly sweeping away old realities and certainties, creating new opportunities and challenges associated with living in a 'shrinking' world. We are now said to be in the midst of a 'new industrial revolution', one that will lead us into a new kind of society, an 'information age' (Webster, 2003). Yet awareness of, and enthusiasm for, these changes have been tempered by fears that the Internet brings with it new threats and dangers to our well-being and security. 'Cyber-space', the realm of computerized interactions and exchanges, seems to offer a vast range of new opportunities for criminal and deviant activities. A decade or so on from the Internet's first appearance in popular consciousness, we can see that the intervening years have been replete with fears about its 'darker', criminal dimensions. Businesses cite threats to economic performance and stability, ranging from vandalism to 'e-fraud' and 'piracy'; governments talk of 'cyberwarfare' and 'cyberterror', especially in the wake of the September 11 attacks; parents fear for their children's online safety, as they are told of perverts

3

and paedophiles stalking the Internet's 'chat rooms' looking for victims; hardly a computer user exists who has not been subjected to attack by 'viruses' and other forms of malicious software; the defenders of democratic rights and freedoms see a threat from the state itself, convinced that the Internet furnishes a tool for surveillance and control of citizens, an electronic web with which 'Big Brother' can watch us all. The development of the Internet and related communication technologies thus appears to present an array of new challenges to individual and collective safety, social order and stability, economic prosperity and political liberty.

Our awareness of the Internet's criminal dimensions has certainly been cultivated and heightened by mass media representations. The news media have played their part in identifying and intensifying public concerns, and hardly a day goes by without some new report of an Internet-related threat. Dowland et al. (1999: 723–4) surveyed two 'quality' UK newspapers over a two and half-year period, and found that, on average, stories about computer-related crime appeared twice a week in each throughout the period. In addition to the print media, we must also consider broadcast media (television, radio) and the Internet itself (which now constitutes a major source of cybercrime reportage). Popular fiction has also picked-up on the Internet's more problematic dimensions, with films such as *Hackers* and *The Net* sharpening the sense that our safety may be under threat from irresponsible individuals and unscrupulous authorities. Perhaps such representations, and the concerns they inform and incite, should not altogether surprise us. After all, while the Internet itself may be new, history shows us that times of rapid social, economic and technological change are often accompanied by heightened cultural anxieties (even 'panics') about threats to our familiar and ordered ways of life (Goode and Ben-Yehuda, 1994). Thomas and Loader (2000: 8) suggest that social transformations wrought by Internet technologies 'makes the future appear insecure and unpredictable', yielding public and political overreaction. Such 'moral panics', fuelled by the media, lead to an excessive and unjustified belief that particular individuals, groups or events present an urgent threat to society (Critcher, 2003). Internet-related instances of such panics include those over the effects of pornography in the mid-1990s, and more recently over threats to child safety from paedophiles (Littlewood, 2003). The proliferation of such anxieties is perhaps best viewed as a consequence in part of the rapid shifts and reconstructions in the midst of which we currently find ourselves. This is not to suggest, however, that the dangers posed by cybercrime can simply be dismissed as wholly unfounded. Nor is it to suggest that such widespread reactions ought to be simply ignored by criminologists. Media representations, both factual and fictional, constitute an important criminological research topic in their own right; their careful examination enables us to uncover how the problem of cybercrime is being constructed and defined, and how this shapes social and political responses to it (Taylor,

2000; Vegh, 2002). Yet the weight of such representations can also serve to obscure the realities of criminal activity and its impacts, hindering rather than facilitating a balanced understanding.

Cybercrime: questions and answers

1.2 For criminologists, making sense of cybercrime consequently presents a significant challenge, as it requires us to take, as best we can, a more sober and balanced view, sifting fact from fantasy and myth from reality. The very existence of this book is testimony to the author's belief that such an examination is both possible and worthwhile. Indeed, numerous scholars have already made considerable strides in this direction. By using a combination of theoretical analysis and empirical investigation they have attempted to get a handle on a range of pressing questions:

- Just what might be meant by 'cybercrimes'?
- What is the actual scope and scale of such crimes?
- How might such crimes be both like and unlike the 'terrestrial' crimes with which we are more familiar?
- Who are the 'cybercriminals'?
- What are the causes and motivations behind their offending?
- What are the experiences of the victims of such crimes?
- What distinctive challenges do such crimes present for criminal justice and law enforcement?
- How are policy-makers, legislators, police, courts, business organizations and others responding?
- How are such responses shaped by popular perceptions of computer crime and computer criminals?
- How is cybercrime shaping the future development and use of the Internet itself?

There now exists a considerable literature addressing such issues, drawn from a wide range of disciplines including criminology, sociology, law and socio-legal studies, political science, political economy, cultural and media studies, science and technology studies, business and management, and computing. The ever-expanding range of such material, along with its dispersal across different disciplinary boundaries, makes it difficult for the newcomer to find an accessible route into current debates. This difficulty is exacerbated by the fact that cybercrime refers not so much to a single, distinctive kind of criminal activity, but more to a diverse *range* of illegal and illicit activities that share in common the unique electronic environment ('cyberspace') in which they take place. Consequently, different academic contributions tend to focus on some selected aspects of the cybercrime problem, to the detriment or neglect of others. Hence the purpose of the present volume, which is conceived as a thorough and up-to-date introduction to the range of issues, questions and debates about cybercrime that have come to characterize it as a field of study. Out of necessity, I draw upon theoretical and empirical contributions from different areas of scholarship, but with the main focus falling upon criminology and sociology, the two areas that comprise my own primary fields of expertise. The following chapters will furnish a critical introduction to a variety of substantive issues. Many of them focus on recognizably different kinds of cybercriminal activity, such as 'piracy', 'hacking', 'e-fraud', 'cyberstalking', and 'cyberterrorism'; each is examined and analysed in light of the social, political, economic and cultural context in which it takes shape. Other chapters consider debates of a more general nature, addressing, for example, the tensions apparent between Internet security and policing, on the one hand, and individual rights, freedoms and liberties, on the other. Given the range of issues to be covered, their treatment cannot be exhaustive. Hence each chapter contains guidance for further, more in-depth reading, which can be found both in conventional print form and online.

However, before we can move on to these more detailed examinations, there are a number of important issues of background and context that must be outlined, and some important conceptual issues that must be tackled. Hence the remainder of this chapter will situate cybercrime in relation to the growth and development of the Internet, and ask questions about how we might best classify cybercriminal activities, and why it is that cybercrime might need to be viewed as qualitatively different from other kinds of criminal and illicit activity.

A brief history and analysis of the Internet

1.3 An examination of cybercrime ought to begin with the Internet, for the simple reason that without the latter, the former could and would not exist. It is the Internet that provides the crucial electronically generated environment in which cybercrime takes place. Moreover, the Internet should not be viewed as simply a piece of technology, a kind of 'blank slate' that exists apart from the people who use it. Rather, it needs to be seen as a set of *social practices* – the Internet takes the form that it does because people use it in particular ways and for particular purposes (Snyder, 2001). 'What' people do with the Net, and 'how' they typically go about it, are crucial for understanding what kind of phenomenon the Internet actually is. Indeed, it is the kinds of social uses to which we put the Internet that create the possibilities of criminal and deviant activity. To give one example, if people didn't use the Internet for shopping, then there would be no opportunities for the kind of credit card crimes perpetrated by 'Curador', mentioned earlier. Similarly, it is *because* we use the Internet for electronic communication with friends and colleagues that the 'Love Bug' worm, which targeted the email systems we use for that purpose, could cause billions of dollars in damage.

The Internet, as its name suggests, is in essence a computer network; or, to be more precise, a 'network of networks' (Castells, 2002). A network links computers together, enabling communication and information exchange between them. Many such networks of information and communication technology (ICT) have been in existence for decades – those of financial markets, the military, government departments, business organizations, universities, and so on. The Internet provides the means to link up the many and diverse networks already in existence, creating from them a single network that enables communication between any and all 'nodes' (e.g. individual computers) within it.

The origins of the Internet can be traced to the development of a network, the ARPANET, sponsored by the US military in the 1960s. The aim was to establish a means by which secure and resilient communication and coordination of military activities could be made possible. In the political and strategic context of the 'Cold War', with the ever-present threat of nuclear confrontations, such a network was seen as a way to ensure that critical communications could be sustained, even if particular 'points' within the computer infrastructure were damaged by attack. The ARPANET's technology would allow communications to be broken up into 'packets' that could then be sent via a range of different routes to their destinations, where they could be reassembled into their original form. Even if some of the intermediate points within the network failed, they could simply be bypassed in favour of an alternate route, ensuring that messages reached their intended recipients. The creation of the network entailed the development not only of the appropriate computer hardware, but also of 'protocols', the codes and rules that would allow different computers to 'understand' each other. This development got under way in the late 1960s, and by 1969 the ARPANET was up and running, initially linking together a handful of university research communities with government agencies.

From the early 1970s further innovations appeared, such as electronic mail applications, which expanded the possibilities for communication. Other networks, paralleling ARPANET, were established such as the UK's JANET (Joint Academic Network) and the US's NSFNET (belonging to the American National Science Foundation). By using common communication protocols, these networks could be connected together, forming an inter-net, a network of networks. A major impetus for the emergence of the Internet as we now know it was given when, in 1990, the US authorities released the ARPANET to civilian control, under the auspices of the National Science Foundation. The same year, 1990, saw the development of a web browser (basically an information sharing application) by researchers at the CERN physics laboratory in Switzerland. Dubbed the 'world wide web' (www), this software was subsequently elaborated by other programmers, allowing more sophisticated forms of information exchange such as the sharing of images as well as text. The first commercial browser, Netscape, was launched in 1994, with Microsoft launching its own

Internet Explorer the following year. These browsers made Internet access possible from personal computers (PCs). In the mid-1990s, numerous commercial Internet Service Providers (ISPs) entered the market, offering connection to the Internet for anyone with a computer and access to a conventional telephone line.

Since the commercialization of the Internet in the mid-1990s, its growth has been incredibly rapid. Between 1994 and 1999 the number of countries connected to the Internet increased from 83 to 226 (Furnell, 2002: 7). In December 1995 there were an estimated 16 million Internet users worldwide; by May 2002, this figure had risen to over 580 million, almost 10 per cent of the world's total population (NUA, 2003). The figure is predicted to rise to 1 billion by 2005, and 2 billion by 2010 (Castells, 2002: 3). However, it is crucial to bear in mind that, despite this phenomenal growth, access to the Internet remains highly uneven both between countries and regions, and within individual nations. The technical capacity enabling Internet access (PCs, software, reliable telecommunications grids) is unevenly distributed – for example, while in the USA there were 65.89 PCs per 100 inhabitants in 2002, and in the UK there were 40.57, the figure for the African continent was only 1.3 (ITU, 2004). Consequently, over 95 per cent of the worldwide total Internet connections are located in the USA, Canada, Europe, Australia and Japan (Furnell, 2002: 6). Unequal access also follows existing lines of social exclusion within individual countries – factors such as employment, income, education, ethnicity and disability are reflected in the patterns of Internet use (Castells, 2002: 208–23). These inequalities are criminologically important, as they tell us something about the likely social characteristics of both potential cybercriminal offenders and their potential victims (a point I shall return to later in the chapter).

It is further worth considering not only what kinds of people are online, where, and in what numbers, but also *what they do* in online environments. As noted earlier, the range of social practices that people legitimately engage in will create distinctive opportunities for offending – what criminologists call 'opportunity structures' arising from people's online 'routine activities' (Grabosky, 2001; Newman and Clarke, 2003). Thus, one of the most important areas of Internet usage relates to its applications in electronic business or 'e-commerce'. Businesses increasingly use the Internet as a routine part of their activities, ranging from research and development, to production, distribution, marketing and sales. These uses create a range of criminal opportunities – for example, the theft of trade secrets and sensitive strategic information (Jackson, 2000), the disruption of online selling systems, and the fraudulent use of credit cards to obtain goods and services (Grabosky and Smith, 2001). Similarly, the Internet is increasingly being mobilized by a range of actors for political purposes – governments use it to inform and consult citizens, political parties use it to recruit supporters, pressure groups use to it organize campaigns and raise funds, and so on. Consequently, we see the emergence of cybercrimes that are political in nature – these range from the sabotage and defacement of official websites, the use of the Internet to instigate 'hate' campaigns by far-right extremists, to the activities of 'terrorist' groups aiming to recruit members and raise funds (Denning, 1999: 228–31; Whine, 2000). Another important area of Internet activity relates to leisure and cultural consumption. People in increasing numbers are turning to the Internet to access everything from music and movies to celebrity gossip and online video gaming. Yet again, the demand for such goods creates opportunities exploited by the criminally inclined – these range from the distribution of obscene imagery, to the trade in 'pirate' audio and video recordings and computer software (Akdeniz, 2000; McCourt and Burkart, 2003; Yar, 2004). These examples suggest that illegitimate online activities must be viewed not in isolation, but as deeply interconnected with their legitimate counterparts.

Defining and classifying cybercrime

1.4 A major problem for the study of cybercrime is the absence of a consistent current definition, even among those law enforcement agencies charged with tackling it (NOP/NHTCU 2002: 3). As Wall (2001a: 2) notes, the term 'has no specific referent in law', yet it is often used in political, criminal justice, media, public and academic discussions. I have already suggested that instead of trying to grasp cybercrime as a single phenomenon, it might be better to view the term as signifying a *range* of illicit activities whose 'common denominator' is the central role played by networks of information and communication technology (ICT) in their commission. A working definition along these lines is offered by Thomas and Loader (2000: 3) who conceptualize cybercrime as those 'computer-mediated activities which are either illegal or considered illicit by certain parties and which can be conducted through global electronic networks'. Thomas and Loader's definition contains an important distinction that warrants further reflection, namely that between *crime* (acts explicitly prohibited by law, and hence illegal) and *deviance* (acts that breach informal social norms and rules, hence considered undesirable or objectionable). Some analysts of cybercrime focus their attention on the former, those activities that attract the sanctions of criminal law (see, for example, Akdeniz et al., 2000). Others, however, take a broader view, including within discussions of cybercrime some acts which may not necessarily be illegal, but which large sections of a society might deem to be deviant. A prime example of this latter kind of activity would be sexually explicit speech and imagery online (see, for example, DiMarco, 2003). Given that the primary focus of this book is crime rather than deviance, discussion will be directed in the main toward those Internet-related activities that carry formal legal sanctions.

9

However, it is important to bear in mind that crime and deviance cannot always be strictly separated in criminological inquiry. For example, the widespread perception that a particular activity is deviant may fuel moves for its formal prohibition through the introduction of new laws. Alternatively, while particular activities may be illegal, large sections of the population may not necessarily see them as deviant or problematic, thereby challenging and undermining attempts to outlaw them (one such instance, discussed in Chapter 4 is that of 'piracy'). Such dynamics, in which boundaries between the criminal and the deviant are socially negotiated, are a recurrent feature of contemporary developments around the Internet.

Starting with an understanding of cybercrime as 'computer-mediated activities that are illegal', it is possible to further classify such crime along a number of different lines. One commonplace approach is to distinguish between 'computer-assisted crimes' (those crimes that pre-date the Internet, but which take on a new life in cyberspace e.g. fraud, theft, money laundering, sexual harassment, hate speech, pornography) and 'computer-focused crimes' (those crimes that have emerged in tandem with the establishment of the Internet, and could not exist apart from it e.g. hacking, viral attacks, website defacement) (Furnell, 2002: 22; Lilley, 2002: 24). On this classification, the main way in which cybercrime can be subdivided is according to the role played by the technology i.e. whether the Internet plays a merely 'contingent' role in the crime (it could be done without it, using other means), or if is it absolutely 'necessary' (without the Internet, no such crime could exist). This kind of classification is adopted by policing bodies such as the UK's National Hi-Tech Crime Unit, which distinguishes between 'old crimes, new tools' and 'new crimes, new tools' (NHTCU, 2004).

While the above distinction is helpful, it may be rather limited for criminological purposes, as it focuses on the *technology* at the expense of the relationships between offenders and their targets or victims. One alternative is to use existing categories drawn from criminal law into which their cyber-counterparts can be placed. Thus, Wall (2001a: 3–7) sub-divides cybercrime into four established legal categories:

1 Cyber-*trespass* – crossing boundaries into other people's property and/or causing damage, e.g. hacking, defacement, viruses.
2 Cyber-*deceptions* and *thefts* – stealing (money, property), e.g. credit card fraud, intellectual property violations (a.k.a. 'piracy').
3 Cyber-*pornography* – breaching laws on obscenity and decency.
4 Cyber-*violence* – doing psychological harm to, or inciting physical harm against others, thereby breaching laws relating to the protection of the person, e.g. hate speech, stalking.

Such classification can be seen to sub-divide cybercrime according to the object or target of the offence: the first two categories comprise 'crimes against property',

..e third covers 'crimes against morality', and the fourth relates to 'crimes against the person'. To these we may also wish to add 'crimes against the state', those activities that breach laws protecting the integrity of the nation and its infrastructure (e.g. terrorism, espionage and disclosure of official secrets). Such a classification is helpful, as it allows us to relate cybercrime to existing conceptions of prohibited and harmful acts.

What's 'new' about cybercrime?

1.5 The classification outlined thus far, while indispensable, may not by itself illuminate all the relevant characteristics of cybercrime. By relating such crime to familiar types of offending behaviour, it stresses those aspects of cybercrime that are continuous with 'terrestrial' crimes. Consequently, it does little in the way of isolating what might be qualitatively *different* or *new* about such offences and their commission, when considered from a broader, non-legal viewpoint. This question of the 'novelty' of cybercrime is an important one for criminologists. Some argue that cybercrime is pretty much the same as 'old-fashioned' non-virtual crime, and just uses some new tools that are helpful for the offender; what Grabosky (2001) dubs 'old wine in new bottles'. Others, however, insist that it represents a new form of crime that is radically different from the kinds of 'real world' crimes that predate it. Among this latter group, many criminologists (especially those with a sociological orientation) focus their search for novelty upon the social-structural features of the environment ('cyberspace') in which such crimes occur. It is widely held that this environment has a profound impact upon how social interactions can take place (both licit and illicit), and so transforms the potential scope and scale of offending, inexorably altering the relationships between offenders and victims, and the potential for criminal justice systems to offer satisfactory solutions or resolutions (Capeller, 2001). Particular attention is given to the ways in which the establishment of cyberspace variously 'transcends', 'explodes', 'compresses', or 'collapses' the constraints of space and time that limit interactions in the 'real world'. Borrowing from sociological accounts of globalization as 'time-space compression' (Harvey, 1989), theorists of the Internet suggest that cyberspace makes possible near-instantaneous encounters and interactions between spatially distant actors, creating possibilities for ever-new forms of association and exchange (Shields, 1996). Criminologically, this seems to render us vulnerable to an array of potential predators who can reach us almost instantaneously, untroubled by the normal barriers of physical distance. Moreover, the ability of the potential offender to target individuals and property is seemingly amplified by the Internet – computer-mediated communication (CMC) enables a single individual to reach, interact with, and affect thousands of individuals at the same time. Thus, the technology acts as a 'force multiplier' enabling individuals with minimal resources to generate potentially huge negative effects (mass distribution of email 'scams' and distribution of viruses being two examples). In addition, great emphasis is placed on how the Internet enables the manipulation and reinvention of social identity – cyberspace interactions give individuals the capacity to reinvent themselves, adopting new virtual personae potentially far removed from their 'real world' identities (Poster, 1990; Turkle, 1995). From a criminological perspective, this is viewed as a powerful tool for the unscrupulous to perpetrate offences while maintaining anonymity through disguise (Snyder, 2001: 252; Joseph, 2003: 116–18), and a formidable challenge to those seeking to track down offenders.

From the above, we can conclude that it is the novel social-interactional features of the cyberspace environment (primarily the collapse of space–time barriers, many-to-many connectivity, and the anonymity and changeability of online identity) that make possible new forms and patterns of illicit activity. It is this difference from the 'terrestrial world' of conventional crimes that makes cybercrime distinctive and original.

How many crimes? Assessing the scale of Internet offences

1.6 Gaining a realistic measure of the scope and scale of cybercriminal activities presents considerable challenges. Some of these problems are well known to criminologists. 'Official statistics' on crime, for example, have been critiqued as 'social constructions' that do not necessarily provide us with an 'objective' picture of the true, underlying levels and patterns of offending (Maguire, 2002). There are a number of reasons for this. First, such statistics depend upon crimes having been *reported* to the police or other official agencies. Studies, however, show that a large proportion of offences simply remain unreported for a wide variety of reasons: victims may be unaware that an offence has been committed; they may consider the offence insufficiently 'serious' to warrant contacting the authorities; they may feel that there is little likelihood of a satisfactory resolution (such as the apprehension of the offender or the return of their property). Second, even if an offence is reported, it may not be *recorded* by the police or other agencies, again, for a variety of reasons. For example, political priorities may lead police to prioritize some crimes as the expense of others (Coleman and Moynihan, 1996); police perceptions of 'seriousness' will affect whether they deem tackling an offence as a worthwhile use of their time and resources; police may have disincentives to record certain types of crime, where they feel that there is little likelihood of a successful investigatory outcome, as a large number of unresolved offences might cultivate the impression that police are failing to maintain 'law and order'. In addition, decisions about whether or not to record a reported offence may depend upon police judgements about the person(s) doing the reporting, such as their perceived status, reliability or trustworthiness. Third, serious problems are evident when we attempt to establish longitudinal measures of crime i.e. the charting of crime trends (decreases and increases) over time. The ways in which crime recording classifies and groups offences is subject to change, making direct comparison over the years difficult. Moreover, it must be remembered that crime is a legal construct (Lacey, 2002: 266–7) – what happens to be illegal is subject to its inclusion in criminal law. Laws change over time – new categories of offence are created, thereby making previously permissible behaviour illegal; conversely, previously prohibited behaviour may be de-criminalized or legalized, removing it from the domain of criminal activity. Consequently, year-on-year measures of crime rarely compare 'like with like', making it difficult to derive reliable conclusions about whether or not particular types of crime (or crime in general) is on the increase or decrease.

These familiar problems with measuring crime are, if anything, exacerbated in relation to cybercrime. For example, the relatively hidden nature of Internet crimes may lead to them going unnoticed. Unfamiliarity with laws covering computer-related crimes may lead victims to be unaware that a particular activity is in fact illegal (Wall, 2001a: 8; Dowland et al., 1999: 715, 721). The very limited allocation of police resources and expertise to tackling computer crime may result in the relevant authorities being unknown or inaccessible to victims for reporting purposes. The extent to which the Internet enables offenders to remain anonymous may lead victims (and police) to conclude that there is little likelihood of a perpetrator being identified (for example, the chance of being prosecuted for computer hacking in the USA is placed at 1 in 10,000 (Bequai, 1999: 16)). The inherently global nature of the Internet (where victim and offender may be located in different countries, with different laws relating to computer crime) renders effective police action particularly difficult and time-consuming, leading such offences to be sidelined in favour of more manageable 'local' problems (Wall, 2001b: 177). Such factors suggest that there may in fact be a massive under-reporting and under-recording of Internet-related crimes, and a correspondingly massive (and by definition unknown) 'dark figure' of cybercrime. The problems for charting cybercrime trends over time are also heightened by rapid innovations in Internet and computer-related law. Recent years have seen the introduction of many new sanctions into criminal law to cover computer-related offences. These have taken the form of national legislation (such as the UK's Computer Misuse Act (1990) and the US Computer Abuse and Fraud Act (1986) and the No Electronic Theft Act (1988)) and a range of criminal sanctions incorporated into national laws as a result of international agreements, treaties and directives (such as the 1994 TRIPS (Trade-Related Aspects of Intellectual Property

Rights) agreement under the WTO (World Trade Organization), the Council of Europe Convention of Cybercrime (2004), and the provisions of European Union law). Such innovations have meant that the range of Internet activities covered by criminal law have been constantly shifting, making trend data about cybercrime as a whole difficult to construct.

One way in which the shortcomings of official crime measures have been addressed is through the development of crime and victimization surveys. These have aimed to uncover those crimes that remain unreported and unrecorded by official statistics, thereby giving a more complete and accurate picture of the scope and patterns of offending (Maguire, 2002: 348–58). Such surveys are particularly important for generating knowledge about cybercrime, since there is by and large little officially collected and collated data specifically relating to Internet crimes. However, we should not conclude that such alternative measures wholly overcome the problems previously identified in relation to official statistics. For example, no reporting is possible where victims are unaware that an offence has been committed; those surveyed may have a different understanding of what counts as an offence from those administering the survey; and they may be unwilling to report an offence even when disclosure is made on an anonymous basis. The problems in relation to cybercrime surveys are, once again, further heightened. First, such surveys as exist tend to be highly selective, focusing mainly upon business and/or public sector organizations, to the exclusion of individual citizens (prime examples include the annual computer crime survey undertaken in the USA by the Computer Security Institute (CSI) on behalf of the FBI, and similar surveys conducted in the UK by the polling organization NOP on behalf of the National Hi-Tech Crime Unit). Moreover, as Wall (2001a: 7–8) notes, there is no consistent methodology or classification across such surveys, making comparison and aggregation of data difficult. Finally, there are serious problems relating to under-reporting, as many organizations may prefer not to acknowledge victimization because of (1) fear of embarrassment: (2) loss of public or customer confidence (as in the case of breaches relating to supposedly secure e-shopping and e-banking facilities): and (3) because of potential legal liabilities (for example, under legislation relating to data protection, which places organizations under a legal duty to safeguard confidential information relating to citizens and customers) (Furnell, 2002: 28, 51). All of the above should lead us to treat statistics about cybercrime, be they official or otherwise, with considerable caution. One of the most basic challenges for both criminology and criminal justice in relation to cybercrime is the need to develop basic, robust measures of the problem itself.

Despite the difficulties outlined above, it would be mistaken to simply ignore the available statistical measures, limited and partial as they might be. If we wish to glean *some* insight into the nature and extent of the 'cybercrime problem' we must make use of such data as are available – a case of relatively weak data being better than absolutely no data at all. So long as we not do 'reify' these measures, taking them to be incontrovertible facts, they can still serve a useful purpose in giving us some preliminary indication of the problem. Indeed, insofar as such data are taken seriously by the various actors who discourse publicly upon cybercrime and take legislative, policing and security decisions on its basis, we need to give these figures due consideration. Subsequent chapters will give more detailed attention to the 'facts and figures' as they relate to different types of cybercriminal activity (such as hacking, viruses, e-fraud, piracy, and so on). For the moment, we can reflect on some 'headline' figures that have appeared in high-profile reports on cybercrime, as these give us an indication of why Internet crime has become the object of concerted concern for a range of public and private actors:

- A survey of 530 public and private sector organizations in the USA revealed that 56 per cent were aware of some form of cyber-attacks against their computer systems in the previous 12 months. The total financial losses incurred from these incidents were estimated at over $200 million (CSI/FBI, 2003: 3).
- A survey of 105 business organizations in the UK revealed that 97 per cent were aware of having experienced 'computer-enabled crimes' in the previous 12 months. Such crimes included virus attacks, disruption of computer systems, sabotage of networks, fraud, information theft, defacement of websites, and eavesdropping or espionage (NOP/NHTCU, 2002).
- According to UK government figures, hacking and viruses cost UK businesses up to $10 billion per annum (Hinde, 2003: 90).
- Worldwide, hacking is estimated to have cost businesses $1.6 trillion in 2000 alone (Newman and Clarke, 2003: 55).
- US 'copyright industries' claim annual losses due to 'piracy' (of goods such as music, films and computer software) to the order of $15 billion per annum (EC, 1998: 4), much of it distributed via the Internet. Film industry sources claim that 125 million films are illegally downloaded from the Internet every year (Valenti, 2002).
- In Russia, computer crime is estimated to be increasing at 400 per cent per annum (Saytarly, 2004).
- By July 2001, there were estimated to be 66,000 computer viruses in existence, with new 'strains' appearing at a rate of 100 per month (Furnell, 2002: 153); another estimate places the figure at over 73,000 by May 2002 (Lilley, 2002: 15).
- A credit card fraud is estimated to occur via the Internet every 20 seconds (Everett, 2003: 1).
- US police sources estimate that 20 per cent of cases of sexual harassment and stalking reported now occur on the Internet (Joseph, 2003: 107).

Figures such as those above furnish an important context for understanding why the media, politicians, law enforcement agencies and business organizations have come to be increasingly exercised by the cybercrime threat. Cybercrime can be viewed as an integral component of those globalized risks that are increasingly coming to define 'contemporary landscapes of crime, order and control' (Loader and Sparks, 2002). Moreover, if we bear in mind estimates that as little as 5 per cent of such crimes may actually be reported to the authorities (Furnell, 2002: 190), then the problems posed by cybercrime may well figure among the most urgent of the early twenty-first century.

Challenges for criminology, criminal justice and policing

1.7 The proliferation of cybercriminal activity poses new challenges not just for criminal justice and crime control, but also for criminology as a discipline. The specific character of such challenges will be considered in more detail in subsequent chapters, but we can identify here some general dimensions.

The challenge for policing and criminal justice

1.7.1   From the discussion thus far it is clear that the Internet has distinctive features that shape the crimes that take place in cyberspace. These features pose difficulties for tackling crime when approached by established structures and processes of criminal justice systems. Not least among these is that policing has historically followed the organization of political, social and economic life within national territories. Moreover, crime control agencies such as the police traditionally operate within local boundaries, focusing attention and resources on crimes occurring within their 'patch' (Lenk, 1997: 129). Yet cybercrime, given the global nature of the Internet, is an inherently de-territorialized phenomenon. Crimes in cyberspace bring together offenders, victims and targets that may well be physically situated in different countries and continents, and so the offence spans national territories and boundaries. While there are ongoing attempts to strengthen transnational policing through agencies such as EUROPOL and INTERPOL (Bowling and Foster, 2002: 1005–9), these are largely focused upon sharing intelligence related to large-scale 'organized crime'. A more focused transnational initiative is the EU high-tech crime agency, ENISA, established in 2004; yet its role is not directly investigatory, but restricted to coordinating investigations into cybercrime by police in member countries (Best, 2003).

Further problems arise when we consider the constraints of limited resources and insufficient expertise. For example, the UK's National Hi-Tech Crime Unit was established in 2001, comprising 80 dedicated officers and with a budget of £25 million; however, this amounts to less than 0.1 per cent of the total number of police, and less than 0.5 per cent over the overall expenditure on 'reduction of crime' (Home Office, 2002a; Wales, 2001: 6). ENISA, the EU agency, labours under similar budgetary constraints, with an annual allocation of just £17 million (€24.3 million) to coordinate transnational investigations spanning the 25 member countries (Best, 2003). Lack of appropriate expertise also presents barriers to the effective policing of cybercrime. Investigation of such crimes will often require specialized technical knowledge and skills, and there is at present little indication that police have the appropriate training and competence (Bequai, 1999: 17). Moreover, research indicates that many police do not view the investigation of computer-related crime as falling within the normal parameters of their responsibilities, undermining attempts to put such policing on a systematic footing (Hyde, 1999: 9).

The difficulties are further intensified once we consider the problem posed by different legal regimes across national territories. The move toward international harmonization of Internet law has already been noted. Yet such developments are in a relatively early stage. Examination of Internet law reveals that many countries lack the legislative frameworks necessary to effectively address Internet-related crimes (Sinrod and Reilly, 2000: 2). Attempts to legislatively tackle cybercrime may also run foul of existing national laws. For example, the US introduction of the Communication Decency Act in 1996, aimed at curbing 'offensive' and 'indecent' images on the Internet, was partly overturned as some of its provisions were held to breach constitutional guarantees relating to the freedom and speech and expression (Biegel, 2003: 129–36). Even where appropriate legal measures have been put in place, many countries (especially in the 'developing world') simply lack the resources needed to enforce them (Drahos and Braithwaite, 2002). In countries facing urgent economic problems, with states that may be attempting to impose order under conditions of considerable social and political instability, the enforcement of Internet laws will likely come very low on the list of priorities, if it appears at all.

Challenges for criminology

1.7.2 The discipline of criminology has been concerned throughout its history with attempts to uncover the underlying causes behind law-breaking behaviour. Thus, theories of crime purport to locate the forces that propel or incline people toward transgressing society's rules and prohibitions. Such explanations have, inevitably, been based upon data relating to criminal activity in 'real-world' settings and situations. The emergence of the Internet poses challenges to existing criminological perspectives insofar as it exhibits structural and social features that diverge considerably from conventional 'terrestrial' settings. It is by no means clear whether and to what extent established theories are compatible with the realm of cyberspace and the crimes that occur within it. Two such challenges for criminology are now considered:

1   *The problem of 'where'*. Many criminological perspectives are based, implicitly or explicitly, upon 'ecological' assumptions. That is to say, they view crimes as occurring within particular *places* that have important defining social, cultural and material characteristics. It is in the distinctive features of such local environments that the causes of the crime are supposedly to be found. Recent decades have seen the development of influential criminologies that focus upon the spatial organization of lived environments, and explain patterns and distributions of offending in terms of the ways in which such environments are configured. Thus, for example, 'routine activity' approaches focus on how potential offenders are able to converge in space and time with potential targets, thereby creating the conditions in which offending is able to take place (Cohen and Felson, 1979; Felson, 1998). Such thinking has also inspired a range of crime mapping, measurement and prevention programmes, again focused on identifying 'criminogenic' environments and localities whose crime-inducing characteristics can then be removed (Fyfe, 2001). However, such approaches run into difficulties when we consider cybercrimes. The environment in which such crimes take place, cyberspace, cannot be divided into distinctive spatial locations in any straightforward manner, in the way we can distinguish in the 'real world' between neighbourhoods and districts, urban and suburban, the city and the country, and so on. Rather, cyberspace can been viewed as basically 'anti-spatial' (Mitchell, 1995: 8), an environment in which there is 'zero distance' between all points (Stadler, 1998), so that identifying locations with distinctive crime-inducing characteristics becomes well-nigh impossible (Yar, 2005). The inability to answer the question of 'where' crimes take place in cyberspace indicates that criminological perspectives based on spatial distinctions may be of limited use.

2   *The problem of 'who'*. Criminological theories have also sought to understand why it is that some individuals engage in law-breaking behaviour, while others do not. Official statistics indicate that offending is not only spatially but also *socially* located; the profile of offenders shows a preponderance of those with certain shared characteristics. One such characteristic has been the over-representation among known offenders of those from socially, economically, culturally and educationally marginalized backgrounds. Thus the fact of 'deprivation' (whether 'relative' or 'absolute') has come to be causally linked to offending behaviour (Lea and Young, 1984; Hagan and Peterson, 1994; Finer and Nellis, 1998). Such inferences have not enjoyed universal acceptance, as Marxist and other 'critical' criminologists have claimed that the association of socio-economic marginality with criminal activity is more a product of the iniquitous class-based prejudices of the criminal justice system than of any real concentration of offending among particular social groups. However, much mainstream criminology gives considerable credibility to the view that the 'crime problem' is one predominantly centred upon those who suffer 'social exclusion' (although controversy continues to rage between those on the 'Left' who find the causes of such exclusion in economic structures and processes (Wilson, 1996), and those on the 'Right' who attribute it to the individual's 'fecklessness' and irresponsibility (Murray, 1984)). Wherever we stand on the

ultimate origins of exclusion, the relationship between marginality and offending is an established feature of criminological explanation. When we come to consider cyber-crime, however, this correspondence appears to break down. It was noted earlier that the capacity to access and make full use of the Internet is unevenly distributed across society, with those in the most marginal positions enjoying *least* access. Conversely, the skills and resources required to commission offences in cyberspace are concentrated among the relatively 'privileged', those enjoying higher levels of employment, income, and education. Consequently, the social patterns of Internet criminality may well turn out to be rather different from those typically identified in the 'terrestrial' world, with cyber-offenders being 'fairly atypical in terms of traditional criminological expectations' (Wall, 2001a: 8–9). If this is the case, then recourse to concepts such as 'marginality' and 'exclusion' to explain the origins of offending behaviour, so prevalent in relation to 'real-world' criminology, might be of extremely limited value when attempting to explain the genesis of cybercrimes.

The foregoing discussion suggests that criminology, as much as criminal justice, faces challenges from the emergence of cybercrime. Rather than simply being able to transpose an existing 'stock' of empirical assumptions and explanatory concepts onto cyberspace, the appearance of Internet crimes might require considerable theoretical innovation. Criminology itself may need to start looking for some 'new tools' for these 'new crimes'.

Summary

1.8 In the past decade or so, cybercrime has become an increasingly widely debated topic across many walks of life. Our understandings of cyber-crime are simultaneously informed and obscured by political and media discussions of the problem. It is clear that the rapid growth of the Internet has created unprecedented new opportunities for offending. These developments present serious challenges for law and criminal justice, as it struggles to adapt to crimes that no longer take place in the terrestrial world but in the virtual environment of cyberspace, which span the globe through the Internet's instantaneous communication, and afford offenders new possibilities for anonymity, deception and disguise. Society's increasing dependence on networks of computer technology renders us ever more vulnerable to the failure and exploitation of those systems. Equally, the emergence of cybercrime poses difficult questions for criminologists and sociologists of crime and deviance. Such academic disciplines have formed their theories of and explanations for crime on the basis of assumptions (about who, what, where, and so on) drawn from offending in the terrestrial world. Insofar as the virtual environment of the Internet may be radically different from its terrestrial counterpart, criminology itself is challenged to adapt its perspectives in order to come to grips with cyber crime, or to develop new concepts and vocabularies which might better fit with the online world which we increasingly inhabit.

Study questions

- *how does public discourse represent the problem of cybercrime?*
- *what kind of questions does the emergence of cybercrime invite us to ask?*
- *how great a problem are cybercrimes when set alongside those terrestrial crimes with which we are more familiar?*
- *what is new or different about cybercrime?*
- *what kinds of cybercrimes do everyday users of the Internet encounter?*
- *who are the 'cybercriminals'? Are they the 'usual suspects' of criminal justice and criminology?*
- *how might the growth of cybercrimes shape the ways in which the Internet develops in the future?*

Further reading

Valuable introductions to a range of cybercrime issues and debates are found in David Wall (ed.) *Crime and the Internet* (2001c) and Doug Thomas and Brian Loader (eds) *Cybercrime: Law Enforcement, Security and Surveillance in the Information Age* (2000). The growth of the Internet and its central place in the development of the 'Information Society' are explored in Manuel Castells' ground-breaking *The Information Age: Economy, Society and Culture: vol. 3 End of Millennium* (1998) as well as his *The Internet Galaxy: Reflections on the Internet, Business, and Society* (2002). For up-to-date and detailed data on the levels and trends in cybercrime, see the Computer Security Institute's annual 'Computer Crime and Security Survey'. The debate about whether or not cybercrime is a new or novel phenomenon is conducted in Peter Grabosky's article 'Virtual Criminality: Old Wine in New Bottles?' (2001), and Wanda Capeller's 'Not Such a Neat Net: Some Comments on Virtual Criminality' (2001). Finally, useful discussions about the governance and regulation of the Internet can be found in Brian Loader (ed.) *The Governance of Cyberspace* (1997).

TWO

Hackers, Crackers
and Viral Coders

Overview

Chapter 2 examines the following issues:

- *how definitions of computer hacking and hackers are constructed and contested;*
- *how political, criminal justice and popular representations of hackers embody wider cultural concerns about technological and social change;*
- *the kinds of activities involved in hacking, and the tools and techniques used to undertake them;*
- *the realities behind the myth of hacking as an expert and elite activity;*
- *the ways in which various actors seek to account for and explain hackers' motivations for engaging in computer intrusions;*
- *the legal responses that have emerged in recent years in response to the perceived threat to society posed by hacking.*

---
key terms

Cracking	Malicious software or	Techniques of neutralization
Denial of service	'malware'	Trojan horses
Differential association	Masculinity	Viruses
Gender	Subculture	Website defacement
Hacking		

Hackers and hacking: contested definitions

2.1 A few decades ago, the terms 'hacker' and 'hacking' were known only to a relatively small number of people, mainly those in the technically specialized world of computing. Today they have become 'common knowledge', something with which most people are familiar, if only through hearsay and exposure to mass media and popular cultural accounts. Hacking provides one of the most widely analysed and debated forms of cybercriminal activity, and serves as an intense focus for public concerns about the threat that such activity poses to society. Current discussion has coalesced around a relatively clear-cut definition, which understands hacking as 'the unauthorised access and subsequent use of other people's computer systems' (Taylor, 1999: xi). It is this widely accepted sense of hacking as 'computer break-in', and of its perpetrators as 'break-in artists' and 'intruders', that structures most media, political and criminal justice responses. Thus we would appear to have a fairly definite and unambiguous starting point for an exploration of this kind of cybercrime.

However, the term has in fact undergone a series of changes in meaning over the years, and continues to be deeply contested, not least among those within the computing community. The term 'hacker' originated in the world of computer programming in the 1960s, where it was a *positive* label used to describe someone who was highly skilled in developing creative, elegant and effective solutions to computing problems. A 'hack' was, correspondingly, an innovative use of technology (especially the production of computer code or programs) that yielded positive results and benefits. On this understanding, the pioneers of the Internet, those who brought computing to 'the masses', and the developers of new and exciting computer applications (such as video gaming), were all considered to be 'hackers' *par excellence*, the brave new pioneers of the 'computer revolution' (Levy, 1984; Naughton, 2000: 313). These hackers were said to form a community with its own clearly defined 'ethic', one closely associated with the social and political values of the 1960s and the 1970s' 'counter-culture' and protest movements. This ethic emphasized, among other things, the right to freely access and exchange knowledge and information; a belief in the capacity of science and technology (especially computing) to enhance individuals' lives; a distrust of political, military and corporate authorities; and a resistance to 'conventional' and 'mainstream' lifestyles, attitudes and social hierarchies (Taylor, 1999: 24–6; Thomas, 2002). While such hackers would often engage in 'exploration' of others' computer systems, they purported to do so out of curiosity, a desire to learn and discover, and to freely share what they had found with others; damaging those systems while 'exploring', intentionally or otherwise, was considered both incompetent and unethical. This earlier understanding of hacking and its ethos has since been largely overridden by its more negative counterpart, with its stress upon intrusion, violation, theft and sabotage. Hackers of the 'old school' angrily refute their depiction in such terms, and use the term 'cracker' to distinguish the malicious type of computer enthusiast from hackers proper. Some would suggest that these differences are of little more than historical interest, and insist that the current, 'negative' and 'criminal' definition of hacking and hackers should be adopted, since this is the dominant way in which the terms are now understood and used (Twist, 2003). Moreover, to shift around between different groups' and individuals' definitions only invites confusion. There is considerable value to this pragmatic approach – throughout this and subsequent chapters, the 'terms 'hacking' and 'hackers' will be used in the current sense to denote those illegal activities associated with computer intrusion and manipulation, and to denote those persons who engage in such activities.

The contested nature of the terms is, however, worth bearing in mind, for a good criminological reason. It shows how hacking, as a form of cybercriminal activity, is actively *constructed* by governments, law enforcement, the computer security industry, businesses, and the media; and how the equation of such activities with 'crime' and 'criminality' is both embraced and challenged by those who engage in them. In other words, the contest over characterizing hackers and hacking is a prime example of what sociologists such as Becker (1963) identify as the 'labelling process', the process by which categories of criminal/deviant activity and identity are socially produced. Reactions to hacking and hackers cannot be understood independently from how their meanings are socially created, negotiated and resisted. Criminal justice and other agents propagate, disseminate and utilize negative constructions of hacking as part of the 'war on cybercrime'. Those who find themselves so positioned may reject the label, insisting that they are misunderstood, and try to persuade others that they are not 'criminals'; alternatively, they may seek out and embrace the label, and act accordingly, thereby setting in motion a process of 'deviance amplification' (Young, 1971) which ends up producing the very behaviour that the forces of 'law and order' are seeking to prevent. *In extremis*, such constructions can be seen to make hackers into 'folk devils' (Cohen, 1972), an apparently urgent threat to society which fuels the kinds of 'moral panic' about cybercrime alluded to in the previous chapter. As we shall see, such processes of labelling, negotiation and resistance are a central feature of ongoing social interactions about hacking.

Representations of hackers and hacking: technological fears and fantasies

2.2 This chapter began by noting that hacking comprises one of the most widely discussed areas of cybercriminal activity; indeed, for many people cybercrime and hacking have become synonymous. The public discourse on hacking appears to evoke fear and fascination in equal measure. The origins of this intense controversy can be understood in a number of different ways. The most straightforward explanation of social sensitivities to hacking stresses the degree of threat or danger that the activity carries. From what Hunt (1987) calls an 'objectivist' view of social problems, the response to hacking is a perfectly understandable and appropriate reaction to the level of social harm that it causes. The constant stream of estimates about financial losses incurred from hacking, and analyses of the dangers it poses to national security and public safety, would appear to give credence to such a view (see, for example, Coutorie, 1995; Bowers, 1998; Boni, 2001). Put simply, this viewpoint states that we are *right* to be extremely alarmed by hacking, because objective assessments show us that hacking *is* an extremely damaging form of cybercriminal behaviour. However, numerous commentators have suggested that social representations of the hacker threat are out of all proportion to the actual harm that their activities cause (Sterling, 1994; Kovacich, 1999). Thus official pronouncements on hacking often tend towards hyperbole – as, for example, when a senior law enforcement official told the US Senate that the nation is facing 'a cyber equivalent of Pearl

Harbor' (cited in Taylor, 1999: 7). Similarly exaggerated responses may be seen in media accounts. Taylor (1999: 7) recounts a story from a UK 'tabloid' newspaper depicting a 17-year-old computer hacker who, while ensconced in his bedroom, had supposedly broken into US military systems and had 'his twitching index finger hover[ing] over the nuclear button'. Such lurid and (literally) apocalyptic representations of hacking suggest that we have to look beyond the 'objective' assessment of threats if we wish to understand why it evokes such a heightened degree of alarm.

Paul Taylor (1999, 2000) situates social representations of hackers and hacking in the context of wider responses to rapid technological change. Historically speaking, such change has often incited anxieties that technology presents a threat to human existence, a fear that the more powerful our creations, the more they can escape our control and do untold damage. Thus, in Mary Shelley's *Frankenstein*, a scientist's desire to 'play God' and generate new life results in the creation of monster that turns on its creator. The theme of technological monstrosities, unwittingly unleashed by 'mad scientists', subsequently became a staple of twentieth-century popular culture (Tudor, 1989). From the 1960s onwards, the computer has come increasingly to the fore as the embodiment of this technological 'Pandora's box'. Thus, in Stanley Kubrick's *2001: A Space Odyssey* (1969) the initially benevolent spaceship computer HAL goes 'insane' and turns to murdering the human members of the crew. In the 1977 film *Demon Seed*, an experiment in artificial intelligence goes awry, creating a 'demonic' computer that even goes so far as to rape a woman in order to create its 'child', a human–machine hybrid. Similar themes are replayed in the popular *Terminator* series of films, in which a sentient military computer called Skynet launches a nuclear war against its human masters. Such representations, it can be suggested, give voice to a wider unease about technological innovation and its potentially uncontrollable catastrophic effects. Films focusing on hacking reinterpret such themes in their own particular way. The 1983 movie *War Games* tells the tale of a teenage hacker who unknowingly breaks in to a military computer and, while thinking he is playing a computer game called 'global thermonuclear warfare', brings the world to the very edge of nuclear oblivion. Such representations also point to a related kind of cultural anxiety, the fear that the more technologically oriented we become, the less human we are, the more we lose touch with a 'normal' existence. Representations of hackers (in both fiction and non-fiction) often allude to this, depicting them as alienated, dysfunctional and isolated loners who are able to interact effectively only with their computers. The fact that hackers are also invariably *young* in popular perceptions is also not a coincidence – the apparent ease with which a 'younger generation' is able to engage with the realm of computer technology, a technology that many older people continue to see as mysteriously daunting, merely serves to sharpen the sense that all manner of extravagant things may be possible for those with the know-how.

The sceptical reader may at this point object that the above examples are 'merely' Hollywood fictions, and that people are sufficiently astute to be capable of distinguishing them from 'reality'. However, such dismissal may overlook the profound ways in which popular representations shape public understandings of the world. Thus, for example, the aforementioned *War Games* was presented before a committee of the US Congress as an example of possible threats from hacking (as, a few years later, was the film *Die Hard II*, in which terrorists hack into an air traffic control computer in order to hold the authorities to ransom by threatening to crash incoming aircraft) (Taylor, 1999: 10). Law enforcement agencies have shown a similar willingness to make inferences about real-life hackers and their activities from depictions of their fictional counterparts (ibid.: 181). Taylor (ibid.: 9) concludes that 'the movies' representations of hacking have had a disproportionately important influence upon the legislative response to the activity' and that 'over-reliance upon fictional portrayals of hacking by the authorities has contributed to help-ing to create a generally fearful and ignorant atmosphere'. In short, cultural anxieties and their popular representation have played a significant role in how the threat from hacking has come to be perceived in both official and wider public domains.

However, social representations of hackers and hacking have not been exclu-sively of a negative kind. Rather, they exhibit considerable ambivalence, with hackers evoking a kind of fascination and even admiration. Studies of public attitudes suggest that among a significant portion of the population, especially the young, hackers and their activities are viewed in a rather positive light (Dowland et al., 1999: 720; Voiskounsky et al., 2000: 69–76). There are a number of ways in which such favourable representations of hacking can be under-stood. First, they can be seen in relation to the aforementioned sense of threat or anxiety evoked by new and seemingly incomprehensible technologies. In such a situation, hackers come to represent a mastery of the arcane new world of computing that others desire or aspire to. Consequently, public perceptions of hackers often stress traits such as unusual intelligence and ingenuity (Voiskounsky et al., 2000: 72–3); news media also propagate similar images of hackers as 'geniuses', 'wizards' and 'virtuosos' (Furnell, 2002: 201). Depictions of hacking as arcane, mysterious and powerful also appear in popular fictions. For example, the sci-fi thriller *The Core* (2003) features a brilliant hacker who demonstrates his abilities to a sceptical audience by 'hacking' a mobile phone by merely whistling tones into the handset through a foil gum wrapper; finish-ing this 10-second piece of hacker virtuosity, he laconically hands the phone back to its owner, claiming that 'You now have free long-distance calls for life!'. The implication here is that, while hackers are seen as threatening insofar as they immerse themselves in an 'alien' and dehumanized world of technology, they also offer a vision of individuals reclaiming their autonomy by taking forceful control of a technological system which they can use for their own human ends (Taylor, 2000: 43). A second kind of threat, to which hackers appear to offer resistance, is the perceived domination of high technology by governmental powers and/or faceless corporations. Concerns about the Internet often coalesce around a kind of Orwellian nightmare of surveillance and manipulation, and hackers are sometimes represented as the resistance to such unaccountable and invasive uses of technological power – what one commentator dubs the 'freedom fighters of the 21st century' (Kovacich, 1999). Popular culture again appropriates and disseminates such interpretations. The film *Hackers* (1995), for example, portrays an idealistic group of young computer outlaws who use their hacking skills to take on corporate conspirators who are intent on causing an ecological catastrophe, which they will blame on our innocent 'heroes'. In a similar vein, public resentments about the domination of computer technology by corporations such as Microsoft are explicitly exploited in *AntiTrust* (2001), another computer crime movie. Here, a (thinly disguised) Bill Gates-like computer tycoon is hell-bent on global domination at any cost, only to be thwarted by young computer 'geeks' who hold fast to the 'hacker ethic' of freedom of information and knowledge. In sum, we can see that socio-cultural fears and fantasies about computer technology shape often ambivalent and contradictory representations of the hacker, who appears as 'a schizophrenic blend of dangerous criminal and geeky Robin Hood' (Hawn, 1996; cited in Taylor, 2000: xii).

What hackers actually *do*: a brief guide for the technologically bewildered

2.3 Having examined the contested definitions and wider representations of hackers and hacking, it is now time to consider in a little detail what it is that hackers actually do when they 'hack', and how they go about it. As will become apparent below, 'hacking' is, in fact, a generic label for a range of distinct activities associated with computer intrusion, manipulation and disruption.

Unauthorized access to computer systems

2.3.1 The most fundamental form of hacker activity is that of gaining access to, and control over, others' computer systems. Once such access and control have been gained (what hackers call 'taking ownership' of a system), a range of further prohibited activities become possible. Such access is made possible by the networking of computer systems, since their inter-connection makes it possible to access a system from the 'outside', from other computers which can connect to it. The Internet has increased the possibilities for such intrusion many-fold since, given the network's 'open architecture', all systems connected to it are 'public facing', i.e. can be communicated with remotely by anyone who can establish an Internet connection (Esen, 2002: 269). As an ever-greater number of systems have become connected to the Internet, the number of such intrusions has increased steadily. For example, in 1998 the FBI reported that computer intrusion incidents had increased 250 per cent over a two-year period (Lilley, 2002: 32). In 2003, 36 per cent of US organizations questioned in the annual CSI/FBI computer crime survey reported having experienced a 'system penetration' attack. The Internet was reported as an increasingly frequent point of attack, with 78 per cent of respondents reporting at least one such incident in the previous 12 months, up from 57 per cent in 1999 (CSI/FBI, 2003: 8–10). The frequency of such intrusions is anticipated to continue rising markedly, as Internet use continues to spread, and an ever greater range of Internet-enabled devices become available (such as personal digital assistants (PDAs) and mobile phones). Moreover, given that as few as 5 per cent of incidents are thought to actually be reported to the authorities (Lilley, 2002: 32), the extent of such intrusions may well be massively greater than official figures reveal.

Illegalities following computer intrusion

2.3.2   Once access to a computer system has been established, hackers are able to perpetrate a further range of criminal acts. These include the following:

- *Theft of computer resources.* Hackers may use the resources of the hacked system for their own purposes, such as the storage of illegal or undesirable materials. In one such incident a hacker from Sweden illegally accessed an American university's systems, and used them to store and distribute a massive array of pirated music (MP3) files (Furnell, 2002: 101).
- *Theft of proprietary or confidential information.* Hackers may exploit unauthorized access in order to steal or copy information including software, business secrets, personal information about an organization's employees and customers, and credit card details which can subsequently be used for fraudulent purposes. Theft of proprietary information is cited as the greatest source of financial losses by business and other organizations (CSI/FBI, 2003: 4). There have even been cases in which seemingly reputable business organizations have allegedly commissioned hackers to steal confidential information from their competitors (Eichenwald, 1998: 157). Incidents also abound in which thousands of customer credit card details have been stolen as a result of hacking incidents, or in which hackers were able to exploit banks' systems to arrange illegal electronic transfers of funds (Riem, 2001: 12–13; Travis, 2001; Wilding, 2003: 4). In one case of the former, a Russian hacker known only as 'Maxim' accessed the systems of an Internet retailer and stole details of some 300,000 credit cards; when the company refused to pay the $100,000 the hacker demanded as part of 'his' blackmail scheme, 'he' posted details of

25,000 of the cards on the Internet (Philippsohn, 2001: 57). In an instance of the latter, a group of hackers, again from Russia, managed to electronically transfer over $10 million from the accounts of Citibank's US customers (Grabosky and Smith, 2001: 34).

- *Systems sabotage, alteration and destruction.* Hackers may exploit access to cause significant amounts of damage to a system's operations. While outright 'trashing' of content is relatively rare (Furnell, 2002: 101), it is not unheard of; there have been a number of documented cases in which disgruntled former employees have unleashed such destruction upon their erstwhile employers in revenge for having been dismissed (Philippsohn, 2001: 55). More frequent is the selective alteration of data held within the system. This may be undertaken by hackers so as to cover their tracks, hiding from administrators the fact that their system has been compromised, thereby allowing the hackers to access the system on an ongoing basis. Systems content may be also be altered or erased by hackers 'as a prank, protest, or to flaunt their skills' (Denning, 1999: 227). (Tampering as a protest or political act will be considered in detail in Chapter 3). Hackers may also alter data so as to gain some personal advantage for themselves, their friends or family. There are a number of cases in which students gained access to school or university computers to alter their own or their friends' grades. There was even one incident in which an inmate of a California jail broke into the prison's information system, and altered his release date 'so that he could be home in time for Christmas' (ibid.,). Overall, some 21 per cent of organizations surveyed in the USA report having experienced some such form of sabotage during a 12-month period (CSI/FBI, 2003: 10); in the UK for the same period, 'sabotage of data or networks' was estimated to have impacted upon 9 per cent of business organizations (NOP/NHTCU, 2002: 4).
- *Website defacement and 'spoofing'.* Such hacker attacks directly target Internet websites themselves, and can take a number of distinct forms. In instances of 'defacement', the website is hacked and its contents altered. These may be viewed as 'pranks' intended to 'amuse' web-surfers, as exercises in self-aggrandizement by hackers who wish to advertise their skills, or as ideologically and politically motivated forms of protest against governments and businesses (Vegh, 2002; Woo et al., 2004). Website defacements are an increasingly prominent form of hacker activity, with recorded attacks rising from just 5 in 1995 to almost 6000 in 2000 (Furnell, 2002: 104). Victims in recent years have included the US, Hong Kong, and Colombian governments, the CIA and the US military, the UK Labour and Conservative Parties, the *New York Times*, the LAPD, as well as (ironically) the sites of companies specializing in providing Internet security solutions (Denning, 1999: 228–31; Furnell, 2002: 103–9; Lilley, 2002: 53–4). The second form of website-centred hack, 'spoofing' does not attack organizations' actual sites. Rather, the hacker establishes a 'spoof' or 'fake' website to which the unsuspecting Internet user is re-directed. Again, this can cause considerable embarrassment to the owner of the legitimate website, since its forged replacement may feature offensive speech, pornographic imagery, or accusations about the victim's supposedly unsavoury business or political practices. Spoofing is also used in the commission of Internet

frauds. In such cases, the forged website is made to appear as similar as possible to its legitimate counterpart, so that the visitor may be unaware that it is a fake. The user will thus proceed to use the site as normal, for example, by attempting to log on using their username and password. In the case of e-commerce and e-banking sites, for example, this has been exploited to acquire access to customers' accounts which can then be raided (Philippsohn, 2001: 60). (Website spoofing for the commission of fraud will be considered further in Chapter 5).

In addition to those activities outlined above, there are a number of important, illicit activities usually associated with hacking, but which do not in fact require unauthorized access or 'break-in' to a computer system; rather, they can be engineered simply via email or Internet connection:

- *Denial of service attacks.* 'Denial of service' basically refers to a cyber-attack 'which prevents a computer user or owner access to the services available on his system' (Esen, 2002: 271). Such an attack can be performed without direct access to a system, by 'flooding' Internet-accessible computers with communications, so that they become 'overloaded' and are rendered unable to perform functions for legitimate users. Such attacks are seen as an increasingly frequent form of hacker activity, with 42 per cent of US-based and 20 per cent of UK-based organizations reporting such attacks during 2002–3 (CSI/FBI, 2003: 10; NOP/NHTCU, 2002: 4). During 2001, in one of the most publicized cases of recent years, a 15-year-old Canadian, going under the hacker pseudonym of 'Mafiaboy', managed to effectively shut down access to leading e-commerce websites such as Amazon.com and eBay.com, as well as the site of the global news service CNN. At his subsequent trial, he was alleged to have caused some $1.7 billion in damages (BBC News, 2001a).
- *Distribution of 'malicious software'.* Malicious software (or 'malware' for short) refers to computer codes and programs, usually distributed via the Internet and email, which infect computers, causing varying degrees of disruption to their operation or damage to data. Malware takes a number of distinctive forms, such as 'viruses', 'worms' and 'Trojan horses'. Computer viruses, like their biological counterparts, need hosts to reproduce and transmit themselves (Boase and Wellman, 2001: 39). Worms, however, are independent pieces of software capable of self-replication and self-transmission (for example, by emailing themselves to others in a computer's address book) (Furnell, 2002: 147). A Trojan horse, as the name suggests, is a program that appears to perform a benign or useful function, but in fact has some hidden destructive capabilities that only become apparent after a user has downloaded and installed the software. Taken together, such forms malware are widely recognized as the most disruptive and destructive kind of cyber-attack (CSI/FBI, 2003: 4). Chapter 1 began with the example of the 'Love Bug' worm that affected millions of computers in May 2001, causing an estimated 7–10 billion dollars of damage. A few months later, on 13 July, the 'Code Red' worm appeared, and infected more than a quarter of a million systems in its first nine hours (CERT/CC, 2002). By 1 August, it had caused an estimated $1.2 billion in losses (BBC News,

01/08/01). In January 2004, a virus dubbed 'MyDoom' became the fastest spreading virus ever, causing an estimated $20 billion of damage to businesses worldwide in just 15 days (Wright, 2004; McCandless, 2004). As I write this, the 'Sasser' worm is in its second week of release, and has already infected millions of machines, including the systems of the South African government, the UK coastguard, the Taiwanese national post office, and the Australian rail network (leaving some 300,000 passengers stranded) (Sophos, 2004). The massive disruption caused by such malicious codes is a consequence of the way in which they can use the Internet to rapidly distribute themselves – the openness of the network and the near-instantaneity of communication enable them to replicate and spread exponentially. Further problems arise as viruses, again like their biological equivalents, are often capable of mutation, thereby evading virus detection and eradication systems programmed to recognize only earlier versions of the code (Boase and Wellman, 2001: 41–2). A piece of malware need be sent to only a single networked machine from which it can automatically spread to millions of others without any further action from its author. This capacity for generating rapid and widespread disruption to the global network of computer systems is now viewed as a key tool for conducting 'information warfare', 'cyberterrorism' and other politically motivated attacks (considered in detail in Chapter 3).

Hacker myths and realities: wizards or button-pushers?

2.4 In Section 2.2, I noted the tendency of social representations of hacking to stress the technical virtuosity and exceptional abilities of its practitioners. Press reporting has propagated such imagery, not least because it enhances the frisson of danger and fascination surrounding the activity, creating around the figure of the hacker a kind of mystique. Popular fiction has similarly stressed the abnormal intelligence and skills of hackers – in films such as *Hackers, The Core* and *The Italian Job* (2003), the hacker appears as a kind of savant, using knowledge and techniques far beyond the comprehension of normal people to achieve the most awe-inspiring control over computerized systems. Such cultural constructions of the hacker as a 'genius' have significantly shaped wider perceptions of hacking as a social practice. If such perceptions are valid, then the actual number of hackers may be very limited, given that only the most gifted and accomplished can acquire the skills necessary to succeed. Estimating numbers is particularly difficult, given the inherently covert nature of the activity, the increasing criminal sanctions that can be brought to bear upon hackers if identified and which serve to drive them further underground, and the capacity for anonymity afforded by the Internet environment. Writing in the relatively early days of mass-networked computing, Sterling (1994: 76–7) estimated that the 'digital underground' of hacking comprised no more than about 5,000 individuals, of whom 'as few as a hundred are truly "elite" – active computer intruders, skilled enough to penetrate sophisticated

HACKERS, CRACKERS AND VIRAL CODERS

systems and truly to worry corporate security and law enforcement'. More recently, TruSecure, a US-based Internet security company, is aware of some 11,000 individuals organized into about 900 different hacking groups (Twist, 2003). While the numbers may have increased over the past decade, the levels of skill and knowledge necessary for effective hacking appear to present a barrier to entry, thereby setting limits on the extent of hacking as a cybercrime problem.

However, the view of hacking as an activity restricted to a small, highly able and motivated 'elite' may be increasingly at odds with reality. Hacking itself has undergone considerable evolution and change over recent years. Perhaps it was true that, for an earlier generation of hackers, crackers and viral-coders, technical knowledge and skills were a prerequisite, since they had to rely on either formal training in computing and/or concerted experimentation, trial and error in order to stage attacks. However, as hacking techniques have evolved, an increasing range of automated software tools have appeared which can perform much of the necessary work. For example, the kinds of unauthorized access and hijacking of computers described earlier can now be performed with a range of tools such as 'Titan', 'SATAN', and 'BO2K' which probe networks to find vulnerable systems and establish remote control over them; programs such as 'Ethereal' and 'L0phtCrack' can be used to capture and decrypt user passwords (Furnell, 2002: 119). Similarly, denial of service attacks can now be launched automatically using software such as 'FloodNet' (Denning, 1999: 237). Such tools are readily available for download from hacker websites. There are also numerous readily available tools for creating viruses and worms (over 100 according to one estimate). Many of these programs come with user-friendly Windows-style interfaces, pull-down menus and even 'help' files to guide the inexperienced user. One such tool, the 'Vbs Worm Generator', allows the user to custom-design a worm with a range of different destructive payloads, all with a few clicks of the mouse (Furnell, 2002: 178–81). Such tools enable even the novice, with little or no existing expertise, to generate cyber-attacks. Thus in 2001, a 20-year-old from the Netherlands, calling himself 'OnTheFly', used the Vbs tool to create the 'Anna Kournikova' worm. When it spread across the Internet with alarming and unexpected rapidity, the terrified author surrendered himself to the authorities. He subsequently revealed that it was his first effort at viral coding and 'it only took me a minute to write it' (Delio, 2001). In the words of 'Sir Dystic', one of the authors of the 'BO2K' hacking tool, 'we made the software easy enough for an eight-year-old to hack with and we think it could do serious damage' (cited in Furnell, 2002: 123). Such technical innovations have effectively 'democratized' hacking, making it increasingly available to anyone with a PC, Internet connection and the curiosity or desire to see if they too can join the 'digital underground'.

2.5 Inquiries into crime have long dwelt on the causes and motivations behind offending behaviour – in the words of Hirschi (1969), one of the most frequently asked questions is 'Why do they do it?' In this respect, deliberations on cybercrime are no different, with a range of actors such as journalists, academics, politicians, law enforcement operatives, and members of the public all indicating what they perceive to be the factors underlying hackers' dedication to computer crime. Many commentators focus upon 'motivations', effectively viewing hackers as 'rational actors' who consciously choose to engage in their illicit activities in expectation of some kind of reward or satisfaction. The motivations variously attributed to hackers are wide-ranging and often contradictory. Among those concerned with combating hacking activity, there is a tendency to emphasize maliciousness, vandalism, and the desire to commit wanton destruction (Kovacich, 1999); attribution of such motivations by law enforcement and computer security agencies is unsurprising, as it offers the most clear-cut way of denying hacking any socially recognized legitimacy. Among the wider public, hackers are perceived to act on motivations ranging from self-assertion, curiosity, and thrill seeking, to greed and hooliganism (Dowland et al., 1999: 720; Voiskounsky et al., 2000: 71). This diversity of attributed motivations may in fact reflect the variety of individuals who engage in hacking and the different aims and goals that such activities satisfy. While some may see hacking as an end-in-itself, others may view it as merely a convenient 'instrumental' means to achieve other goals. Such goals may be related to economic self-interest (as, for example, in cases of computer-enabled fraud) or to political ideas and ideologies (as in cases of 'cyberterrorism' and 'hacktivism'). From a 'rational choice' viewpoint, such variety is to be expected, as computer criminals (like their terrestrial counterparts) are deemed to be driven by a range of motivations 'as old as human society, including greed, lust, revenge and curiosity' (Grabosky and Smith, 2001: 35).

One way in which commentators have attempted to refine their understandings of hacker motivations is to elicit from hackers themselves their reasons for engaging in computer crimes. There now exist a number of studies, both 'popular' and 'scholarly' in which hackers have been interviewed about their illicit activities (for example, Clough and Mungo, 1992; Taylor, 1999; Verton, 2002). In addition, hackers themselves have authored texts and documents in which they elaborate upon their ethos and aims (see, for example, Dr K, 2004; Mitnick and Simon, 2005). Such 'insider' accounts cite motivations very different to those cited by 'outsiders'. In fact, they consistently invoke a rationale for hacking that explicitly mobilizes the 'hacker ethic' of an earlier generation of computer enthusiasts. In hackers' self-presentations, they are motivated by factors such as intellectual curiosity, the desire to expand the boundaries of knowledge, a commitment to the free flow and exchange of information, resistance to political authoritarianism and corporate domination, and the aim of *improving* computer security by exposing the laxity and ineptitude of those charged with safeguarding socially sensitive data. However, such accounts 'straight from the horse's mouth' do not necessarily furnish insights into hacker motivations that are any more objectively true than those attributed by outside observers. As Taylor (1999: 44) notes, 'it is difficult ... to separate clearly the *ex ante* motivations of hackers from their *ex post* justifications'. In other words, such self-attributed motivations may well be rhetorical devices mobilized by hackers to justify their law-breaking and defend themselves against accusations of criminality and deviance. Viewed in this way, hackers' accounts can be seen as part of what criminologists Sykes and Matza (1957) call 'techniques of neutralisation'. According to Sykes and Matza, 'delinquents' will make recourse to such techniques as a way of overcoming the inhibitions or guilt they may otherwise feel when embarking upon law-breaking activity. These techniques include strategies such as 'denial of injury', 'denial of the victim', 'condemnation of the condemners' and 'appeal to higher loyalties'. The view of hackers' self-narrations as instances of such techniques can be supported if we examine hacker accounts. A clear illustration is provided by a now famous (or infamous) document called 'The Conscience of a Hacker' authored by 'The Mentor' in 1986, now better known as 'The Hacker's Manifesto'. In the 'Manifesto', its author explains hackers' motivations by citing factors such as: the boredom experienced by 'smart kids' at the mercy of incompetent school teachers and 'sadists'; the desire to access a service that 'could be dirt-cheap if it wasn't run by profiteering gluttons'; the desire to explore and learn which is denied by 'you' who 'build atomic bombs, ... wage wars, ... murder, cheat and lie' (The Mentor, 1986). Such reasoning clearly justifies hacking activities by re-labelling 'harm' as 'curiosity', by suggesting that victims are in some sense 'getting what they deserve' as a consequence of their greed, and turning the tables on accusers by claiming the 'moral high ground' through a citation of 'real' crimes committed by the legitimate political and economic establishment. Just as agents of 'law and order' present hacker motivations in manner that supports criminalization, insiders' accounts of hacking serve to resist deviant and criminal labels by legitimating hacker activities; both are part of the process through which the social and political meanings of hacking are constructed and contested.

A second strand of thinking about hacking downplays 'motivations' and 'choices', and emphasizes instead the psychological and/or social factors that seemingly dispose certain individuals or groups toward law-breaking behaviour. In such accounts, 'free choice' is sidelined in favour of a view of human actions as fundamentally *caused* by forces acting within or upon the offender.

From an individualistic perspective, some psychologists have attempted to explain hacking by viewing it as an extension of compulsive computer use over which the actor has limited control. So-called 'Internet Addiction Disorder' is viewed as an addiction akin to alcoholism and narcotic dependence, in which the sufferer loses the capacity to exercise restraint over his or her own habituated desire (Young, 1998; Young et al., 1999). Some accounts of hacking draw explicit parallels with drug addiction, going so far as to suggest that engagement in relatively innocuous hacking activities can lead to more serious infractions, just as use of 'soft' drugs like marijuana is commonly claimed to constitute a 'slippery slope' leading to the use of 'hard' drugs like crack cocaine and heroin (Verton, 2002: 35, 39, 41, 51). This 'medicalization' of hacking as a psychological disorder has gained sufficient purchase so as to have played a role in the prosecution and sentencing of a number of hackers: in the USA the notorious hacker Kevin Mitnick was ordered by the sentencing judge to attend an Alcoholics Anonymous-style '12 step' recovery program for his purported computer addiction; and in the UK, Paul Bedworth was acquitted of hacking charges on the grounds of computer addiction (Grossman, 2001: 1–13).

Both psychological and social explanations of hacking have focused in particular upon *masculinity* and *youth* as key issues, since hackers appear to have a distinctive gender and age distribution. In terms of gender, studies of hacking reveal it to be an overwhelmingly male activity, with some authors estimating a male:female ratio as high as 99:1 (Taylor, 1999: 32). In terms of age, studies again reveal hackers to be predominantly young, often adolescents and teenagers. Thus, Sterling (1994: 76) claims that 'most hackers start young', and 'drop out' by their early twenties; Taylor (1999: 32) found that those who continued to hack into their mid-twenties complained that they were viewed as 'has-beens' by the youthful majority of the hacker 'underground'. Attempts to explain the domination of hacking by male youth will be considered below, with the dimensions of gender and age being tackled in turn.

'Boys will be boys'? Masculinity and hacking

2.5.1 Explanations for the massive over-representation of males among hackers variously emphasize psychological and/or socio-cultural factors. Some commentators attribute the appeal of hacking for males (and its lack of appeal for females) to innate psychological differences between the genders, claiming that males are more oriented toward, and fascinated by, mathematical and logical problem solving (Taylor, 1999: 35). An objection to such approaches is, however, that they conflate 'nature' and 'nurture'; that is, they attribute to individuals' innate biological heritage what in fact may be socially learned behaviours, dispositions and inclinations. Consequently, others instead view

HACKERS, CRACKERS AND VIRAL CODERS

such psychological differences as the outcome of cultural influences. Thus, Turkle (1984) claims that males are culturally socialized into a desire for what she calls 'hard mastery', seeking to impose their will and control over machines, thereby furnishing them with attitudes particularly suited towards hacking (see also discussion in Taylor, 2003). A slightly different aspect of gendered psychology is stressed by those who emphasize the ways in which teenage boys turn to hacking in order to satisfy a desire for power in the face of their actual powerlessness in 'real-world' social relations (Sterling, 1994: 19). In sociological and criminological terms, this disposition may be viewed as a consequence of the domination in our culture of what Connell (1987) calls 'hegemonic masculinity'. This is seen as an ideology that presents being a 'real man' in terms of the ability to exercise authority, control and domination over others (see also Messerschmidt, 1993; Jefferson, 1997). Given the pressures and expectations placed upon boys to demonstrate their 'manliness' in such terms, hacking (and crime more generally) may be seen as an appealing avenue for those striving to negotiate their way towards a socially recognized status as 'real men'. A final strand of explanation places less emphasis upon factors disposing males to engage in hacking, and instead focuses upon those factors that actively *discourage* female participation in such activities. Taylor (1999: 36–40; 2003: 136–8) notes how the culture of hacker groups, websites and online forums exhibits strong sexist and misogynistic dimensions; the flow of sexist and demeaning speech and harassment of women issuing from male hackers may also be actively encouraged by the anonymity of online interaction which loosens inhibitions which may apply in 'real-world' settings. This 'locker room' or 'bar room' culture may discourage women from involvement in hacker circles and activities in spite of any genuine interest they might have.

Hacking: just another case of 'juvenile delinquency'?

2.5.2   The second area upon which explanations of hacking focus is related to the over-representation of youth among its practitioners. Given that most hackers appear to be teenagers (Verton, 2002), this inevitably raises questions about the relationship between age and the disposition to participate in such computer-related offences. As with discussions of gender, reflections on youth and hacking take a range of different approaches, some psychological and some more sociologically oriented.

One tendency in explanations of hacking departs from the widely held view of adolescence as a period of inevitable psychological turmoil and crisis (Muncie, 1999: 92–3), suggesting that such disturbance helps account for youthful participation in hacking alongside other forms of 'delinquent' and 'anti-social' behaviour. In particular, it has been suggested that 'juveniles appear to have an ethical "deficit" which disposes them toward law- and rule-breaking behaviour when it comes to computer use' (DeMarco, 2001). This view is backed up by citation of surveys about youth attitudes towards computer crimes, which claim that significant numbers of young people participate in computer-related offences and that many deem it acceptable to do so (Bowker, 1999: 40). Such accounts may be seen to implicitly side with theories of developmental psychology that claim that individuals, as they move from childhood to adulthood, pass through a number of stages of moral learning; it is only with 'maturity' that individuals are fully able to appreciate and apply moral principles to regulate their own and others' behaviour. As such, juveniles occupy a space of moral 'immaturity' in which they are likely to act upon their hedonistic impulses with limited regard for the impact of their actions upon others (Hollin, 2002: 159–60). When applied to computer crime, such understandings attribute youthful participation in hacking to a combination of adolescent 'crisis' and ethical 'underdevelopment'; and, conversely, they can be used to explain why most individuals 'drop out' of hacking as they reach psychological maturity in their twenties.

A more socially oriented explanation of youthful involvement in hacking stresses the problematic family backgrounds of offenders. There is an established tradition of 'developmental criminology' that claims a strong correlation between youth offending and experiences of parental neglect, parental conflict, and family disruption and breakdown (see, for example, Loeber and Stouthamer-Loeber, 1986). While accounts of hackers and hacking seldom make explicit reference to such scholarly literature, they nonetheless can be seen to reproduce its association between offending and familial problems. Thus, for example, Verton (2002), in his study of teenage hackers, makes repeated references to the 'troubled' family backgrounds of his subjects, citing biographical details relating to parental conflict, divorce, 'dysfunctional family environment', parents' alcoholism, and physical abuse (ibid.: xvii, xviii, 37, 86, 102, 105, 142, 145, 170, 188). Of one hacker, dubbed 'Explotion', he notes that 'his mother died when he was 13, and his father liked to practice his left jab on his face'; of another, Willie Gonzalez, Verton opines that 'Willie was heading down a dangerous path that a lot of teenage hackers ... find themselves on. He was an outsider, a loner with no escape from a dreadful home life' (ibid.: 105, 146). The clear implication here is that involvement in hacking, like other forms of 'delinquent' behaviour, is explicable by the teenagers' lack of 'caring, loving, stable families' (ibid.: 188). However, such reasoning can be criticized for falling prey to what Felson (1998) calls the 'pathological fallacy', the idea that forms of 'pathological', 'deviant' or 'abnormal' behaviour must be explained by reference to some other 'pathology' or 'abnormality' in the individual's personal and social circumstances. Writers on hacking such as Fitch (2004: 7) also contest this view of hackers as 'alienated, angsty teens', seeing them instead as 'normal kids, muddling through everyday life issues', and hence largely indistinguishable from their peers.

An alternative socially oriented explanation for youth involvement in hacking emerges from 'subcultural' and 'differential association' perspectives on delinquency. Subcultural criminology starts by rejecting the depiction of offenders and offending in individualistic terms. Rather, analysts stress that crime and delinquency are situated in the context of social group membership; the groups to which 'delinquent' individuals belong will have distinctive shared beliefs, attitudes and values, and it is this distinctive 'subculture' that both licenses and rewards behaviour that may be at odds with 'mainstream' social norm and rules (Cohen, 1955; Cloward and Ohlin, 1961). Similarly, 'differential association' theory views crime and delinquency as socially learned behaviour, and sees close personal groups and peer milieu as the main context for such learning. Through association with others, individuals will learn not only the techniques for carrying out crimes but also the attitudes and values that support and validate such behaviour (Sutherland and Cressey, 1974). Social-psychological perspectives such as 'social learning theory' similarly stress how individuals are socialized into rule-breaking behaviour through peer-association (Bandura, 1977; Fitch, 2004). Such perspectives can be mobilized to explain youth involvement in hacking and other forms of computer crime, as studies clearly show the ways in which such behaviour takes place in a distinctive socio-cultural context and 'communal' structure (Fream and Skinner, 1997; Taylor, 1999: x, 26). Peer association in the hacking subculture takes places in both 'real' and 'virtual' worlds (Fitch, 2004: 8–9). In the 'terrestrial' world, hackers participate in organized conferences, such as the annual DefCon hacker gathering, at which knowledge, tools and tales are exchanged; similarly, chapters of the '2600' hackers organization meet weekly in towns and cities across the USA (Rogers, 2000: 12). In 'virtual' or online settings, peer groups are formed and sustained via computer-mediated interaction in 'chat rooms' and via 'bulletin boards'. Such groups not only provide opportunities for novice or would-be hackers to learn the 'tricks of the trade' from their more experienced counterparts, but also socialize new members into the distinctive ethos and attitudes of hacker culture (Denning, 1991: 60). This culture includes those values (noted earlier) which legitimate hacking, and counter outsider accusations of deviance and criminality; it also includes broader 'life style' codes about dress, speech and leisure pursuits that serve to symbolically unite hackers and demarcate them from the despised non-hacker culture. Moreover, such groupings provide social and symbolic rewards for their members in terms of the peer recognition and esteem granted to those who successfully carry off 'hacks' (Taylor, 1999: 59–60); such recognition becomes crucial in sustaining members' ongoing commitment to the hacker ideology and lifestyle. From a subcultural perspective, participation in and identification with hacking culture may be viewed as a strategy of boundary formation through which 'youth' is produced as a distinctive and oppositional category of social membership, one which its participants experience as a form of resistance to 'mainstream' adult society (Muncie, 1999: 158–69).

Hacking and the law: legislative innovations and responses

2.6 The appearance of any supposedly new and pressing criminal threat typically instigates a process of social 'innovation' in which authorities and agents of social control take steps to curtail the perceived danger presented by the 'offending' individuals or groups (Cohen, 1972; Goode and Ben-Yehuda, 1994). The threat from hacking, be it real or imagined, has incited a range of legislative and criminal justice responses that have driven an ongoing 'crackdown' on activities of computer intrusion and manipulation. This domain of reaction and innovation will be considered below.

As Walker et al. (2000) point out, the expansion of Internet-related crimes has generated a range of legislative and legal responses, many of which seek to adapt existing laws to the novel environment of cyberspace. Particularly significant challenges are presented by the inherently transnational nature of Internet interactions. Consequently, legal innovations at the national level, while considered essential, have of necessity been complemented by both a burgeoning number of international agreements, as well as 'informal' regimes of governance and regulation implemented by a range of non-governmental actors (ibid.: 6, 19). Below we will focus on the more specific question of legal innovations in response to the perceived threat of hacking and computer intrusion.

It would appear that, in the 'early years' of computer crime, there was a tendency to rely upon existing legislation covering offences of trespass, theft and fraud to tackle hacking and related offences. However, a number of landmark cases proved that these innovative computer crimes could 'slip through the net' of existing legislation, resulting in failure to successfully prosecute offenders. Thus in 1988, for example, in the case of Gold and Schifreen, the UK House of Lords ruled that unauthorized access to a computer system did not constitute an offence under existing criminal law (Wasik, 2000: 274; Esen, 2002: 273). This apparent gap in the law led to the publication of a working paper on computer misuse by the Law Commission in 1988; Parliament, following the Commission's recommendations, subsequently introduced the Computer Misuse Act in 1990 to specifically cover offences such as hacking and computer viruses. Numerous countries have now established similar legal provisions to cover hacking and related offences. While there is not the space here to review even a significant portion of relevant provisions from around the world, we can briefly examine the legal measures instituted in the USA and the UK in order to establish a preliminary understanding of how such laws are framed, the kinds of penalties they provide for, as well as some of the criticisms that have been levelled at them.

The USA introduced one of the earliest national laws specifically oriented to computer crime in the form of the Computer Fraud and Abuse Act (CFAA) of 1984. This act made it a crime to 'knowingly access computers without authorization, obtain unauthorized information with intent to defraud, or "cause damage" to "protected computers"' (Biegel, 2003: 236). The law made provision for a range of punishments according to the particular offence, including a custodial sentence of up to five years for first-time offenders, up to ten years for repeat offenders, as well as significant fines. In response to technological innovations and new forms of computer crime, the Act was subsequently amended on numerous occasions (1986, 1989, 1990, 1994, and 1996), and there are continued calls to adjust its provisions further to close perceived 'loopholes' (ibid.: 236–9). Indeed, a number of particularly significant amendments to the CFAA were introduced by the US PATRIOT Act of 2001, in the wake of the September 11 attacks; these included the increase of maximum penalties from five to ten years for first offenders and from 10 to 20 years for repeat offenders (Milone, 2003: 85). In addition to this federal law, a number of individual US states have their own laws covering unauthorized access to computers (Lilley, 2002: 245–6).

The UK Computer Misuse Act also makes provisions covering unauthorized access and damage to computer systems. These provisions fall under three main sections. Section 1 makes it an offence to intentionally attempt to gain unauthorized access to a computer system, and makes such an offence punishable by up to six months imprisonment and/or a fine of up to £5000 (Wasik, 2000: 274–9). Section 2 covers unauthorized access 'with intent to commit or facilitate the commission of further offences', and is punishable by up to five years imprisonment and/or an unlimited fine (Furnell, 2002: 211). Section 3 covers the 'unauthorised modification of computer material', and so encompasses the distribution of viruses and other forms of malicious software, and is again punishable by up to five years imprisonment and/or an unlimited fine (ibid.).

Both the US and UK laws have, however, been criticized from a number of angles. Critics in the USA have complained that, in reality, the legal provisions are seldom invoked to their full extent, so that prosecution 'frequently translates into a slap on the wrist' and that 'few cybercriminals ever see the inside of a US jail' (Bequai, 1999: 17). This failure to bring 'the full force of the law' to bear on hackers is held to undermine any deterrent effect that the provisions might have, a problem further exacerbated by the relative scarcity of prosecutions brought to bear (attributed in part to the problems of identifying perpetrators, the lack of appropriate law enforcement expertise and resources, and the lack of appropriate technical knowledge on the part of judges and juries alike). Similarly, critics of the UK law have bemoaned its lack of effectiveness as a deterrent, given the infrequency of successful prosecution and the tendency toward 'lenient' sentences (Coleman, 2003: 132). The law has also been criticized for requiring too heavy a burden of proof, as prosecutors are required to prove intent on the part of the offender for the more serious offences under Sections 2 and 3 of the Act. It has also been criticized for being outdated, as it does not cover newer forms of crime such as denial of service attacks which do not require unauthorized access to a system to interfere with its operations, nor do they require modification of system's contents (ibid.). However, from the other side, some commentators have suggested that the scarcity of successful prosecutions has meant that in those cases where convictions *are* secured, there is a tendency to impose excessive and unwarranted penalties so as to 'make an example' of hackers, and that this excessiveness is fuelled by the tendency to grossly exaggerate the amount of damage that the perpetrator's activities have caused (Kovacich, 1999: 574; Furnell, 2002: 215). Thus, Furnell (2002: 214–5) notes that while hacker Kevin Mitnick was sentenced to five years' imprisonment for computer intrusion, the average term of imprisonment in the USA for manslaughter is only two years and ten months; this would suggest that the cases of high-profile hackers are liable to turn into 'show trials' resulting in sentences out of all proportion when compared with those for other, arguably more serious crimes.

Another serious challenge for legal provisions against hacking relates to the international rather than national context. While numerous countries have now established laws to tackle hacking, many as yet lack any such provisions; one survey of 52 countries found that 33 as yet had no special legal provisions for tackling cybercrime (McConnell International, 2000: 4). Even where countries have such legal measures in place, there is currently little in the way of harmonization or consistency across territories. For example, while US law allows for custodial sentences of up to 20 years, the laws of Greece and Ireland only allow for a maximum custodial sentence of three months (Lilley, 2002: 218, 223–4). These cross-national variations, it is suggested, can encourage what is referred to as 'regulatory arbitrage', with individuals and groups committing offences from those territories where they are assured of facing little or nothing in the way of criminal sanctions. The need to establish cross-national consistency in cybercrime laws has consequently stimulated the development of international treaties and agreements, such as the Council of Europe Convention on Cybercrime. The Convention was signed by 30 countries in November 2003 (including four non-European states that participated in the negotiations and drafting of the convention – the USA, Canada, Japan and South Africa), and came into force in 2004. The Convention aims to

HACKERS, CRACKERS AND VIRAL CODERS

harmonize national laws on cybercrime, to establish criminal laws and sanctions, and to establish a regime for international cooperation (Coleman, 2003: 132). While the process of implementation is currently in the very early stages of what will likely be a long-drawn-out process, the Convention establishes an international framework for the legal and criminal justice response to hacking and other forms of cybercriminal activity.

Summary

2.7 In the public mind, cybercrime is perhaps associated most clearly with computer hacking. This chapter explored how images of hackers and hacking have been constructed in popular media, and how this has shaped legal and criminal justice responses. It was suggested that the concern over hackers and hacking can be seen as part of wider social tensions and anxieties about technological change and its threat to familiar ways of life. These representations are contested by hackers themselves, who often give a range of justifications for their activities, and claim hacking is far from the 'mindless vandalism' with which it is often associated. Debates over hacking thus exemplify what criminologists and sociologists dub the 'labelling process' and the 'social construction of deviance'. A wide range of hacking activities are apparent on the Internet today, ranging from computer intrusion and the distribution of viruses, to website defacement and denial of service. Such activities appear to be on the increase, facilitated by the availability of numerous tools that enable even the unskilled novice to engage in hacking. Participation in such activities appears to follow a distinctive social profile – the overwhelming majority of hackers are young and male. There are a number of explanations that can be suggested for this pattern, relating to masculine ideologies, juvenile delinquency, and subcultural association.

Study questions

- *how do representations of hackers in movies, books and press reports construct hacking as a deviant and dangerous activity?*
- *how do these representations connect with wider social anxieities about technology?*
- *what kinds of harm are caused by hacking activities?*
- *why do so many young males find hacking so appealing?*
- *what kinds of measures are being put in place to counter the growth of hacking?*

Further reading

The best sociological study of hacking is Paul Taylor's *Hackers: Crime in the Digital Sublime* (1999). Other more popular, but nevertheless interesting reads include Bruce Sterling's *The Hacker Crackdown: Law and Disorder on the Electronic Frontier* (1994) and Dan Verton's *The Hacker Diaries: Confessions of Teenage Hackers* (2002). A user-friendly introduction to the more technical aspects of hacking is provided by Steven Furnell's *Cybercrime: Vandalizing the Information Society* (2002), and Dorothy Denning's *Information Warfare and Security* (1999). A rare and powerful defence of hackers from within the computer security industry is Kovacich's article 'Hackers: Freedom Fighters of the 21st Century' (1999). For more on youth and hacking see Bowker's 'Juveniles and Computers: Should We Be Concerned?' (1999), as well as Verton (above). For anyone interested in how images of hackers and hacking are constructed in popular culture, Hollywood movies such as *War Games, Hackers, AntiTrust* and *The Core* are essential viewing, and William Gibson's pioneering novel *Neuromancer* is an indispensable read.

THREE

Political Hacking

From hacktivism to cyberterrorism

Overview

Chapter 3 examines the following issues:

- *the development of hacking as a form of political resistance and protest;*
- *the emerging debate about terrorist uses of hacking;*
- *the ways in which hacking might enhance terrorists' abilities to achieve their goals;*
- *the ways in which cyberterrorism is being constructed as part of the 'war on terror' in the wake of September 11 2001;*
- *other ways, apart from hacking, in which the Internet may prove useful to terrorist organizations.*

---

key terms

Anti-globalization movement	Hacktivism	War on Terror
Cyberterrorism	Terrorism	

Introduction

3.1 The previous chapter introduced a range of cybercriminal activities associated with computer intrusion and manipulation, which are generally identified under the label of 'hacking'. In this chapter we will critically explore claims that hacking is evolving in a new and distinctively *political* direction, taking the form of activities variously described under labels such as 'hacktivism' and 'cyberterrorism'. It was noted in the previous chapter that the early development of hacking was seemingly characterized by a distinctive ethos or ethic, and that this outlook might be seen to have contained a political element. In particular, the ethic stressed a 'democratic' vision of free and unfettered access to new technology, and a corresponding distrust of corporate and governmental domination or control of computing resources. However, as Paul Taylor (2004a) notes, this political potential remained largely unrealized, for two main reasons. First, the hacker ethic tended to focus upon access to technology itself as a primary goal, rather than seeing it as a tool or stepping stone for realizing other social and political aims and as such, the political dimension of hacking culture remained limited. Second, the counter-cultural aspirations of pioneering hackers were largely incorporated by corporate capitalism, turning hackers increasingly into consumers of computing resources on the one hand, and appropriating their skills and drive for commercial purposes on the other (ibid.: 488–9). However, since the mid-1990s, there has been a surge of political activity that mobilizes the tools and techniques developed by hackers and crackers. First of all, this period has seen the development of what is commonly known as 'hacktivism', the mobilization of hacking in the service of political activism and protest. Second, since the September 11 attacks in the United States, there has emerged an increasing political and public focus on the threat posed by 'cyberterrorism', the exploitation of electronic vulnerabilities by terrorist groups in pursuit of their political aims. It is this range of explicitly politicized uses of hacking that will provide the focus for discussion in the present chapter. However, it should be noted from the outset that the boundaries between these forms of political activity remain fluid and deeply contested, so that hacktivists often find themselves positioned as 'information terrorists' (ibid.: 487). Equally, the nature and extent of any cyberterrorist threat remain obscured behind an often overly dramatic rhetoric that may hinder rather than help us in developing a sound assessment of the nature, scope and scale of the problem. Indeed, we shall see that the use of labels such as 'terrorist' to characterize certain actors is best viewed as itself a profoundly political activity, bound up with wider social tensions and conflicts.

Hacktivism and the politics of resistance in a globalized world

3.2 Considerable attention has been devoted in the past decade to the Internet's potential for transforming political life. In Western, liberal-democratic countries, the expansion of the online environment has been grasped as a means for revitalizing a political culture increasingly characterized by public cynicism and disengagement. Governments have seized the Internet as a tool for political communication: the state can mobilize it to inform citizens, while citizens can be drawn into a consultative process whereby they voice their opinions, needs and concerns through mechanisms of online consultation (Castells, 2002: 137–64). More pragmatically, political parties and other political organizations (such as pressure groups) have used the Internet for purposes of campaigning and recruitment. The Internet has also been seen as a means for stimulating citizen participation and involvement in civic life at the local level (Carter, 1997: 136–7), and for revitalizing community cohesion seemingly undermined by industrialization, urbanization and the individualization processes (Evans, 2004). However, the area in which perhaps the greatest impact has been seen is the mobilization of the Internet by social and political resistance movements of various kinds; in both the West and elsewhere, since the mid-1990s there has been an upsurge in online activism. This activism has moved in step with a growing awareness of the impacts of globalization (Taylor, 2004a: 486), the rise in Western military interventionism (for example, in Kosovo and the two Gulf Wars), and ongoing pro-democracy struggles around the world.

The upsurge in Internet activism has been understood in a variety of political and ideological terms, depending upon the viewpoint of the commentators. For the advocates of Western political values, it is welcomed as a resource for 'protecting human rights and spreading democratic values' (Milone, 2003: 75). For others, it is a tool of resistance to Western capitalist domination and US-led 'neo-imperialism'. Whatever the stance taken on such activism, some key features can nevertheless be identified. Much online political activism has taken the form of non-violent civil disobedience and protest, modelled on the traditions of past social movements (such as the labour movement, the civil rights movement, women's liberation, gay liberation and radical environmentalism). A substantial proportion of such engagements have mobilized the tools and techniques developed by hackers, appropriating them for explicitly political purposes. Such activities have attracted the label of 'hacktivism' a combination of 'hacking' and 'activism'. We can see that such interventions take a number of distinct forms:

- *Virtual sit-ins and blockades.* Virtual sit-ins can be seen as the cyber-equivalents of the traditional protest method by which a particular site, associated with opposing or oppressive political interests, is physically occupied by activists. History is replete with such instances, including: suffragettes chaining themselves to the railings outside the British Parliament in support of the women's vote; the famous 'freedom rides' of the US civil rights movement, where Black protesters would occupy the 'whites only' seating at the front of buses; and the student occupations of university campuses during the anti-war movement of the 1960s. The virtual counterparts of these protests take the form of a coordinated and simultaneous request to access a particular website. The deluge of such requests from thousands of activists overloads web servers, making the site unavailable. One of the most memorable uses of this technique occurred in 1998, when the so-called Electronic Disturbance Theatre (EDT) organized a sit-in of Mexican government websites in support of the Zapatista land-rights movement, whose participants were being forcibly and violently suppressed by the Mexican police and military. The sit-in garnered worldwide publicity, raising awareness of the Zapatista cause, and adding pressure upon the Mexican authorities to end the suppression. These denial of service attacks were notable for using the Flood Net hacking software (discussed in Chapter 2.4) in order to overload the web servers (Taylor, 2004b: 118). Similar attacks were used in 1995 by the 'Strano Network', an anti-nuclear group that targeted French Government websites (Taylor, 2004a: 488).
- *Email bombs.* The email bomb is a tool used to overload email systems by sending mass mailings, which has the effect of overwhelming the system, thereby blocking legitimate traffic. There are numerous instances in which this simple technique has been used successfully by political activists to disrupt the communications capacity

48

of target organizations and governments. In 1998, a group called themselves the 'Internet Black Tigers' (associating themselves with the Tamil Tigers, the ethnic guerrilla-cum-liberation movement in Sri Lanka) swamped Sri Lankan embassies with 800 emails every day over a period of weeks. In the same year, Spanish hacktivists tied up the email systems of the Institute for Global Communications (IGC), in protest over the IGC's hosting websites for the *Euskal Herria Journal*, a publication supporting Basque independence from Spain. Similarly, during the NATO military intervention in Kosovo in 1999, activists objecting to Western involvement in the war email-bombed NATO websites (Denning, 2000a: 5).

- *Website defacements.* Hacktivists have also had recourse to defacing and altering websites as a form of protest. This form of cyber-attack (already discussed in Chapter 2.3) is not always politically motivated by any means; it is estimated that some 70 per cent of all defacements are 'pranks', in which the choice of target is indiscriminate (Woo et al., 2004). However, the remaining 30 per cent can be seen as attacks targeting specific sites in order to make a political, social or moral point. Such web hacks appear to be often triggered by offline conflicts, such as war or a rise in political tensions between nations. Thus, for example, we see instances of tit-for-tat defacements as part of the Israel–Palestine conflict, as well as between hacktivists in Japan and Korea, China and America, and India and Pakistan (ibid.: 64). Other defacements are undertaken in protest against governments' handling of particular issues, such as human rights. Figure 3.1 illustrates a typical hack of this kind, in which US-based hacktivists defaced a Chinese government human rights website, in protest both against that country's record of ongoing human rights abuses, and against the US government's 'hypocrisy' in granting China favoured trading status.
- *Viruses and worms.* Viruses, worms and other forms of malicious software (discussed in Chapter 2.3) are of limited use to hacktivists, since they tend to be indiscriminate by nature, spreading across the web in an uncontrollable manner. For hacktivists aiming to target specific organizations, agencies and states, the inability to restrict the impact of such software means that it is not a widely favoured tool of choice. However, there have been a number of notable instances in which hacktivists have used viruses and worms. The earliest such attack was staged by anti-nuclear activists against NASA (the US National Aeronautics and Space Administration) in 1989; NASA computers were targeted with the so-called 'WANK' worm (standing for Worms Against Nuclear Killers). During the first Gulf War, Israeli hackers launched virus attacks at Iraqi government systems in an effort to disrupt their communications capacity during the US-led invasion.

The use of such hacking techniques by activists offers a number of advantages over more traditional forms of terrestrial protest. They enable participants who may be dispersed across cities, nations and countries to converge in the virtual environment in potentially large numbers to make themselves felt. They also offer protesters a considerable degree of protection from suppression by police and security forces, unlike terrestrial protesters whose access to physical sites and locations may be blocked, or who may be forcibly and

BOYCOTT CHINA

I simply can not believe the total bullshit propaganda on this web site. Chinas people have no rights at all, never mind Human RIghts. I really can't believe our government deals with them. They censor, murder, torture, maim, and do everything we take for granite left the earth with the middle ages.

The Chinese communist government, is made out a gang of 100+ year old thugs and bullies who hide in seclusion. This pitiful effort of trying to change the hearts and minds of of the world is a joke!

How can the United States trade millions and millions of dollars with them and give them most favored trade status when they know what is happening? Two wrongs do not lead to a right, no matter what twisted world you live in.

Get informed!

Amnesty International – China
Human Rights in China
The Murder of an Innocent Man
A Brave Man Stands Alone

Figure 3.1 A defaced website

violently removed through use of crowd dispersal means such as water cannon and C.S. gas. However, it must be noted that by no means all observers view the rise of hacktivism as a benign phenomenon or as a legitimate development of free speech and political participation. Many, especially those in law enforcement and state circles, make little distinction between political and non-political uses of hacking, and view all such activities as instances of vandalism and criminal damage. Like the hacks undertaken by their non-politicized counterparts, hacktivist incursions on the web fall foul of increasingly stringent computer crime laws, and as such are punishable by substantial financial penalties and/or lengthy custodial sentences. Indeed, as we shall see below, the climate of fear generated around 'terrorism' is recent years has led hacktivism to be labelled by many as a form of 'information terrorism'.

The spectre of cyberterrorism

3.3 'Cyberterrorism', as the term suggests, basically connotes a convergence between terrorism and cyberspace. It is claimed that the growth and increasing social, political and economic dependence upon the Internet affords terrorist organizations a new arena in which to pursue their goals by staging attacks or threats against computer networks and information systems (Milone, 2003: 75). The definition of what counts as 'terrorism' is, of course deeply contested – the term is slippery in the extreme (Embar-Seddon, 2002: 1034; Grabosky, 2003: 1), and the label can be seen in part as a *rhetorical* device by which particular political projects are delegitimated by those who oppose them (Furedi, 2005). Conventional understandings of terrorism nevertheless take it to denote a distinct form of criminal action, characterized by the marriage of *violence* and *politics* (Crozier, 1974). Schmid (1993: 8) understands terrorism as the use of 'repeated violent action' for achieving particular ends; such violence, or the threat of its use, is mobilized by the terrorist to incite anxiety and thereby manipulate, intimidate or coerce its targets (a population, a government) into acceding to the terrorist's political demands. A further salient feature of the conventional understanding of terrorism is its association with non-state and sub-state actors (which may or may not be 'state sponsored' or supported). On this basis, 'cyberterrorism' has been defined as: 'the execution of a surprise attack by a subnational foreign terrorist group or individuals with a domestic political agenda using computer technology and the Internet to cripple or disable a nation's electronic and physical infrastructures' (Verton, 2003: xx).

In a similar vein, Denning (2000a: 1) takes the term to denote:

> unlawful attacks and threats of attack against computers, networks, and the information stored therein when done to intimidate or coerce a government or its people in furtherance of political or social objectives. Further, to qualify as cyberterrorism, an attack should result in violence against persons or property, or at least cause enough harm to generate fear. Attacks that lead to death or bodily injury, explosions, or severe economic loss would be examples. Serious attacks against critical infrastructures could be acts of cyberterrorism, depending on their impact. Attacks that disrupt nonessential services or that are mainly a costly nuisance would not.

This notion of cyberterrorism has, in recent years, been enshrined in law. For example, the UK Terrorism Act of 2000 makes provision for those who 'seriously interfere with or seriously disrupt an electronic system'. In the wake of the September 11 2001 attacks in New York and Washington, the USA has taken the lead in making legal provision to protect the nation's computer systems against 'terrorist' attack. The USA PATRIOT Act (an acronym for Uniting and Strengthening America by Providing Appropriate Tools Required to Intercept and Obstruct Terrorism) was passed into law on 26 October 2001, barely six weeks after the attacks on the Twin Towers and the Pentagon. The Act considerably strengthens penalties under the Computer Fraud and Abuse Act of 1984 (discussed in Chapter 2.6), including provision for the life imprisonment of convicted 'cyberterrorists' (Milone, 2003: 79; Hamm, 2004: 288–9); the Act also eases restrictions on electronic surveillance by the state and law enforcement agencies (Milone, 2003: 79). Thus, we can see that, as part of the growing political and ideological momentum behind the so-called 'War on Terror', the notion of terrorist attacks using the Internet have come increasingly to the fore of the political agenda.

The perceived threat from cyberterrorism needs to be understood not only in the political context of the post-September 11 world, but also in terms of the concept of 'critical infrastructure' which has been developed in recent decades by those working in the quasi-military field of 'resilience studies'. Critical infrastructure (CI) is defined as: 'an infrastructure or asset the incapacitation or destruction of which would have a debilitating impact on the national security or economic or social welfare of a nation' (Dunn and Wigert, 2004: 18). CI includes a range of material systems such as those used to provide communications (mail, telephones), energy (oil, electricity, gas), water, food (production, import, processing, distribution and sale), emergency services (police, ambulance, fire, rescue) and health care provision (Milone, 2003: 76). CI also includes material assets whose *symbolic* content or inherent meaning are deemed important to national cohesion and welfare, for example, the Statue of Liberty or the Twin Towers. Attacks on symbolically significant targets can be seen to yield valuable publicity, which terrorist organizations need if they are to succeed in mobilizing fear to secure their aims (Gerrits, 1992: 450–8; Paletz and Vinson, 1992: 2). As the threat of terrorist attack has been seemingly amplified, the question of protecting these key social systems has commanded greater attention. 1996 saw the establishment of the Presidential Commission on Critical Infrastructure Protection (PCCIP) under the Clinton administration, and in the wake of September 11 the Office of Homeland Security was established in 2001, which includes the National Infrastructure Advisory Council (NIAC) and the President's Critical Infrastructure Protection Board (CIPB) (Dunn and Wigert, 2004: 201–3). The UK established the National Infrastructure Security Coordination Centre (NISCC) in 1999 (ibid.: 189–90). These and a plethora of other state agencies are charged with formulating strategies to protect critical infrastructure against terrorist attack, with coordinating activities between state agencies and with non-state actors (e.g. energy suppliers, water authorities, etc.), with establishing systems for early warning against threats of terrorist attack against the CI, and so on. The sums being invested in CI protection are vast by any standard, for example, President Bush signed a $37.4 billion appropriations bill for Homeland Security in 2004 (ibid.: 201).

To a significant degree, the debate about terrorist threats to critical infrastructure have been concerned with what is termed the critical *information* infrastructure (CII). CII is taken to comprise 'the information and telecommunications sector, and includes components such as telecommunications, computers/ software, the Internet, satellites, fibre-optics, etc. The term is also used for the totality of interconnected computers and networks and their critical information flows' (ibid.: 20). This 'totality of interconnected computers and networks' is seen as an essential element of critical infrastructures for two main reasons. First, the growth of the Internet and allied systems plays an increasingly central role in the economic, political and social lives of Western industrialized nations. For example, electronic communications networks are used increasingly for commercial transactions (e-commerce), and banking and finance (e-banking, financial transfers, stock markets); consequently, a serious attack on these networks would 'have a debilitating impact on the ... economic ... welfare of a nation'. Second, and perhaps even more seriously, electronic information networks are increasingly integrated with conventional critical infrastructures, for example, they are now used to control and coordinate essential services such as power, water, air traffic, emergency services, national defence, and so on. This dependence upon networked technologies, while enabling greater speed and efficiency, simultaneously renders these essential services vulnerable; hijacking these information systems via Internet connections could enable key infrastructures to be manipulated and controlled; disruption of the information infrastructure (for example, via viruses, worms, logic bombs, or denial of service attacks) would seriously undermine critical infrastructural operations. Consequently, common scenarios in cyber-terror threat assessments include:

- loss of power via attacks on systems that control power grids (Denning, 2000a: 1);
- disruption of financial transactions, bringing economic systems to a halt (Denning, 2000a: 1; Gordon and Ford, 2003: 7);
- crippling transport systems such as air and rail by corrupting or crashing the computers used to control them (Verton, 2003: 8);
- theft of top-secret information relating to defence and national security by hacking government computers.

Such threat assessments have stimulated extensive investment in programs to secure information infrastructures against cyber-attack, especially in the wake of the September 11 attacks. In 1999, the Clinton administration committed $1.46 billion to combat the threat of cyberterrorism (Hamblen, 1999; Miyawaki, 1999). In 2000, they issued the first comprehensive plan for protecting the US critical information infrastructure, *Defending America's Cyberspace: National Plan for Information Systems Protection*. In the wake of September 11, the Bush administration earmarked a further $839.3 million for cybersecurity as part of the Homeland Security appropriations bill (Dunn and Wigert, 2004: 201). Similarly, other nations have substantially increased the resources allocated to protecting information infrastructures after the September 11 attacks: for example, Australia's CIIP budget was set at $ 2 million in May 2001, but tripled the following year to $6 million, and was allocated a total of $24.9 million over four years (ibid.: 43).

Why *cyber*terror? Terrorist advantages of utilizing Internet attacks

3.4 Assessments by official and academic commentators that cyberterrorism presents a substantial and growing threat are based upon a number of factors. The transition from terrestrial to virtual attacks is deemed to offer a number of advantages to terrorist groups:

- *The Internet, by its nature, enables 'action at a distance'.* Terrorists no longer need to gain physical access to a particular location, as they can access electronic systems from anywhere in the world (Gordon and Ford, 2003: 6). This is held to be of particular importance in the wake of September 11, as many countries have instituted increasingly rigorous border and travel controls so as to prevent terrorists from entering national territories and/or bringing weapons material (such as explosives) across borders. For example, the USA now routinely records fingerprint IDs and other personal details of foreign nationals entering the USA (Adey, 2004: 508). The use of the Internet for staging terrorist attacks bypasses such security measures, along with the risks of apprehension at airports, ports and border checkpoints. Moreover, by staging cyber-attacks from within the borders of so-called 'rogue states' (which may well endorse or directly support the terrorist actions), it is possible to exploit a 'safe haven' lying outside the reach of security and criminal justice agencies in the target nations.
- *The Internet turns actors with relatively small numbers and limited financial and material resources into what have been called 'empowered small agents'.* The empowerment reaped by actors is a result of the fact that the Internet can function as a so-called 'force multiplier'. A force multiplier is something that can 'increase the striking potential of a unit without increasing its personnel' (White, 1991: 18). One instance of such force multiplication is the impact of computer viruses – small pieces of malicious code can spread rapidly across the global network of the web, reproducing exponentially and corrupting systems as they goes. Thus, for example, the 'MyDoom' virus (discussed in Chapter 2.3) managed to cause an estimated $20 billion of damage in just 15 days. Moreover, the potential effects of cyber-attacks are further multiplied due to the high levels of *interdependence* between ostensibly separate technological systems; as Rasch (2003: vii) puts it: 'Without electricity, there is no telephone service; without either there is no usable Internet.' Thus, disabling one element of this infrastructure can yield a 'cascade effect' that spreads through other systems with which it is inter-connected and co-dependent. The 'cost–benefit' ratio of using electronic disruption (small investment, massive damage) can make it a desirable weapon of choice for those intent on causing mayhem and spreading fear. Indeed, the global nature of the Internet means that

cyber-attacks are likely to be highly visible and impact upon a large number of users, thereby assuring a significant impact in terms of publicizing the attack (Embar-Seddon, 2002: 1038).

- *Anonymity.* It has already been noted that one of the greatest challenges presented by cybercrime to law enforcement is the extent to which the Internet environment affords perpetrators a degree of anonymity or disguise (Flemming and Stohl, 2000: 38, 46). Such anonymity can be achieved by staging cyber-attacks through use of 'proxies', where activities are routed through a range of intermediate systems and servers, making it difficult to trace the point of origin of the attack. It can also be achieved through what is know as 'identity theft', where the perpetrator uses an identity stolen from an innocent third party (such as an account access password) in order to stage an attack in his/her name (identity theft is discussed further in Chapter 5.4.1).

- *Lack of regulation.* One of the greatest problems in securing the Internet against potential cyber-attack is the absence of any centralized and coordinated regulation of the virtual environment. The Internet has evolved as an open, decentred network, with 'nodes' distributed worldwide across legislative and territorial boundaries. While this is considered one of its great strengths, it also constitutes one of its greatest weaknesses, insofar as there will inevitably be innumerable weak points at which the security of the network can be compromised. Moreover, while responsibility for national security falls to the state and its agencies, the vast bulk of the world's critical information infrastructure is held in private hands (more than 85 per cent of the US critical information infrastructure is estimated to be privately owned and operated (Verton, 2003: xxiii)); this renders it well-nigh impossible for any government to effect centralized control (Grabosky, 2003: 3).

Rhetorics and myths of cyberterrorism

3.5 The foregoing discussion paints a vivid picture of a technologically dependent world which is ever more vulnerable to terrorist groups who might cause massive economic and social damage should they choose to exploit the opportunities readily available. However, perhaps even more so than any other form of cybercrime, Internet terrorism is bound up with, and often obscured by, a great deal of rhetorical embellishment and myth-making. It has been suggested by more sceptical commentators that there is little empirical evidence to warrant the level of concern currently being generated over cyber-terrorism, nor to justify the sweeping enhancement of state powers that are being instituted in order to respond to the supposed threat. Professor Dorothy Denning (recognized as a leading world authority on Internet security) states that 'there are few if any computer network attacks that meet the criteria for cyberterrorism', and that there 'is little concrete evidence of terrorists preparing to use the Internet as a venue for inflicting grave harm' (Denning, 2000b: 23–4). Donoghue (2004) goes further and claims that 'there has never been a recorded act of cyberterrorism pre- or post September 11th' (see also Buxbaum, 2002: 1). There are numerous cases *cited* as examples of 'cyberterror' (see, for example, Lawson, 2002; Embar-Seddon, 2003; Verton, 2003). However, upon closer examination, such incidents turn out to be cases of either 'hacktivism', or of opportunistic disruption supported by no discernible political, social or other agenda. Establishing whether or not cyber-attacks by terrorist organizations are in fact occurring is becoming more, not less, difficult in a climate of growing state secrecy. Thus in October of 2001, the Bush administration supported a bipartisan Congressional proposal to limit government disclosures about successful cyber-attacks (Milone, 2003: 90, 101).

We have already identified those factors (such as action-at-a-distance, anonymity, etc.) that lead many government, computer security and media commentators to perceive the Internet as a desirable target for terrorists. However, we can conversely see that there are numerous reasons why terrorist groups might be *disinclined* to turn their hands to virtual engagements. First, many of those systems which regulate critical infrastructure (power, air traffic control, stock markets, etc.) are largely isolated from the public Internet on private networks, so access is not nearly as straightforward as might be supposed. While the prospect of al-Qaeda hackers misdirecting aircraft toward midair collisions might make spectacular media copy and mobilize public concern with national security issues, the likelihood of such an action is slim, precisely because air traffic control systems operate in isolation from the Internet. Second, it has been suggested that the very *virtuality* and immateriality of the Internet make it an unsuitable target for those whose acts are intended to generate *terror*. As Denning (2000a: 9) notes, 'unless people are injured, there is ... less drama and emotional appeal', and images of the visible consequences of bomb blasts and shootings are inevitably more visceral in their impact than more abstract reports of damaged data and monetary losses. Consequently, she concludes that 'for now, the truck bomb poses a much greater threat than the logic bomb' (ibid.: 9; see also discussion in Green, 2001).

Given that there is at present little evidence to support claims of an imminent cyberterrorist threat, we must ask why so much political energy, institutional innovation and financial resources are being expended to counter the perceived threat. One possible explanation is that current efforts to institute counter-measures for cyberterrorist attacks are *anticipatory* in character. That is to say, while there is deemed to be little likelihood of an immediate attack of this kind against the critical infrastructure, the possibility of such incidents manifesting in the future cannot be excluded; therefore, a responsible government is duty-bound to take such preventative measures as are possible. This would seem to chime with the position of the UK government, whose threat assessment about cyberterrorist attacks appears considerably more realistic than that of their US counterparts. David Blunkett, the former British Home

Secretary, stated in 2002 that 'The risk is assessed to be low, but growing. It could change rapidly at any time and our response will need to adjust to remain proportionate' (UK Parliament, 2002).

However, a more critical perspective sees the current discourse on cyber-terrorism as fundamentally disproportionate; the scale of the response cannot be explained in a 'realist' manner by looking to the actual, or potential future, level of threat. Rather, the whole treatment of cyberterrorism must be under-stood as a *social construction*. Furedi (2005) notes that the category of 'terror-ism' as a distinct and morally reprehensible form of political violence has been understood by some scholars as a means of delegitimating particular political struggles and thereby legitimating the authority of the state and its monopoly over the use of political violence (see also Oliverio, 1998). The same can be claimed for the current discussion of cyberterrorism. On this view, character-izing those resisting the hegemony or control of the state as 'cyberterrorists' serves to undermine any popular support that such oppositional forces might enjoy, and to justify further criminalization and social control of 'suspect' popu-lations. It is in this context that Vegh (2002: 1) discerns a growing pressure on 'anti-hegemonic forms of Internet use' in the wake of September 11; the lan-guage of cyberterror enables authorities to re-label hackers and hacktivists as 'information terrorists', and to win popular and political support for otherwise controversial controls over Internet use, such as bans on the use of encryption and steganography technologies, and the monitoring of electronic communi-cations. In response to the measures instituted by the Bush administration in the US, Vegh (2002: 10) writes:

> In the name of national security, the government now openly supports the control and containment of these liberating technologies, even at the price of curtailing the consti-tutional civil liberties it had so proudly protected. It is now claimed, through news media reports, that terrorists ... plan to carry out cyberattacks ... that will cripple the U.S. econ-omy. All these technologies ... are now fully vilified in the war against terror'.

However, it must be noted that 'government' is not a homogeneous entity, but an array of institutions, each of which may well have its own agenda and its own self-interest to pursue. Thus, we may understand the development of the discourse on cyberterrorism as a form of 'moral entrepreneurship' (Becker, 1963), an attempt to generate public and political concern via the media so as to secure sectional interests. It is in this vein that McCullagh (2001) notes how: 'Some administration critics think the FBI and CIA are using potential terrorist attacks an attempt to justify expensive new proposals such as the National Homeland Security Agency.' If true, then it would certainly not be the first instance in which law enforcement agencies have constructed a 'moral panic' in order to secure greater powers and to capture greater resources (see, for example, Hunt, 1987). Moreover, other actors, such as those in the computer security industry, may also have a vested interest in promulgating the idea of an urgent and imminent cyberterrorist threat. The commercial sector in the provision of computer security is now worth an estimated $27 billion per annum (Grow, 2004), and state and private sector provisions to tackle cyberterrorism will inevitably result in a significant expansion of commercial opportunities for such businesses.

Alternative conjunctions between terrorism and the Internet

3.6 The foregoing discussion has suggested that the threat of cyberterrorist attack on critical infrastructures is more a case of strategically useful fancy than hard fact. However, this does not necessarily mean that there are no significant convergences between terrorist activities and the Internet. In contrast to the computer-focused crimes discussed thus far, it has been argued that the Internet plays a significant and growing role in *computer-assisted* terrorist offences. In other words, terrorist groups make use of the Internet in support of their conventional, terrestrially based activities. Such uses of the Internet can be seen to fall into a number of distinct types:

- *Communication and coordination.* The Internet may be used as an efficient means of intra-organizational communication and coordination of terrorist activities, through use of technologies such as email and bulletin boards (Shelley, 2003: 305; see also Conway, 2002). Here, terrorist groups (like other organizations, be they political, commercial or criminal) use the Internet to help secure their goals (Fleming and Stohl, 2000: 38). Use of online tools offers a number of advantages over conventional communications: they enable ease of communication on a transnational basis; they afford greater anonymity; and they afford security. The last of these points is considered particularly important, given the ready availability of so-called 'strong encryption' software (such as the free PGP or 'Pretty Good Privacy' developed by an American programmer, Phil Zimmermann). Encryption (derived from the term *cryptography*, meaning 'hidden writing') is a technique which enables communications to be encoded prior to transmission, so that they are unreadable if intercepted; only the intended recipient has a 'key' which enables the message to be decoded and restored to its original legible form. Encryption technologies are now widely used in legitimate Internet exchanges, permitting the secure transmission of sensitive data such as financial information and systems access passwords. This same technology is allegedly used by terrorists and other organized criminal groups to protect their communications from identification and interception by security and law enforcement agencies. There are a number of documented instances of terrorist groups using encryption technologies. For example, the Aum Shinri Kyo cult (which staged the Sarin nerve gas attacks in Tokyo in 1995) stored their records on computer in encrypted form; Ramsay Yousef, who participated in the 1993 bombing of the World Trade Center, was later discovered to have used a laptop with encrypted files containing plans for further bombings (Denning and Baugh, 1997: 1–2). Another variant on encryption is the use of *steganography* (from the Greek meaning 'compartmentalized writing'). Steganography works by hiding data within the digital code used to construct images; unless one knows where to look, the hidden data will be virtually undetectable. Kelley (2001) claims that groups such as al Qaeda are using steganographic techniques to hide messages within images (including hard-core pornography) posted or transmitted via the Internet. However, claims about such uses of steganography have proved controversial, with one group of US research scientists claiming that a comprehensive study of web images 'found no evidence of steganography on the Net' (Vegh, 2002: 13).

- *Propaganda, publicity and recruitment.* As already noted, publicity (be it about a group's attacks, ideology, aims or demands) is an essential component of terrorism. Terrorist groups have traditionally been dependent upon established news media (newspapers, radio, television) for dissemination of their messages (note, for example, al Qaeda's use of the Arab satellite news channel Al Jazira to broadcast warnings, demands, and statements from Osama Bin-Laden). However, this arrangement creates, from the terrorists' point of view, an unwelcome dependence upon actors over whom they may have no control, and who may be actively hostile to the group's agenda. The Internet offers an inexpensive means to address a worldwide audience, bypassing the dependence on intermediary news organizations. Numerous terrorist organizations now maintain their own websites, including: Hamas and Hezbollah in the Middle East; ETA (Basque separatists) and the IRA in Europe; the Shining Path (Peru) and FARC (Colombia) in Latin America; Aum Shinri Kyo (Japan), al Qaeda, the Tamil Tigers (Sri Lanka), and the Japanese Red Army in Asia (Weimann, 2004: 3–4). Such sites typically provide:

> a history of the organization and its activities, a detailed review of its social and political background, accounts of its notable exploits, biographies of its leaders, founders, and heroes, information on its political and ideological aims, fierce criticism of its enemies, and up-to-date news ... Hezbollah and Hamas, whose sites feature updated statistical reports of their actions ('daily operations') and tallies of both 'dead martyrs' and 'Israeli enemies' and 'collaborators' killed.
>
> (ibid.: 4)

As well a targeting international public opinion and enemy publics, such sites can be used to reach potential supporters and recruits. Recruiters may also use interactive web technologies such as chat rooms and bulletin boards in search of sympathetic individuals who may prove potential future members and supporters (ibid.: 8).

- *Information gathering.* The billions of pages of the Internet constitutes a massive repository of potentially useful information for terrorist groups. Large amounts of surprisingly sensitive information is routinely made available on the Internet by governments, public bodies and businesses (especially in countries which have freedom of information provisions in place intended to increase government transparency and hence accountability). Systematic exploration of the Internet (known as 'data mining') can enable groups to gather information on potentially exploitable targets, their location, and so on (such techniques are routinely used *by* law enforcement in their intelligence-gathering on terrorist groups and organized crime groups). Hacking techniques can also be used to access confidential information. For example, Denning (2000a: 6) reports that the IRA hired hackers to obtain personal details about law enforcement and security operatives in order to formulate plans for an assassination programme. Moreover, the Internet can be seen as a freely accessible library of technical information on methods useful for perpetrating terrorist attacks. Documents readily available for download include *The Anarchist's Cookbook* and *The Terrorist's Handbook* which include instructions for making explosives from household items such as bleach; the *Sabotage Handbook*, which offers instructions on planning assassinations and anti-surveillance methods; and the *Mujahedeen Poisons Handbook*, with detailed information on manufacturing homemade poisons and poison gases (Weimann, 2004: 9).

- *Fund-raising and financing.* The Internet provides a valuable tool for terrorist fund-raising. Websites are used, for example, to post details of bank accounts via which sympathizers can make payments to organizations. The web also provides a useful means for soliciting donations. Internet user demographics are used to identify potential supporters who can then by approached via email. Solicitations are typically made via a front organization (such as a charity) that can then be used to channel finance to the terrorist organization (Weimann, 2004: 6–7). More generally, the expansion of Internet banking makes it more difficult for authorities to detect suspicious transactions (Fitzgerald, 2003: 21), and its transnational nature enables prohibited organizations to exploit international inconsistencies and gaps in the legal regulation of finance (Shelley, 2003: 304). Finally, a range of cybercriminal activities can be mobilized in order to raise direct finance for groups' activities, for example, online copyright theft and 'piracy' (discussed in Chapter 4) and Internet frauds (discussed in Chapter 5) can furnish valuable avenues for high-profit and low-risk acquisition of monetary resources. Recent studies have presented evidence for such connections between terrorist organizations, organized crime groups, and media 'piracy' (TraCCC, 2001; AACP, 2002).

All the above intersections suggest a clear convergence between terrorism and the Internet. This should not be surprising, since terrorists (just like other social actors and organizations) are liable to adopt new technologies where they offer strategic advantages and efficiencies in the pursuit of their goals. What renders the use of the Internet in this way particularly challenging are the difficulties in monitoring and regulating its illicit use.

3.7 This chapter has explored the convergence between politics and the Internet. The first part examined the ways in which various forms of political activism and protest have appeared online, and the ways in which they have mobilized techniques originally developed by hackers. This 'hacktivism' offers a number of advantages over traditional terrestrial protest activism, including the Internet's ability to bring together spatially separated individuals, anonymity, and protection from both state and private security agents who might otherwise be able to disrupt protests. The second part of the chapter focused upon the issue of cyberterrorism, something which has acquired an intensified political and media profile in the wake of the September 11 attacks. It was noted how our increasing dependence on networks of information and communication technology apparently renders social, political and economic systems vulnerable to technological disruption. Moreover, the Internet's relative anonymity, its enabling of 'action at a distance', and its function as a 'force multiplier' are held to make cyber-attacks an appealing option for terrorists. However, it was noted that there are a number of drawbacks in engaging in virtual as opposed to terrestrial terrorist actions, and which might disincline such groups from going online to pursue their aims. Indeed, it was argued that the empirical evidence offers little concrete support for the claim that cyberterrorism is an immediate or significant threat. Rather, the current upsurge in concern on this issue ought to be situated critically and politically as a form of 'moral entrepreneurship' on the part of government, law enforcement and/or the computer security industry in pursuit of their sectional aims and interests. However, despite this deconstruction of the cyberterrorist threat, the chapter concluded by examining the more prosaic but nevertheless highly effective ways in which terrorists can and do use the Internet.

Study questions

- what is the difference between hackers and hacktivists?
- is hacktivism a legitimate form of political protest, or a criminal activity that should be discouraged?
- what are the implications of increasing dependence upon information technology for national security and social and economic stability?
- is cyberterrorism a 'clear and present danger' or merely a 'phantom menace'?
- is it possible to curtail the uses of the Internet by terrorist organizations for the purposes of publicity, recruitment, information gathering, or financing? If so, what effects might such counter-measures have upon legitimate and legal uses of the Internet?

Further reading

The best available accounts of hacktivism are Paul Taylor's article 'Hacktivism – Resistance is Fertile?' (2004) and Paul Taylor and Tim Jordan's book *Hacktivism and Cyberwars: Rebels with a Cause?* (2004). An exhaustive survey of issues relating to critical information infrastructure protection policy can be found in Dunn and Wigert's *International CIIP Handbook* (2004). For the view of cyberterrorism as a serious threat, see Verton's, *Black Ice: The Invisible Threat of Cyber-Terrorism* (2003). For a more balanced assessment, Dorothy Denning's writings provide a valuable point of reference (most can be accessed online at her website: http://www.cs. georgetown. edu/~denning/publications.html). An excellent critique of the construction of cyberterrorism in political and media discourse can be found in Sandor Vegh's article, 'Hacktivists or Cyberterrorists? The Changing Media Discourse on Hacking' (2002). Finally, useful overviews of terrorist uses of the Internet in support of their conventional activities can be found in Weimann's *www.terror.net* (2004) and in Shelley's article 'Organized Crime, Terrorism and Cybercrime' (2003).

FOUR
Virtual 'Pirates'

Intellectual property theft online

Overview

Chapter 4 examines the following issues:

- the nature of 'intellectual property' and 'piracy';
- the extent and growth of 'piracy' in relation to software, music and movies;
- the relationship between technological change and Internet 'piracy';
- the relationship between 'youth' and 'piracy';
- the kinds of legal, enforcement and campaigning activities that have emerged in response to 'piracy';
- the problems with official estimates of the 'piracy problem';
- the rhetorical and ideological dimensions of the 'piracy' debate.

---

key terms

Copyright	Intangible goods	Piracy
Downloading	Intellectual Property	Property rights
File sharing		

Introduction

4.1 At first glance, the notion that the Internet may be used as a conduit for stealing property may strike the reader as somewhat improbable. After all, we normally take 'property' to mean a variety of *material* goods; and when criminologists talk about 'property crimes', they are usually referring to theft of everyday personal possessions such as automobiles, consumer electronics, clothing, alcohol and tobacco, and so on. The Internet might seem an unlikely tool for property theft, given that such material goods cannot be transmitted via its electronic networks; by its very nature, the Internet deals in the transmission of *information*, the immaterial electronic signals of digital communication. Nevertheless, the focus for this chapter falls upon the ways in which the Internet is now identified as an arena for the theft of property and its worldwide distribution. The property in question is of a very particular, but increasingly common, kind – what is known as *intellectual property*. The most familiar kinds of intellectual property include goods such as books, computer software, musical recordings, and motion pictures. In legal terms, such goods are owned by their creators or manufacturers, who make a profit by selling copies to consumers. In recent years, the Internet has become implicated in the massive increase in theft of such intellectual properties. Indeed, given that such property itself is nothing more than forms of information (the arrangement

---

of words in a book, the sequence of codes making up a program, the succession of images comprising a movie), the Internet is the most powerful medium ever for its theft and distribution – computers and the Internet enable such information to be almost instantaneously copied without limit, and transmitted equally quickly anywhere in the world. Consequently, the web has become almost synonymous with the problem of 'intellectual property theft', also commonly referred to as 'copyright theft' or 'piracy'. Today, some of the world's leading industries claim that they lose billions of dollars every year due to theft of their intellectual property via the Internet. This chapter will explore what is known about such 'copyright crimes' – how widespread they actually are, what is being stolen, by whom, and at what cost. It will also examine how crime control and criminal justice initiatives are being mobilized to challenge Internet 'piracy' worldwide. However, we will also turn a critical lens upon the current debates about intellectual property theft, and consider why there is an increasingly vocal movement to allow, rather than repress, the free flow of information and cultural goods in the online environment.

Intellectual property, copyright and 'piracy': an overview

4.2 In order to appreciate why the copying and distribution of information may be considered a form of criminal activity, we must establish what is meant by terms such as 'piracy', 'intellectual property', and 'copyright'. Settling upon a precise and internationally agreed definition of 'piracy' has proved remarkably difficult. However, all legal and economic uses of the term have their basis in intellectual property (IP) law and protection. IP law is itself immensely complicated, spanning as it does national, regional, and international laws, treaties, conventions, and directives, as well as judicial rulings and other precedents. Moreover, as Bently and Sherman (2001) note, it is a field in radical flux, the past decade having seen far-reaching revisions in IP rights, beginning from the TRIPS (Trade-Related Aspects of Intellectual Property) Agreement, which was finalized under the auspices of the World Trade Organization in 1994. While it is not necessary to revisit the long history and detailed development of IP law in the present context[1], a basic definition of intellectual property, and especially of copyright, is necessary if we are to grasp the current legal grounds upon which the problem of Internet 'piracy' is constituted.

At its most fundamental, intellectual property takes the form of so-called 'intangibles', such as ideas, inventions, signs, information and expression. Whereas laws covering 'real' property establish rights over 'tangibles', IP laws establish proprietary rights over 'original' forms of intellectual production (ibid.: 1–2; WIPO, 2001: 3). IP can take a number of recognized forms – patents, trademarks, trade secrets, industrial designs and, crucially for us, copyright.

Copyright, in essence, establishes the holder's (e.g. an author's) rights over a particular form of original expression (WIPO, 2001: 40–1). Typical objects of copyright include writing, music, paintings, drawings, audio-visual recordings, and (most recently) computer software. As the term suggests, copyright grants the holder rights over the copying, reproduction, distribution, broadcast and performance of the designated 'work' or content. In essence, the holder retains ownership of the expression and the right to exploit it through, for example, licensing its copying, distribution, or performance in return for some financial compensation (e.g. the payment of a royalty or fee). Thus, for example, if I purchase a CD recording of songs, I have ownership over the tangible object (the CD), *but not of the musical content* of the CD, whose ownership remains with the copyright holder. Therefore, I am legally prohibited from copying, distributing or performing the content without authorization from the holder and the payment of some agreed compensation. In essence, 'piracy' amounts to just such an infringement of copyright. In current uses, 'piracy' refers to the unauthorized copying and distribution (often, though not necessarily, for commercial gain) of copyrighted content.[2]

Scope and scale of 'piracy' activity

4.3 According to the copyright industries, 'piracy' (the unauthorized copying, distribution and/or sale of copyrighted content) is approaching near-epidemic levels. Much of the available data emanates from US sources, reflecting that country's preeminent position in the global market for media and software goods. According to the International Intellectual Property Alliance (henceforth IIPA), 'piracy' of US copyrighted materials results in $20–22 billion in losses to rights-holder, excluding growing levels of 'piracy' via the Internet (IIPA, 2005). The major sectors affected are those producing computer software, music and motion pictures; each will be considered below in turn.

In the area of musical recordings, the International Federation of Phonographic Industries (IFPI) claims that the global production of 'pirated' recordings now amounts to 1.8 billion units per annum, the bulk in the form of CDs; this means that 1 in 3 CDs sold is an unauthorized copy. In financial terms, this amounts to $4.6 billion (IFPI, 2003: 2). These figures cover only commercial 'piracy', and do not include copying by consumers and distribution via peer-to-peer 'file sharing' Internet sites. It is claimed that 81.5 million people (4.98 per cent of the world's Internet users) illegally downloaded music in the course of 2003. This 'piracy' is deemed to have lead to an average *monthly* loss of $450 million to copyright holders throughout 2004 (DIG, 2004).

In the area of motion pictures, the Motion Picture Association of America (MPAA) claims that the US film industry loses in excess of $3 billion per annum worldwide as a result of 'piracy' (MPAA, 2005). In 2002, over 7 million 'pirate'

DVDs were seized worldwide (Valenti, 2003). The MPAA further estimates that more than 350,000 unauthorized Internet movie downloads take place every day (Valenti, 2002); if true, this would amount to a staggering *125 million* film downloads per annum. The UK film industry, while dramatically smaller than its US counterpart, claims losses in the region of £400 million per annum, a piracy rate of some 30 per cent (effectively, almost 1 in 3 British movies purchased in the UK is 'pirated') (FACT, 2003a). In 2002, UK seizures of 'pirated' films on optical disk (DVD) exceeded 1 million units, a three-fold increase on the previous year, while seizures of 'pirated' films on VHS videocassette (a 'piracy' format previously thought to be in decline) rose 100 per cent (FACT, 2003b).

The computer software industry claims the largest financial losses to 'piracy'. Global losses were pinned at $13.08 billion for 2002 (BSA, 2003: 3). Eastern-Central Europe is deemed to have the highest 'piracy' rate, where 71 per cent of all software is claimed to be an illegal copy; however, rates are also high for North America (24 per cent) and Western Europe (35 per cent) (ibid.: 2). Internet piracy of software can take a number of forms. First, the software may be made available for download, often via bulletin boards or so-called 'warez' sites (short for 'softwares'). Second, such sites may make available activation codes for software packages. This practice is of growing significance, as software is increasingly being retailed online. Sellers permit Internet users to download the software, but it can only be activated using a code that is provided once the potential user has made the appropriate online payment for the program. By providing such codes online, users can install and run the software without making the necessary purchase payment to the copyright holder.

Explaining the growth of Internet 'piracy'

4.4 A major factor in explaining this growth of Internet 'piracy' is the rapid expansion of the Internet itself. Worldwide, there are now an estimated 605 million Internet users, with over 190 million in Europe, and well over 180 million in both Asia-Pacific and North American regions (NUA Internet Statistics, 2003). In the USA, 61 per cent of households have Internet access (MPAA, 2003: 50), and penetration rates are as high or higher in a number of European countries (such as the UK, Denmark, Sweden, the Netherlands); Asian countries such as Singapore, Taiwan, Japan and Hong Kong have penetration rates in excess of 50 per cent (NUA Internet Statistics, 2003). The growth of 'broadband' Internet access in particular enables users to quickly download large quantities of digital content in compressed format (over 33 per cent of US Internet users have broadband access and over 53 per cent in Canada (Comscore Media Metrix, 2003)). The Internet abounds with 'file-sharing' sites that enable home computer users to exchange the digitized content on their hard drives (there are a number of readily available tools for bypassing copyright protection systems, enabling movies and music to be converted into digital files suitable for download – see Rassool, 2003: 5–6; Vaidhyanathan, 2003: 176–7). The scale of such 'file sharing' on peer-to-peer (P2P) networks is hinted at by the fact that, in an 18-month period from 2001 to mid-2002, US copyright holders issued *100,000* cease-and-desist orders to online movie sharers (Ananova, 2002). And, as industry representatives admit, the 'increasingly decentralized, fragmented and anonymous' nature of these services makes litigation a severely limited tool for curtailing file sharing (Valenti, 2002). In addition, there are numerous commercial 'pirate' download operations which, for a minimal monthly fee (around $1–2), give subscribers access to thousands of films,[3] many of them still showing in US cinemas, and not yet even released in other markets. For example, at the time of writing, major Hollywood films such as *Just Like Heaven, Lord of War*, and *Red Eye* (all awaiting theatrical release in Europe) were readily available for download.

The Internet can be seen to offer a number of advantages over more 'traditional' methods for the illegal copying and distribution of copyrighted content. First, it bypasses the costs involved in recording the software, music or movies onto physical media such as CDs, DVDs, videotapes, and cassettes, since the content can be transmitted and stored directly using computer hard drives. Second, while the distribution of 'hard copies' is slow, the distribution of content via the Internet is rapid. Third, while giving or selling such content to consumers in physical form entails making a copy for each user, the Internet allows an unlimited number of copies to be made by consumers from a single copy hosted on the web. Fourth, the worldwide distribution of 'pirate' content in the form of hard media entails certain risks, such as the confiscation of shipments by customs officials, or the detection of attempts to sell such goods at markets, shops, car boot sales, and such like. In contrast, the Internet bypasses border controls, and affords distributors and sellers a degree of anonymity and protection. If their activities are detected, identifying and apprehending the individuals responsible are considerably more challenging in the online environment, where identity can be more easily disguised. Moreover, by locating the point of distribution in countries with little or no enforcement of copyright laws, the distributors can effectively evade the reach of law enforcement agencies elsewhere in the world, or at least make it very difficult indeed for them to the brought before the law.

Who are the 'pirates'?

4.5 One of the most notable features of Internet 'piracy' is its apparent ubiquity. Far from being confined to a small class of 'professional criminals', 'piracy' activity appears to be socially widespread, and undertaken on a regular basis by individuals who would otherwise consider themselves 'law-abiding citizens'. Participation in the illegal downloading of copyrighted materials appears to span persons from various social classes and walks of life. Some insight into the social distribution and engagement in Internet 'piracy' is afforded by recent surveys and self-report studies; particularly noteworthy among such findings is the disproportionate involvement of young people in such offending.

A recent US-based survey of professional workers revealed that only 26 per cent oppose software 'piracy' 'in principle' (IPSOS, 2004). A UK-based poll in 2004, conducted on behalf of the Business Software Alliance, found that 44 per cent of 18–29-year-olds owned 'pirated' intellectual property; the figure for the 30–50-year age group was 28 per cent, and 17 per cent for the over-50s. The survey further found that 'there is little stigma to owning counterfeit goods' (Thomson, 2004). The findings of the UK Government's 2003 Crime and Justice Survey reports that 9 per cent of people over 18 years old in the UK admit to committing 'technology offences' such as 'illegally downloading software or music' (Budd et al., 2005: 25). Significant, then, is the apparent inverse relationship between age and propensity to commit 'copyright offences' – the younger the age group, the more likely their involvement. Thus surveys of young people's attitudes toward computer-related activities such as downloading show high levels of participation and minimal reservation about doing so (Bowker, 1999: 40). A 2004 poll in the USA found that 'more than half of all 8–18 year olds have downloaded music, a third have downloaded games and nearly a quarter have downloaded software illegally from the Internet' (Snyder, 2004: 1). A number of studies worldwide have found high levels of 'softlifting' (downloaded copyrighted software from the Internet) among college students, and little weight attached to the 'legal and moral' objections (see discussion in Kini et al., 2003: 63–4). A 2004 survey of young people in Canada found that 47 per cent of 12–21-year-olds intended to 'download music, video or software from the Internet over the next six months' (Jedwab, 2004: 1). It further found that 70 per cent of respondents 'deemed [it] acceptable to download music, video or software from the Internet' (ibid.). This relationship between youth and 'piracy' has, as we shall see, shaped in significant ways the development of 'anti-piracy' campaigns and initiatives.

The development of anti-piracy initiatives

4.6 The recent rise to prominence of Internet 'piracy' as a crime problem has stimulated a range of responses from legislators, law enforcement agencies, and private sector organizations that represent the copyright industries. This range of interventions will be considered below.

- *The criminalization of 'piracy'*. In the past, copyright violations have been largely tackled through a range of *civil* remedies available to copyright holders – such as injunctions, 'delivery up' or destruction of infringing articles, and the payment of damages (Bently and Sherman, 2001: 1008–23). Even where the law has made provision for criminal prosecution of IP violations, there tended to be few such actions, for example, between 1970 and 1980 there were less than 20 prosecutions for copyright offences in the UK (Sodipo, 1997: 228). This may be attributed to a range of factors, including the relatively low priority accorded to IP crimes by over-stretched and under-resourced criminal justice agencies; the public concern and political emphasis on more visibly 'harmful' offences, such as 'street crimes' and violent crime; difficulties in policing and intelligence gathering; and the reluctance of public prosecutors to involve themselves in a notoriously complex and specialized domain of law. However, recent years have seen moves to criminalize copyright violations, bringing them increasingly under the sway of criminal sanctions. This has taken two main forms.

First, there has been increased willingness to use existing criminal sanctions against 'pirates', encouraged both by greater political sensitivity to IP rights and their economic importance, and by concerted application of pressure through lobbying by the copyright industry. One key means in achieving this has been the formation of industry organizations (such as the Alliance Against Counterfeiting and Piracy (AACP) and the Federation Against Copyright Theft (FACT) in the UK) that conduct investigations and gather information on 'piracy' activities, and lay complaints before public prosecuting authorities (Sodipo, 1997: 229; Bently and Sherman, 2001: 1030–1). Recent years have seen a number of high-profile 'piracy' cases in which such procedures have led to criminal convictions carrying substantial custodial sentences, for example, in 2002 a FACT investigation led to a four-year prison sentence for the convicted 'pirate' (Carugati, 2003). The overall number of criminal prosecutions for copyright violations has also increased massively – in 2000 alone, there were over 500 such cases in the area of music (CD) counterfeiting alone (Home Office, 2002b: 2).

At a second level, recent years have seen the incorporation of additional provisions for criminal sanctions into both international treaties and national laws. At the national level, we can note for example Section 107 of the Copyright, Designs and Patents Act (1988) in the UK, which places local administrative authorities (such as Trading Standards departments) under a duty to enforce criminal copyright provisions, and significantly strengthens the penalties available in comparison to the previously existing Copyright Act of 1956 (Dworkin and Taylor, 1989: 121–2; Bently and Sherman, 2001: 1031). In the USA, the No Electronic Theft Act (1988) makes provision for up to three years' imprisonment for convicted 'pirates'; it also extends the applicability of sanctions beyond those engaging in 'piracy' for commercial gain, to include, for example, the not-for-profit digital trading engaged in by file-sharers (Drahos and Braithwaite, 2002: 185). At the international level, Article 61 of the TRIPS agreement establishes a *mandatory* requirement for signatories to make criminal provisions against commercial copyright violations. Hence the extensions of available criminal sanctions and the greater willingness to pursue them have, taken together, significantly reconfigured 'piracy', rendering it more grave in an attempt to stem its growth.

- *Policing, enforcement and 'piracy'.* I have already noted the recent increase in policing and enforcement activity, in which industry organizations are playing a leading role. It is worth noting here the proliferation of industry-financed 'anti-piracy' organizations whose *raison d'être* combines research, intelligence gathering, policing, education and lobbying activities. The past two decades has seen the creation of the Counterfeiting Intelligence Bureau, the International Intellectual Property Alliance, the International Anti-Counterfeiting Coalition, the Alliance Against Counterfeiting and Piracy, the Coalition for Intellectual Property Rights, the Artists Coalition Against Piracy, the aforementioned AACP and FACT, as well as numerous existing trade organizations that have established specialist groups and initiatives to combat 'piracy' (such as the Motion Picture Association (MPA) and the Recording Industry Association of America (RIAA)). Such organizations purport to 'lift the burden of investigation from law enforcement agencies' (AACP, 2002: 2) by engaging in a range of increasingly intensive policing activities. Where public agencies have been reluctant to invest time and resources in tackling IP violations, industrial and commercial interests have 'filled the void'. In addition to intelligence gathering and undercover operations, they have attempted to bring IP crime into the criminal justice mainstream through, for example, the appointment of specialist liaison personnel to 'assist' and 'advise' responsible agencies in the detection and prosecution of 'copyright theft'. Governments have themselves responded to concerted pressure from these groups by establishing specialist units within criminal justice agencies to address IP violations (for example, the UK now has the National High-Tech Crime Unit and the National Technical assistance Centre (NTAC), and the USA has the FBI's Internet Fraud Complaint Centre (IFCC); Interpol has established an Intellectual Property Crimes Unit (2002), and there are concerted efforts at the EU level to strengthen EUROPOL's powers of enforcement in the area of IP).
- *Anti-piracy education campaigns.* A third area of response has been the development and implementation of 'anti-piracy education' campaigns, involving both copyright industries and public agencies. Particular focus has fallen upon young people, given their apparently disproportionate involvement in illegal Internet downloading, copying and distribution of copyrighted materials.

Recent years have seen numerous 'educational' programmes produced by umbrella organizations that represent various sectors of the copyright industries – software, music and/or motion pictures. Such programmes typically provide a range of materials, exercises and gaming activities that are intended for use in the classroom, thereby incorporating 'anti-piracy' into the school curriculum. Programmes typically target younger children between the ages of 8 and 13. For example, there is the FA©E (Friends of Active Copyright Education) initiative of the Copyright Society of America – their child-oriented program is called 'Copyright Kids'. Also notable is the SIIA's (Software and Information Industry Association) 'Cybersmart! School Program'. A third is the BSA's (Business Software Alliance) 'Play It Cybersafe' program featuring the cartoon character Garret the Ferret, aka 'The Copyright Crusader'. A fourth campaign is produced by the Government of Western Australia's Department of Education and Training, and is called 'Ippy's Big Idea'. A fifth campaign is the MPAA's 'Starving Artist' schools' road show. This is a role-playing game designed for school children, which was taken 'on tour' in 2003 in 36,000 classrooms across the USA. The game invites students 'to come up with an idea for a record album, cover art, and lyrics' (Menta, 2003). Having completed the exercise, the students are told that their album is already available for download from the Internet, and are asked 'how they felt when they realized that their work was stolen and that they would not get anything for their efforts' (ibid.). All such campaigns attempt to create a moral consensus that unauthorized copying is a form of theft, and as such as immoral as stealing someone else's material possessions; moreover, they also target the children's parents in an attempt to warn them of the possible legal repercussions if their children are caught engaging in 'piracy'.

Thinking critically about 'piracy' statistics

4.7 Thus far, we have followed official understandings of the 'piracy' problem, and considered the ways in which legal and crime control initiatives have emerged as a response. However, we also need to examine the discourses of copyright industries and law enforcement agencies with a critical eye. As noted in previous chapters, crime (that which is criminalized) is not a politically neutral category; rather, it inevitably reflects patterns of interest and relations of power in society. Therefore, we cannot simply take the facts and figures about 'piracy' at face value. Rather, we must reflect upon them as social constructions that may represent a partial point of view, and which may be used by powerful social groups in pursuit of their own interests and agendas.

The figures for software and media 'piracy' that currently circulate within commercial-industrial-media-criminal justice discourses are typically the product of a set of inferences and calculative techniques that are open to methodological challenge. First, there is a problem in that estimates of overall 'piracy' levels and trends are often extrapolated from detection and conviction rates. An obvious problem with this is that the levels of 'piracy' detected, and the number of criminal cases brought and convictions secured, will depend upon the level of policing activity. Therefore, apparent increases in the levels of 'piracy' may in fact be the result of more intensified enforcement activity, as greater attention from enforcement agencies will inevitably lead to a greater proportion of offences being uncovered. Further problems arise with other attempts to quantify the scope and scale of the problem. For example, the allocation of monetary measures to losses from 'piracy' often take the 'legitimate product price' as their baseline – so, for example, in calculating the MPAA figures for losses to film 'piracy', the assumption is that each unauthorized copy deprives the copyright holder of the sale of one unit of the legitimate product, for example, the loss of revenue from a ticket to see the film in a movie theatre, or the purchase of an authorized VCR or DVD copy of the film. As Drahos and Braithwaite (2002: 93–4, 97) point out, this is based upon the erroneous assumption that every consumer of an unauthorized copy would have chosen, had the 'pirate' not been available, to pay the price asked for the authorized exhibition or distribution of that same film. Quite simply, it may well be that while consumers are prepared to pay the lower prices demanded for 'pirate' versions of software, music or movies, they are not prepared to pay the higher prices attached to the legitimate offering – there is no inevitability that the consumers of the 'pirate' would otherwise have paid to purchase an authorized copy.

A more general problem arises from the official reliance on partial industry sources for 'piracy' figures. Industry bodies have a vested interest in maximizing the figures (whether in the form of the number of copies, lost revenues or profits, lost jobs, or lost taxation for the public purse). The larger the figures are, the greater the pressure that can be brought to bear on legislators and enforcement agencies in the drive for more rigorous action (the US government, for example, derives its figures for 'piracy' directly from those provided by industry bodies, with little in the way of independent corroboration). As the CEBR (2002: 29) succinctly puts it, there is 'nothing preventing the companies from overstating their losses through counterfeiting for lobbying purposes'. Yet these industry 'guesstimates' usually become reified into incontrovertible facts, and provide the basis for further discussion and action on the 'piracy problem'. From the industry's viewpoint, the inflation of the figures is the starting point for a 'virtuous circle' – high figures put pressure on legislators to criminalize, and enforcement agencies to police more rigorously; the tightening of copyright laws *produces* more 'copyright theft' as previously legal or tolerated uses are prohibited, and the more intensive policing of 'piracy' results in more seizures; these in turn produce new estimates suggesting that the problem continues to grow unabated; which then legitimates industry calls for even more vigorous action. What the 'true' underlying levels and trends in 'piracy' might be, however, remain inevitably 'obscured' behind this process of socio-statistical construction.

Thinking critically about intellectual property rights

4.8 The emergence of Internet 'piracy' as a crime problem depends in a fundamental way upon the claim that people can, and ought, to have property rights in relation to the expression of ideas. The very language of 'piracy' is emotive, as it draws an equivalence between copying and bloodthirsty sea-faring brigands. Yet we must consider the partial and one-sided character of this viewpoint. By no means all commentators, or creators of music, software, etc., agree with the claim that such copying practices are harmful, or that they should be made the subject of criminal sanctions. Some of the critical counter-arguments to the 'demonization of piracy' (Litman, 2000) are considered below.

First, it can be noted that the criminalization of 'piracy' turns upon the idea that 'property rights' are something natural and unquestionable. This notion of property rights is often associated with the philosopher John Locke (1632–1704), who argued that property rights emerge when 'man' adds 'his' 'honest labour' to nature, generating a product over which 'he' has not only rights of possession and use, but also of transfer (Lemos, 1975). The property 'he' has created is 'his' to do with as 'he' pleases. However, historical and cross-cultural investigations illustrate many alternative conceptions of property. For example, Erich Kasten's fieldwork among the First Nation tribes of the Canadian Pacific Northwest reveals conceptions of property radically different from those dominant in the West; among these peoples, primacy is given to obligations to ancestors to preserve and transmit the group's shared heritage intact to future generations, not to individuals claiming proprietary rights which can be exploited for commercial gain (Kasten, 2004: 10; also Onwuekwe, 2004: 66). Other examples of 'non-Western' approaches to property include the *adat* customary laws of Indonesia and the collectivization of Yoruba art in Nigeria, to name but a few (Story, 2003: 795–6). This anthropological diversity in conceptions of property has recently inspired in the West alternative notions of intellectual property, based on the idea of the 'commons'. The commons refers to 'a wide variety of creations of nature and society that we inherit freely, share and hold in trust for future generations' (Bollier, 2003: 2). As such 'creative works' are seen as constitutive of 'our common culture' rather than the private property of individuals or organizations (ibid.). Advocates of the 'natural rights' position may respond by mobilizing the moral principle that one who creates something by virtue of his or her 'honest labour' justly deserves to enjoy benefits from that labour. However, as Martin (1998: 38) points out, while we may agree that the individual concerned deserves some 'fitting reward', this in no sense entails that this reward should comprise the full market value of that which is produced, nor does it in any way entail that the individual should have a right to determine under what conditions others may make use of what has been created (see also Hettinger, 1989: 34–5; Epstein, 2004). The notions that products are naturally the property of individuals, and that production naturally confers rights to control subsequent uses, may be viewed as a myth which functions primarily to 'facilitate the increasing consolidation of ownership' (McLeod, 2001: 2) by the copyright industries.

A second way in which 'piracy' is criminalized is by asserting a straightforward equivalence between tangible (material) and intangible (ideative) properties. Thus, for example, 'anti-piracy' campaigns place great emphasis upon the claim that 'violating copyright laws … is equivalent to stealing' (Play It Cybersafe, 2005: 3). By recourse to everyday conceptions of 'stealing' and 'theft', and by drawing analogies between tangible and intangible goods, copyright holders justify the criminalization of 'piracy'. However, this equation between tangible and intangible goods can seen as unpersuasive and misleading. Material objects are limited by nature as to their use – if one person is using an object, this means others cannot. As Martin (1998: 30) puts it: 'If one person wears a pair of shoes, no one else can wear them at the same time.' A tangible object 'can only be in one place at a time' (Kasten, 2004: 21), and only utilized by one party at a time. This limit to use justifies the prohibition on unauthorized use – if you take my shoes and wear them, I am denied their use. However, intangibles are fundamentally different. The particular expression of an idea can be taken and used by someone else, but this in no way deprives the possessor of the original expression – they still have the original and can make full use of it. Thus, in the case of digital content (music, movies, software), it can be endlessly reproduced, but this does not entail dispossessing anyone. Through copying there is no limit to sharing the good, without encroaching upon any owner's possession of their version of the good (Bunz, 2003: 8). Hence it is impossible to 'steal' copyrighted content in the way in which it is possible to steal a physical object. It can be argued that in instances of 'piracy', no one is deprived of their property, but only of possible opportunities to exploit proprietary control over forms of expression for commercial gain. As we shall see below, whether or not individuals *ought* to in fact be accorded such rights of control is a hotly contested issue.

A third way in which 'piracy' is criminalized is by recourse to the idea that individual authors, creators, artists, etc. will be materially harmed by the practice of 'piracy'. Hence, for example, the aforementioned 'Starving Artist' role-playing game, which links 'piracy' to the impoverishment of those who create cultural works. This notion of harm is backed up by aggregate numerical claims, such as the BSA's assertion that software 'piracy' has resulted in 'more than 111,000 jobs lost' (BSA, 2005: 1). Yet the claim that 'piracy' does direct material harm to individual 'creators' can be seen to rest upon a significant factual inaccuracy. In today's cultural economy, 'authors' and 'artists' seldom retain control over copyright but routinely assign those rights to corporate entities who then have virtual *carte blanche* over decisions as to the work's commercial exploitation. In 2000, rock musician Courtney Love launched what has been dubbed the 'Love Manifesto', a critical reflection on 'intellectual property theft', artists, and the recording industry. Love begins her 'Manifesto' thus: 'Today I want to talk about piracy and music. What is piracy? Piracy is the act of stealing an artist's work without any intention of paying for it. I'm not talking about Napster-type software … I'm talking about major label recording contracts' (Love, 2000). She goes on to demonstrate how standard practice within the recording industry deprives musicians of copyrights, and the monies advanced to artists are largely recouped from them by the industry under 'expenses' for recording and promotion. As a consequence, the musicians see little return from their efforts and, she opines, 'the band may as well be working at a 7-Eleven' (ibid.). The appeal to artists' well-being as an 'anti-piracy' strategy is based upon the erroneous claim that royalties earned from authoring provide anything like a viable living. Critic and activist Brian Holmes points out that, of the 100,000 members of the world's best established composers' rights organization, only 2500 have a vote on organization policy, since the privilege of voting is reserved for those who earn more than €5000 per annum from their compositions; in fact, he claims, only 300 members of the organization make a viable living from royalties derived from copyright (Holmes, 2003: 13). In fact, it has been argued that 'piracy' is in the financial interests of most recording artists; most performers make their living from concert performance, and this is best supported and promoted by having their music circulated as widely as possible, including via copying. As musician Ignacio Escolar puts it: 'Like all musicians, I know that 100,000 pirate fans coming to my shows are more profitable than 10,000 original ones' (Escolar, 2003: 15).

The foregoing discussion is intended to draw attention to the ways in which Internet 'piracy', like other forms of criminalized cyber-activity, draws its rhetorical power from some commonplace ideas and ideologies. As the drive to clamp down on copying via the Internet builds apace, criminologists need to pause and reflect upon whether the claims about its harmfulness are justified, and whether curtailing practices such as file sharing is in the interests of consumers, or artists, or just of those large corporations who increasingly control access to cultural goods.

Summary

4.9 This chapter has explored what is perhaps the most common form of Internet-related crime, that of 'piracy' or illegal downloading of software, music and movies. The growth of the Internet, combined with the move to digital media, has created a medium through which copyrighted content can easily be duplicated and distributed worldwide. Copyright industries now claim that illegal copying results in multi-billion dollar losses every year, and threatens the jobs and livelihoods of those working in the creative sectors of the economy. Young people in particular appear to be enthusiastic participants in 'piracy' activities, and have increasingly become the focus of both legal action and 'anti-piracy' education campaigns. A wide array of industry-financed 'anti-piracy' organizations now exists, and they are increasingly involved in policing activities. Recent years have also seen major legislative innovations at both national and transnational levels in an effort to curtail copyright offences. However, critical voices have been raised against what is perceived as the incremental criminalization of cultural communication and exchange, and have argued in favour of the free circulation of knowledge and ideas. The issue of 'piracy' is thus becoming a political and ideological battleground on which the meanings of crime and deviance are negotiated and contested.

Study questions

- *what* is 'intellectual property' and what kinds of forms does it take?
- *how* does the Internet facilitate 'piracy'?
- *how* have copyright industries, governments and law enforcement bodies responded to the growth of illegal copying online?
- *how* might we explain the high levels of involvement in such practices by young people?
- *whose* interests does the criminalization of copying serve? Is there a case for decriminalizing 'piracy'?

Further reading

An accessible introduction to intellectual property and IP law is the World Intellectual Property Organization's *WIPO Intellectual Property Handbook: Policy, Law and Use* (2001). A comprehensive and detailed guide is Lionel Bently and Brad Sherman's *Intellectual Property Law* (2001). For discussions of copyright in relation to music, see Simon Frith and Lee Marshall (eds) *Music and Copyright* (2004). For a critical take on intellectual property generally, see Peter Drahos and John Braithwaite's excellent *Information Feudalism: Who Owns the Knowledge Economy?* (2002); equally useful (and engaging) is Siva Vaidhyanathan's book *Copyrights and Copywrongs: The Rise of Intellectual Property and How it Threatens Creativity* (2003). For the copyright industry perspective on 'piracy', consult the websites of the Motion Picture Association of America (http://www.mpaa.org), the Recording Industry Association of America (http://www.riaa.org) and the Business Software Alliance (http://www.bsa.org). For a critical analysis of claims about the piracy problem, see Majid Yar's 'The Global Epidemic of Movie "Piracy": Crime-Wave or Social Construction?' (2005).

Notes

1 For such a detailed account of both the development and current parameters of IP law, see Bently and Sherman (2001) and Letterman (2001).
2 Distinction is sometimes made between 'piracy' and 'counterfeiting', where the latter refers to products infringing copyright that also replicate the original product

in terms of appearance, packaging, graphics, etc., and can thus be passed off as authorized copies (see Kounoupias, 2003: 3–4; BPI, 2002: 4). Hence, while unauthorized copies of copyrighted material may or may not be 'counterfeit' (replicate in appearance the legitimate product), they are all 'pirated' in that they violate copyright. In reality, the two categories are often combined or used in conjunction to cover the range of copyright thefts (see, for example, the European Commission Green Paper on counterfeiting and piracy – 2 COM(98)569 Final (1998).

3 A 5-minute Internet search was sufficient to locate 15 such sites.

FIVE

Cyber-Frauds, Scams and Cons

Overview

Chapter 5 examines the following issues:

- *the nature and extent of online frauds;*
- *the various forms taken by frauds, such as auction fraud, advanced fee frauds, and website spoofing;*
- *the ways in which the move to the Internet proves advantageous for fraudsters and presents problems for law enforcement and policing;*
- *the emerging strategies for combating Internet-fraud, along with their limitations*

---

key terms

Advances fee fraud	Internet auctions Phishing	Spoofing

Introduction

5.1 Gottfredson and Hirschi (1990) make a valuable distinction between crimes according to the means by which they are perpetrated – while some crimes resort to *force* (for example, 'breaking and entering' or 'mugging'), others proceed by *fraud* or deception. Frauds (know more colloquially as 'scams' and 'cons') are a far from new phenomenon. History is replete with examples of such crimes, ranging from the large-scale and audacious to the small-scale and petty (Maurer, 2000; Moore, 2000). In legal terms, fraud can be defined as: 'A false representation by means of a statement or conduct made knowingly or recklessly in order to gain material advantage' (Martin, 2003: 211). Frauds thus part victims from their money or property by recourse to misinformation and deception. One may be deceived as to the true value of something that one is purchasing, as to its authenticity, as to whom it actually belongs, and so on. One may also be deceived as to who the individual is with whom one does business – they may fraudulently present themselves as someone else, as representatives of some legitimate organization, as the holder of some occupational or professional role to which they in fact have no claim, and so on. The deception furnishes the critical tool with which the victim is induced to *voluntarily* part with their money or goods (as opposed to being *compelled* to do so as in instances of crimes of force). This chapter explores such offences taking place in online environments, something that is proliferating rapidly – as one commentator puts it, the Internet 'can be viewed as a breeding ground for fraud' (Fried, 2001: 1).

5.2 As with many other kinds of cybercrime, analysis of Internet fraud is hindered by a relative lack of systematic and/or official data. The only such source currently available emanates from the Internet Crime Complain Centre (ICCC) in the USA. The ICCC (formerly the Internet Fraud Complaint Centre (IFCC)) is an organizational collaboration between the FBI and the National White Collar Crime Centre (NW3C), whose primary role is to receive public reports of cybercrimes and refer them to the relevant criminal justice agencies for action.[1] The ICCC publishes an annual survey of online frauds, compiled from the public complaints they receive. These surveys can serve to provide a series of snapshots of the scope, scale and characteristics of online frauds, as well as the trends in such offences over time.

In 2004, the ICCC received some 207,000 complaints, the vast majority of which related to frauds of various kinds (other, much smaller categories of complaints received related to issues such as computer intrusion and child pornography) (ICCC, 2004: 3). This figure comprised a 66.6 per cent increase over 2003 (with 124,000 complaints received) and an increase of almost 700 per cent on 2000 (when 30,000 complaints were filed) (Fried, 2001: 4). Such figures must of course be treated with caution, as some (unknown) proportion of the increase may well be attributable to greater reporting of offences, rather than solely to the increase in their prevalence. Nevertheless, a 700 per cent increase over a four-year period suggests that Internet fraud can be reasonably be taken as a problem on the increase.

An array of different kinds of Internet fraud are reported to the ICCC, including Internet auction frauds, banking frauds, investment frauds and advanced fee frauds; these will each be considered in detail in the next section.

Varieties of online fraud
Internet auction frauds

5.3.1 By far the largest proportion of reported Internet frauds involve online auction sites such as eBay. Such online auctions have expanded rapidly in recent years; eBay now has some 20 million items available for sale, with 3.5 million items being added each day (Prigg, 2004). Auction sites provide a forum for bringing together buyers and sellers of a bewildering array of goods (cars, clothes, consumer electronics, books, movies, music, antiques, art, collectibles such as stamps, coins and other memorabilia, DIY equipment, home furnishings, sport and leisure goods, concert and theatre tickets, office equipment, cosmetics, land and properties, food and drinks, and so on). Internet auction frauds accounted for 71.2 per cent of all fraud complaints received by the ICCC in 2004. This figure suggests that auction sites currently comprise the major locus for online frauds. Auction sites themselves, however, deny that fraud is an extensive problem. Hani Durzy, an eBay spokesperson in the USA, claims that frauds account for only 0.01 per cent of transactions undertaken using the site – yet this would still amount to 3000 frauds per day (over 100,000 per annum), given that more than 30 million auctions take place on eBay daily (Cha, 2005). Interestingly, Durzy's UK counterpart, Gareth Griffiths, places the eBay fraud rate at 0.1 per cent of all transactions – a *ten-fold* increase on Durzy's figure (Prigg, 2004). This would result in *30,000* auction frauds every day, or more than *one million* per annum. Outside commentators and law-enforcement experts suggest that even the 0.1 per cent figure grossly under-estimates the level of fraud taking place – computer crime analyst Vincent Rakoczy believes auction sites provide 'a wide-open field' for frauds (Cole, 2004). The varieties of auction fraud are outlined below.

The 'fencing' of stolen goods   Criminologists have argued that finding a viable market for stolen goods is crucial for the success of criminal enterprises involving property theft. Finding a buyer for stolen goods may in fact be more challenging than perpetrating the theft itself. Sutton (1998: 1), a pioneer of the 'market reduction approach' to crime control, claims that 'success or failure to convert stolen property into cash appears to play an important part in whether they [thieves] continue to offend'. Thus success in finding a market for such goods may actively stimulate theft, whereas failure may act as a disincentive, since previous thefts have failed to yield a financial return. Traditionally, stolen goods have been 'fenced' locally, with buyers being sought among friends, workplace colleagues, neighbourhood acquaintances, and in pubs and clubs (Sutton et al., 2001). Transporting stolen goods outside the locality runs the risk of interception by police, customs and other authorities, as well as the problem of doing business with people one does not know from previous personal contact. Subsequently, the locally focused markets provide sites for policing and surveillance – pubs, clubs and street corners can be watched, local informants can alert police to the presence of hawkers of stolen merchandise, and so on. The development of Internet auction sites, however, provides thieves with a global market through which to sell stolen items to unsuspecting customers. A growing number of such cases have been documented, some involving large-scale organized thievery, and sophisticated Internet auction operations for their disposal. Recent examples include:

- an employee of a New York camera store who stole $250,000 worth of photographic equipment and sold it on eBay over a six-month period (Cole, 2004);
- a group of amateur motorcycle thieves in Austin, Texas, whose bikes were dismantled and sold online as spare parts for $15,000 (Cha, 2005);
- an employee of a Silicon Valley electronics company who stole more than $210,000 worth of computer memory cards and sold them via eBay (Ostrom, 2004);

- an 11-person theft ring in Chicago that stole more than $2 million worth of home improvement equipment from retail stores and sold them via Internet auctions (USDOJ, 2003: 1);
- three 17-year-old high school students who successfully auctioned off more than $100,000 worth of computer equipment stolen from local businesses (Lee, 2005);
- instances involving the Internet auction of, among other stolen items: antiquarian books, M29 air guns, high school band equipment, car parts, dinosaur fossils, and archaeological finds (Scuka, 2005; ZDNet, 2005; ABC News online, 2005)

Non-delivery of items   The most common form of Internet auction fraud reported by victims is the non-delivery of items for which they have paid. 67.3 per cent of complainants in the USA were victimized by this method (Dolan, 2004: 12). In such cases, the putative seller advertises non-existent items for sale. Bidders are informed that they have won the auction in which they have participated, and are requested to forward the appropriate payment. However, they receive no goods in turn. Fraudulent 'sellers' typically register themselves with the auction site under a bogus ID, thereby frustrating attempts by defrauded customers and law enforcement agencies to bring them to book (Curry, 2005: 2).

Product inauthenticity and misrepresentation   Some 24.5 per cent of reported frauds involve the sale of goods that have in some sense been misrepresented on the auction site (Dolan, 2004: 12). Such misrepresentation can take a number of forms. For example, it may involve attributing inflated retail values to items, so as to represent the auction prices as substantial savings; it may also involve misrepresenting the condition of the item (Fried, 2001: 4), as when used goods are advertised as new, or items in poor working condition are advertised as fully functional. One of the most common forms of misrepresentation takes the form of selling counterfeit goods that are advertised as authentic items. There is growing evidence that auction sites are extensively used for trading counterfeit DVDs, CDs, and computer software packages, as well as counterfeit clothing, perfumes and other items (Enos, 2000; MPAA, 2003b: 3).

Shill bidding   In cases of shill bidding, the seller places false bids by either (a) using multiple fake identities or aliases to place bids on their own items, or (b) arranging for associates to place bids for the items with no intention of actually purchasing them. Such 'shilling' serves to artificially force up the price of the item, so as to maximize the money that can be extracted from legitimate bidders (Fried, 2001: 4). Only 2 per cent of fraud complaints concern this type of deception (Dolan, 2004: 12). However, it must be borne in mind that it is very difficult for legitimate bidders to detect whether or not other persons bidding for the same items are genuine buyers or 'shills' for the seller. Consequently, the vast majority of such frauds may well pass undetected by buyers, unlike cases of misrepresentation of goods (which will be detected upon delivery) or cases of non-delivery of purchased items. Therefore, shill bidding may well be far more prevalent than reported incidents suggest.

Other types of auction fraud involve methods such as: 'fee stacking', where the seller adds on additional fees after the auction has been completed, thereby increasing the agreed price for the item; failing to deliver the item, giving the seller a refund, but deducting some money on the grounds of 'administration costs'; 'buy and switch', where a winning *bidder* will swap the purchased item for a damaged but otherwise identical item they already possess, and claim a refund – so that they will be end up with *both* an undamaged item *and* their money, while the seller is left with damaged goods (Curry, 2005: 2–3). In all, these and the other auction frauds already discussed are estimated to cost their victims an average of $200 each (ICCC, 2004: 8); however, this median figure disguises the wide variations, with some individuals being defrauded of just a few dollars, while others lose thousands or even tens of thousands.

Auction sites use various mechanisms that in theory make transactions reliable and minimize the possibility of fraud. For example, eBay and other sites invite sellers and buyers to leave feedback and ratings on the transactions that they have undertaken – was the buyer/seller with whom they dealt satisfactory? Was the product as advertised and expected? Were the goods delivered promptly? Feedback for each user is readily available to others contemplating doing business with them, so they can check out the individual's or company's track record according to past customers. If a buyer/seller has positive feedback, then this supposedly reassures others that they are safe and reliable (Boyd, 2002). However, this feedback mechanism is easily exploited – for example, the fraudster can register with the site using multiple false identities and leave positive feedback for him/herself, or arrange for accomplices to do the same. This then creates a positive track record that will help encourage potential victims to enter into a transaction. Moreover, in cases involving the sale of stolen goods, buyers may have no reason to complain as they are likely to be blissfully unaware that the item they have purchased at a bargain price is in fact stolen property. Thus, in the case of the individual who sold cameras stolen from his employer (noted earlier), one of the reasons cited for his ability to trade undetected over a long period was the overwhelmingly positive feedback he received from his unsuspecting victims (Cole, 2004).

Advanced fee frauds or the Nigerian scam

5.3.2 One of oldest and best-known frauds or 'cons' goes by the name of 'the Spanish Prisoner', so-called since it first dates back to the time of Francis

Drake, the Anglo-Spanish war and the Spanish Armada in the sixteenth century. The fraud took the following form. A well-to-do young English gentleman is approached by a man purporting to be an exiled Spanish noble. He tells the Englishman he has been forced to flee his political enemies at home. He then produces a portrait of a beautiful young woman, saying that this is his sister, who is being held prisoner in Spain. The nobleman says he needs the help of a principled Englishman who will help him arrange for his sister's escape from her captors, since he was forced to flee Spain without money and has no resources of his own. He then tells the Englishman that his sister has in her possession a fortune in jewels and gems, the family's inherited riches. The man who is willing to help with the sister's escape will be given a substantial share of the jewels in return for his help; moreover, his beautiful sister will be 'eternally grateful' to the foreign gentleman for helping to free her. The Englishman, dazzled by the prospect of instant riches and the adoration of a beautiful Spanish noblewoman, readily agrees to advance the Spaniard the funds he needs. Subsequently, the Spaniard may well return on a number of occasions and relate how further problems have arisen, and that more money is needed to ensure the sister's safe release. The Englishman continues to furnish further funds, until he has no more to give; at this point, the fictional Spaniard nobleman simply disappears, taking the Englishman's money with him. This fraud has, over the centuries reappeared in various forms; for example, in the early twentieth century, numerous wealthy Americans were defrauded in the 'Mexican prisoner' scam, a reworking of the Spanish con in a new setting.

In recent decades, the latest incarnation of this fraud has been the so-called 'Nigerian Letter Scam', otherwise known as the '419 fraud' (named after the relevant section of the Nigerian penal code prohibiting this kind activity) (USDS, 1997: 4). In the Nigerian fraud, the potential victim is contacted by mail, fax, and more recently via email. The communication purports to come from a former or current government official or his son, daughter or widow. It tells how the individual has a fortune (often ill-gotten) in Nigerian bank accounts, but the money cannot be safely extracted because of the turbulent political situation in the country. A trustworthy foreigner is needed to whom the funds can be transferred. In return for making his/her account available, the foreigner will be given a substantial share of the millions of dollars that will be extracted from Nigeria. However, since all the Nigerian's resources are trapped in this account, he or she needs the foreigner to advance some money to make the transfer possible (hence the term 'advance fee fraud'). A typical example of a Nigerian Scam email is presented in Figure 5.1. The victim may well give substantial sums repeatedly to the fraudster, in hope of becoming an instant millionaire once the monies have been successfully released. Needless to say, there are no millions, and having 'taken' the victim for large sums, the 'Nigerian' simply disappears.

CYBER-FRAUDS, SCAMS AND CONS

FROM: Dr Ibrahim Quattara.
Chairman Contract Review Panel,
Abidjan, Côte D'Ivoire.
West Africa.
Tel:008821633310239

DEAR FRIEND.
LETTER FOR URGENT ASSISTANCE ON FUND TRANSFER
First, I must solicit your strictest confidence in this transaction. This by virtue of its nature as being utterly confidential and TOP SECRET.

I got your contact in our search for a foreign partner who has the ability and reliability to prosecute a transaction of great magnitude involving a pending business transaction requiring maximum confidence.

We are top officials of the Federal Government contract review panel who are interested in investment in your country with funds which are presently trapped here in Côte d' Ivoire. In other to commence this business we solicit your assistance to enable us transfer into your account the said trapped funds.

The source of this fund is as follows: During the last regime here of General Robert Guei in Côte d' Ivoire some government officials set up companies and awarded themselves contracts which were grossly over-invoiced in various ministries. The government set up a contract review panel and we have identified a lot of inflated contracts funds which are presently deposited in a BANK here in Abidjan, Côte d' Ivoire .

However, by virtue of our position as civil servants and members of the panel, we cannot acquire this money in our name. I have therefore, been delegated as a matter of trust by my colleagues to look for an overseas partner into whose account we would transfer the total sum of US$25,500,000.00 [TWENTY FIVE MILLION, FIVE HUNDRED THOUSAND UNITED STATES DOLLARS].

Hence we are writing you this letter. We agreed to share the money
thus:
[1] 20 per cent FOR THE ACCOUNT OWNER [YOU]
[2] 80 per cent FOR US [THE OFFICIALS]

It is from the 80 per cent that we wish to commence investments in your country as you will also stand as our foreign agent over there. Please note that this transaction is 100 per cent safe and we hope to commence the transaction latest seven [7] days from the date of the receipt of the following information bellow.

[A] COMPANY'S NAME BENEFICIARY OF ACCOUNT.
[B] YOUR PERSONAL TELEPHONE NUMBER AND FAX NUMBERS.
[C] BANK ACCOUNT/SORT/ABA/ROUTING NUMBERS
WHICH THE FUND WILL BE TRANSFERRED TO.
[D] YOUR BANK ADDRESS, TELEPHONE NUMBERS/FAX NUMBERS.

The above information will enable us commence the transfer of this
funds into your account in your country without delay.

We are looking forward to doing this business with you and solicit your confidentiality in this transaction.

(Continued)

Figure 5.1 The 'Nigerian Fraud' email

In the period between 1989 and 1999, the US Secret Service estimates that victims worldwide were defrauded of $5 billion by means of the Nigerian Fraud (Smith et al., 1999: 3). Since the rapid expansion of the Internet from the mid-1990s onwards, the fraudsters have moved from using mail and fax to mass emailings as a means of contacting their potential victims. According to the ICCC (2004: 3), the median dollar losses for those victimized by Internet variants of the Nigerian fraud was $3000 per complainant in 2004.

Phishing and spoofing

5.3.3 One of the most recent types of Internet fraud takes the form of bogus emails and/or websites intended to induce victims to voluntarily disclose passwords and other details that can then be used to access their bank and credit card accounts. These take two forms which are usually used in combination to perpetrate the fraud: 'phishing' (from 'fishing') for information via email, and 'spoofing' via bogus versions of legitimate financial services websites.

Phishing typically proceeds through the mass distribution of emails that purport to originate from banks, credit card companies, and e-sellers (such as Amazon). The mails typically request that the account holder needs to visit the bank, credit card company or other website in order to refresh their personal and other details in order to update their account. The more sophisticated variants of these mails use logos and wording associated with the legitimate company in order to cultivate the impression that the email is genuine (for a typical example of a phishing email, see Figure 5.2). The account holders will be provided with a hyperlink that supposedly takes them to the company's website where they can log on and enter the appropriate information. The hyperlink will in fact direct them to a bogus website that looks identical to the legitimate company website which account holders are accustomed to using. Here they will log on and enter their details. The fraudsters thus gain access to the users' passwords and other security and authentication information (date of birth, etc.), which can then be used to empty bank accounts or steal from credit cards.

87

citi WELCOME | MY citi

Account Suspended

Dear Citibank® Customer,

Citibank® is currently performing regular maintenance of our security measures. Your account has been randomly selected for this maintenance, and placed on Hold status. Protecting the security of your Citibank® account is our primary concern, and we apologize for any inconvenience this may cause.

You can reset your password by entering the correct account information or by answering your security questions.

Enter information:
* - Required fields

User ID*

Password*

Email
jessiem@purdue.edu

Card #/CIN*

PIN*

Account #*

Any account linked to your Citibank Banking Card

cancel | continue

OR

Your Full Name*

Address*

Zip*

State*

Email
jessiem@purdue.edu

Social Security #*

Date of Birth*

Mother Maiden Name*

Card # (Citibank® Visa/Mastercard)*

CVV2/CVC2*

3-digits in reverse italic to the right of the card number in the signature area on back

Expiry Date*

cancel | continue

citi
Citi.com

A member of citigroup.
Citigroup Privacy Promise
Terms & Conditions
Copyright © 2004 Citicorp

Figure 5.2   'Phishing' email

Complaints about fraud using phishing and spoofing have been on the increase in recent years (ICCC, 2005: 4). By 1999, spoofing or 'page-jacking', wherein web users are redirected to bogus but authentic-looking versions of genuine websites, was thought to affect some 25 million pages, or 2 per cent of the total sites then available on the Internet (Grazioli and Jarvenpaa, 2000: 3). According to the Anti-Phishing Working Group (APWG), there were over 2500 such sites reported on the Internet for January 2005 alone, a 100 per cent increase on the number in the previous October (APWG, 2005: 1). They also report almost 13,000 new phishing emails appearing in January 2005, a

42 per cent increase on the previous month, and an average monthly rate of increase of 30 per cent (ibid.: 2). The phishing and spoofing emails and websites identified in January 2005 hijacked the brands and credentials of 64 companies such as banks and e-retailers (ibid.). The sophistication of these emails and sites is such that even experienced Internet consumers are usually unable to identify them as fraudulent; in one empirical study, 82 per cent of experienced users failed to detect that the sites they were using were in fact bogus (Grazioli and Jarvenpaa, 2000: 22).

Such frauds are effective and difficult to detect because they exploit the ways in which *trust* is socially organized, in both terrestrial and virtual settings. In our dealings with others, we normally make inferences as to their trustworthiness on the basis of their appearance or 'self-presentation' (Goffman, 1969; Rutter, 2000: 4). If others conform to our typical understandings of trustworthiness (i.e. they look and behave according to our expectations of appropriate appearance and conduct), we take them to be exactly what they claim to be. So, for example, if we encounter on the street an individual dressed in a police uniform, and behaving according to our expectations about how a police officer normally acts, we take it as given that this person is in fact a police officer and not someone merely pretending to be one. Fraudsters and con artists are adept at borrowing the tools of self-presentation so as to convince others that they are someone they are in fact not (Bergmann, 1969; Nash, 1976). Phishing and spoofing effectively appropriate the markers we use to make judgements about trustworthiness and authenticity (the logos, the brand names, the 'professional' appearance of the websites) in order to deceive us into believing that they are legitimately what they purport to be. It is only after the victim has been defrauded does it become apparent that their trust in the other's appearances was fundamentally misplaced.

Investment fraud   A further prominent form of online fraud involves the trading in stocks and shares. By 2001, over 7 million Americans were using the Internet to buy and sell shares; almost 25 per cent of all share trades undertaken by individual investors were taking place online (Fried, 2001: 4). The growth of online share trading has created unprecedented opportunities for fraudsters to exploit.

Investment frauds can take a number of forms. The first and most straightforward is the solicitation of investments in non-existent companies. As early as 1996, the US Securities and Exchanges Commission (SEC), the stock market regulatory body, had brought several cases to court involving such fraudulent online investment schemes. One involved an individual who persuaded Internet users to invest in two non-existent Costa Rican coconut companies; another involved the online marketing of shares in a non-existent eel farm (English, 1996: 8). Fraudsters contact potential investors by means such as mass email, online investment newsletters, bulletin boards and chat rooms (Beresford, 2003: 2). Another common form of investment fraud are so-called 'pump-and-dump' schemes. In such cases, the fraudster contacts the victim claiming to have 'inside information' about a stock-market listed company (usually a small enterprise with a limited market capitalization) which he/she claims is about to 'go through the roof', i.e. its share values will imminently rise rapidly once the 'secret' information goes public. The investor is induced to buy stock in the company in expectation of a rapid and spectacular return. The sudden purchasing of stock by victims pushes up the company's share price ('pumping' the stock). Once the price has risen, the fraudster 'dumps' his or her own stock in the company in order to cash in on the temporary rise. The stock then inevitably falls following the dumping, often to below the price at which the victims purchased it, leaving them out of pocket, while the fraudster reaps a healthy profit at their expense (Fried, 2001: 6; Beresford, 2003: 2–3).

Of the complaints about online fraud received by the ICCC during 2004, 0.6 per cent involved investment scams. While this represents a small proportion of overall Internet frauds, the amounts lost are relatively high when compared to other kinds of scams such as auction fraud. Of those filing complaints about investment fraud, 75 per cent reported having incurred financial losses, the average amount being $625 per victim.

Online fraud: perpetrators' advantages and criminal justice's problems

5.4 The perpetration of frauds in online, rather than terrestrial, environments offers a number of advantages to the fraudster, and a number of corresponding difficulties for law enforcement agencies.

Anonymity and disguise

5.4.1 From the point of view of fraudsters, the Internet offers valuable opportunities to disguise themselves and their identities. They can present themselves under false aliases, or steal the identity of some other unsuspecting and innocent person for the purposes of committing their offences (what is commonly called 'identity theft' – see Smith 2003; Cabinet Office, 2002; Gordon et al., 2004). They can effectively change their personal and social characteristics, such as age, gender, ethnic group, country of residence, and so on. They can also adopt multiple fictitious identities that can be used in frauds to present themselves as previous satisfied customers in order to win the trust of their victims. Even when the commission of a fraud has been detected, identifying the individual(s) responsible may prove extremely difficult; the trail may lead to an innocent third party whose identity has been stolen, or it may simply prove impossible to find the party behind the aliases and false personae (Fried, 2001: 9).

Jurisdiction

5.4.2 A second area in which the Internet offers advantages for fraudsters is their ability to exploit the problems of policing across national jurisdictions. The identification of, and bringing criminal sanctions against, fraudsters located outside the jurisdiction in which the victim is located are beset with problems. First, it is time-consuming and costly for law enforcement agencies, who are often struggling to meet other crime and order issues that take public and political priority over fraud. Second, taking such action requires the cooperation of law enforcement agencies in other countries; while there have recently been moves to institutionalize transnational agreements for such cooperative investigation of cybercrime, they are at a nascent stage. Third, websites such as online auction houses may prove uncooperative, fearing that negative publicity about frauds may deter customers, or that they may themselves be held legally liable for facilitating the offences (as happened in June 2004 when the jewellers Tiffany & Co. filed suit against eBay for allegedly facilitating and participating in counterfeiting and false advertising (Flahardy, 2004: 1)). Fourth, the ability for particular countries to take effective action against online fraud through regulation and legislation is severely hampered by the transnational character of the offences. Thus, for example, in 2001 the Japanese National Police (NPA) floated a range of legislative proposals in response to growing problems of Internet auction fraud, particularly the sale of stolen goods. However, the proposed laws quickly came in for criticism. Gohsuke Takama, a Japanese Internet security expert stated:

> Applying one country's local laws to any Internet industry will cause problems – especially international jurisdiction issues – and the people who put this legislation together clearly didn't consider that. How can a used-goods broker law in Japan be applied to an Internet auction company which is registered outside of Japan, owned by non-Japanese, has transactions processed through a credit card company located outside of Japan, operates on web servers located outside of Japan, but has Japanese pages?
>
> (Quoted in Scuka, 2005)

This case exemplifies the problem of transnational regulation and policing when it comes to Internet fraud. Taken together, the above problems are likely to severely hinder the possibility of a satisfactory resolution for the victim. Hence it comes as no surprise that victimization surveys relating to online fraud reveal high levels of dissatisfaction with the law-enforcement outcomes following the lodging of complaints; Dolan's (2004: 16) survey of victims of auction fraud found that 51 per cent were 'not satisfied with the response they received from law enforcement agencies'.

Under-reporting

5.4.3 As with other forms of cybercrime, there are significant issues related to the under-reporting of offences. Victims of online frauds may be reluctant to report their victimization for a number of reasons:

- They may decide that the relatively small amounts of money involved does not make pursuing the matter worthwhile.
- They may feel embarrassed about having been 'taken in' by a fraudster.
- In cases where the scheme in which they participated involved seemingly illegal activity (such as trading in shares on the basis of insider information), they may fear that they themselves will be charged.
- They may not know to whom to report the offence, or there may be no authority which has been allocated responsibility.
- They may judge that there is little likelihood of a successful outcome, especially if the person who has defrauded them is seemingly located in another country.

All these factors may give fraudsters a sense of security in the expectation that they are unlikely to suffer legal consequences and sanctions as a result of their schemes.

Cost efficiencies and savings

5.4.4 A final factor to be considered is the considerable cost advantages garnered by using the Internet in fraud schemes. For example, while in the past advance fee fraudsters would seek potential victims through the relatively costly and time-consuming practice of posting letters and sending faxes, now they are able to compose and distribute emails to tens of thousands of Internet users in a matter of minutes and at virtually no cost. Similarly, those engaging in investment fraud no longer need to produce expensive, glossy brochures to send to potential victims, or laboriously 'cold call' individuals via telephone; instead, emails and professional-looking investment newsletters can be cheaply and quickly composed on any PC and rapidly disseminated via free email accounts. Such factors considerably reduce the 'start-up' costs for frauds and massively extend the number of potential victims that can be approached. The Internet also has advantages for those fencing stolen goods, as they no longer need to go to the expense (and indeed risk) of transporting the goods to various locations where they can be hawked; instead, they can be kept in storage until a sale has been made online, when they can be sent via post at the expense of the purchaser.

Strategies for policing and combating Internet frauds

5.5 There are a number of emerging and potential strategies by which the growing problem in Internet fraud may be tackled. These are considered below.

Legislative innovation and harmonization

5.5.1 There is apparent a pressing need to update national fraud legislation in order to take account of the innovative forms of fraud that occur in online environments. Some of the crucial areas include the need to establish appropriate criteria for electronic evidence, and for the redefinition of evidentiary categories traditionally used in prosecuting fraud cases, such as the understanding of what constitutes a 'document', 'writing', a 'signature', and so on (Smith and Urbas, 2001: 5). While many countries have taken concerted steps in this direction, others lack appropriate legal instruments for effective action. There is an equally urgent need to internationally harmonize such provisions so as to enable prosecution of Internet fraudsters in cross-national cases. The establishment of international treaties and conventions (such as the European Convention on Cybercrime) will assist in this regard, but there remains at present a limited degree of symmetry between Internet fraud provisions worldwide.

Centralized reporting and coordination

5.5.2 As already noted, one of the difficulties facing the policing of Internet fraud is the widespread absence of relevant agencies to whom victims can make a complaint. In this regard, the ICCC in the USA may be viewed as a model for institutional innovation. The ICCC model offers a two-fold benefit. First, it proved a centralized, national point of contact for complainants, enabling reported frauds to be passed on to the most appropriate law enforcement agency for investigation and action. Second, its recording activities fulfil a strategic function, helping to detect trends and patterns in online fraud, such as the appearance of new kinds of scams. However, at present, the ICCC model remains the exception rather than the rule. Even where national Internet crime agencies have already been established, online fraud may not necessarily be included within their present remit (as in the case of the UK's National Hi-Tech Crime Unit (NHTCU), which does not deal with fraud complaints).

Specialized training and coordination in law enforcement

5.5.3 One of most pressing issues for the policing of online fraud is the lack of specialized expertise and training. Resources need to be made available for the recruitment and retention of staff with the necessary technical skills, such as computer forensics (Smith and Urbas 2001: 4). Similar problems arise with the lack of adequate procedures for inter-agency cooperation and coordination, at both national and transnational levels. In the latter area, the establishment of international cybercrime law enforcement bodies, such as Europol's ENISA marks a move toward more focused partnership between national-level agencies and investigations.

CYBER-FRAUDS, SCAMS AND CONS

Technological anti-fraud innovation

5.5.4 A final area of action relates to the development of new technologies to curtail the perpetration of online fraud. Emerging measures include the following:

- innovations in user authentication technologies, such as the use of biometrics and digital signatures (Wright, 1998: 10; Lawson, 2002: 2–3);
- the use of web traffic analysis and visitor profiling so as to provide early warning about suspicious and potentially fraudulent patterns of use on websites such as auction houses (Experian, 2002: 12);
- schemes for website certification and endorsement, such as the WebTrust programme pioneered in the USA (Smith, 2003: 16).

However, the deployment of any or all of the above cannot be seen as a technological panacea, as each entails its own problems and limitations. The use of more stringent authentication technologies can prove expensive and may deter legitimate customers from using e-commerce facilities, particularly as they raise concerns about excessive intrusion and surveillance (van der Ploeg, 2000). Similarly, the deployment of web traffic analysis and profiling is resource-intensive and may only be viable for the largest e-business sites (such as Amazon, which already utilizes such systems). A problem with certification and endorsement schemes is that there is no agreed standard by which users can judge whether or not a site is legitimate – for example, by 2002 there were already some 20 different 'Webseals' or certification schemes in circulation in Australia alone (Smith, 2003: 14–15). Moreover, past experience with the use of technological e-crime countermeasures has shown that determined offenders are highly adept at finding ways to circumvent and exploit such safeguards. Consequently, technical solutions may only offer a temporary respite from the problems of Internet frauds.

Summary

5.6 This chapter introduced a range of fraudulent activities that are perpetrated by using online facilities such as emails, websites and auction houses. Such frauds can take a range of more or less sophisticated forms, and can prove difficult to tackle. Problems encountered include the under-reporting of victimization for a variety of reasons; the difficulties in identifying perpetrators who usually make recourse to using false or stolen identities; the lack of centralized and coordinated laws enforcement agencies with adequate resources to tackle the problem; and problems of jurisdiction arising from the transnational character of many of the offences. It has been noted that the move from the terrestrial to virtual environment offers many advantages for fraudsters, encouraging them to participate in what can be an increasingly lucrative and relatively low-risk form of criminal enterprise. Strategies for responding to cyber-fraud have been explored, but it is clear that there is no simple tool, technique or policy that can curtail fraudulent activities online. As an ever-greater amount of commercial transactions is being undertaken in online environments, so we can expect a corresponding ongoing growth in cyber-frauds, scams and cons.

Study questions

- what is the distinctive nature of fraud, and how does it differ from other kinds of criminal activity?
- how do fraudsters exploit mechanisms of trust in order to successfully defraud their victims?
- how might characteristics of the Internet such as its global reach and online anonymity assist fraudsters and frustrate law enforcement?
- what are the drawbacks of turning to technology as a 'quick fix' for Internet fraud?
- what might Internet users themselves do in order to reduce their risk of victimization?

Further reading

A useful overview of the issues surrounding online fraud is provided by Peter Grabosky and Russell Smith, in their article, 'Telecommunication fraud in the digital age: the convergence of technologies', in D. Wall (ed.) *Crime and the Internet* (2001). For more detailed and up-to-date information about the patterns and levels of online fraud, see the ICCC's annual *Internet Fraud – Crime Report*. For a detailed study of auction frauds, see Kyle Dolan, 'Internet auction fraud: the silent victims' (2004). Current data on trends in phishing and spoofing can be found on at the Anti-Phishing Working Group's website at www.antiphishing.org, which also contains an interesting archive of past emails. A valuable theoretical exploration of issues relating to online trust is Jason Rutter's 'From the sociology of trust towards a sociology "E-Trust"' (2000). Detailed discussion of legislative and technological counter-measures to combat online fraud can be found in Russell Smith's paper, 'Travelling in cyberspace on a false passport: controlling transnational identity-related crime' (2003). The journal *Computer Fraud and Security* is a valuable resource for reports on the latest research and anti-fraud initiatives as they emerge.

CYBER-FRAUDS, SCAMS AND CONS

Note

1 Canada has recently established a counterpart organization, RECOL (Reporting Economic Crime Online), a partnership between the Canadian White Collar Crime Centre and the Royal Canadian Mounted Police (RCMP). However, RECOL deals with fraud of all kinds, unlike the ICCC which specializes in Internet-related crimes; moreover, it currently makes available only very limited data relating to the scope, scale and nature of online frauds. See www.recol.ca

SIX

Illegal, Harmful and Offensive Content Online

From Hate Speech to Child Pornography

Overview

Chapter 6 examines the following issues:

- *the debate surrounding the criminalization of 'hate speech;*
- *the proliferation of such speech online, and the legal and law enforcement challenges it presents;*
- *the prevalence of pornographic material online;*
- *criminal justice issues around Internet pornography, such as children's access to sexually explicit online content;*
- *the problem of Internet child pornography;*
- *the challenges of eradicating such pornographic material, especially those raised by legal and moral differences across different countries.*

---

key terms

Child	Hate speech	Obscenity
Child pornography	Indecency	Pornography
First Amendment rights	Legal pluralism	

Introduction

6.1 The growth of the Internet has been hailed by many as a powerful medium for free speech and open communication. The online environment enables individuals and groups to share ideas, experiences, and information in ways previously impossible using existing media. This free flow and exchange are viewed as the lifeblood of democratic cultures (McGonagle, 2001: 21), and the Internet as an invaluable means by which citizens can bypass restrictions on speech imposed by authoritarian and repressive governments. The political and social value of such Internet communication is indicated by the burgeoning of online civic and community groups, and by the rise of direct action movements pursuing goals such as global social justice and human rights. However, the liberation of communication enabled by the Internet also has much darker and problematic dimensions. The celebratory attitude toward Internet speech inevitably runs into difficulties when confronted with online content that may be illegal, or deemed offensive and harmful to individuals, communities, or the social fabric. This chapter explores the complex web of issues that arise in relation to illegal, offensive and/or harmful content online. Three forms of online content will be examined. First, there are the various forms of discriminatory 'hate speech' which target individuals or groups on the grounds of their 'racial', ethnic, religious, gender, sexual or other characteristics. Second, there are those forms of (visual and written) representation that might be considered sexually offensive, such as so-called 'hardcore' and violent pornography. Third, there are those online communications that specifically entail the sexualized representation of minors ('child pornography'), much discussed in recent years. Such online content raises a range of thorny issues. For example, in relation to the first two types of content, some forms of representation are illegal and some are not; the same representation may be permissible in one country but not in another; regulating access to such content online can prove difficult (as when young children may be exposed to highly explicit adult sexual content). Arguments may be made for the prohibition of such content on the grounds of harm, while others may resist such restriction in the name of freedom of speech. Even where the content is illegal, the transnational nature of the Internet presents serious challenges for law enforcement. In relation to the third area, child pornography, there is much greater legal and social consensus about its prohibition; nevertheless, there arise serious jurisdictional and practical issues when it comes to enforcing anti-child pornography laws in the online environment. Debates relating to offensive and harmful content are, in short, among the most contentious issues relating to the Internet. As we shall see, the legal and social regulation of Internet speech presents a variety of challenges that are only just starting to be addressed.

Thinking about 'hate speech'

6.2 The term 'hate speech' has emerged in recent decades, initially in response to concerns about the ways in which the use of racist language contributes to discrimination against, and incites hatred and violence towards, minority ethnic individuals and groups. In this context, hate speech can be defined as: 'speech that (1) has a message of racial inferiority, (2) is directed against a member of a historically oppressed group, and (3) is persecutory, hateful and degrading' (Nielsen, 2002: 266). Concern about the social consequences of such language emerged in a number of countries out of various historical and political contexts. For example, in Germany the political and cultural trauma of Nazism and anti-Semitism served to focus attention upon forms of expression that might contribute towards the revival of racial intolerance and hatred (Brugger, 2002; Timofeeva, 2003: 260); the issue was further intensified from the 1970s onwards in Germany with the arrival of large numbers of so-called *Gastarbeiter* or 'guest workers' from countries such as Turkey. In the UK, the tensions and conflicts arising from extensive post-war immigration from British Commonwealth countries (especially from the West Indies and South Asia) created political pressures to address the discrimination and hostility directed towards 'newcomers' by segments of the majority white population; similar developments occurred in France in the context of migration from former French colonial countries in North Africa (Bleich, 2003: 2–3). In the USA, the Civil Rights movement of the 1960s inspired a range of anti-discrimination measures aimed at realizing the goal of social inclusion for African-Americans and overcoming a legacy of prejudice emanating from the era of slavery (McCormack, 1998). From the 1970s onwards, other social constituencies which had historically suffered varying forms of discrimination, exclusion and violence also started to campaign for action against demeaning, hateful and prejudicial forms of representation. From these movements, there emerged an understanding of hate speech that encompassed derogatory representations not just on grounds of 'race' or ethnicity, but also including dimensions such as religion, gender, sexual orientation and disability. Thus the definition cited above can be extended to include 'messages of gender, sexual, religious, physical and mental inferiority' within its scope. Recognition of the need to take legal and institutional action against such forms of expression has, however, been far from universal. Thus, for example, recent years have seen in many Western countries a heated and acrimonious debate about so-called 'political correctness' and the regulation of language use (see for example, Hughes, 1993; Schwartz, 2003).

The pressure to legally prohibit hate speech is founded on a perception that such utterances are actively harmful to the individuals and communities that they target. The harms issuing from hate speech can be understood in two distinctive ways, each of which will be considered briefly below.

First, hate speech is seen as harmful in that it plays a pivotal role in inciting and condoning acts of violence and discrimination against target populations. Thus, for example, US law prohibits 'those words that are directed to inciting or producing imminent lawless action and are likely to incite or produce such action' (Steinhardt, 2000: 253; also Biegel, 2003: 330–1). Hence threats of violence 'consisting of a serious expression of intent to commit an imminent act of violence against an identified individual or group, may be punished' (Wendel, 2004: 1410). In the UK, legal provision goes much further, with legislation such as the Race Relations Act (1965) and the Public Order Act (1986) effectively prohibiting the incitement of racial hatred and defamation on grounds of ethnic or national origin, even in the absence of any likelihood of imminent lawless action following the utterance (Steinhardt, 2000: 253, 258). Most recently, the law has been extended under the Serious Organised Crime and Police Act (2005), providing for criminalization of incitement to *religious* hatred; this was deemed necessary to close the loophole where incitement to racial hatred could be undertaken under the disguise of criticizing an individual's or group's religious beliefs. These more wide-ranging provisions can be seen to enshrine the view that hate speech lays the groundwork for violence through its non-immediate but nevertheless significant impacts on social beliefs by contributing to a culture of bigotry. Hate speech is seen here as part of an inter-connected array of mechanisms of subordination, both symbolic and physical which support each other (Lederer and Delgado, 1995: 5). Thus, Tsesis (2002) draws attention to many historical instances in which hate speech has legitimated and encouraged a climate in which violence and abuse can take place – examples include the upsurge of anti-Semitic language preceding the Nazi Holocaust and the dehumanizing representation of Africans that supported the slave trade (Tsesis, 2002: 51–2, 101–6). More recently, we can note the demonization of the Tutsi ethnic group in Rwanda, which played an integral part in the 1994 genocide that led to the massacre of 800,000 people by their fellow citizens from the Hutu ethnic group (Wendel, 2004: 1404). In all these cases, the gradual build-up of hate speech created a structure of beliefs that supported violence on a near incomprehensible scale. It is the desire to forestall the development of such a culture that legitimizes the restriction of hateful speech and representation.

The second way in which the harmfulness of hate speech is understood turns not so much on its ability to incite acts of violence and abuse, as upon the view that such utterances are themselves *intrinsically* harmful to those who are targeted. Patterns of abusive speech directed at individuals and groups do damage to those targeted, undermining their selfhood and violating their human dignity. Exposure to such speech can lead the victim to internalize the insults directed at them, and produce negative psychological effects such as feelings of humiliation and emotional distress (McGonagle, 2001: 3–4; also Delgado, 1982). In one of the few empirical studies of the impact of (racist and sexist) hate speech upon individuals, Nielsen (2002) found that the experience of insults delivered by strangers in public places left victims feeling fearful, intimidated and threatened. From this perspective, insults are themselves forms of injury, with effects every bit as real as those resulting from acts of physical violence.

Hate speech online

6.3 Online hate speech is by no means a unique phenomenon, rather an extension of utterances (both written and verbal) that occur in the terrestrial world. The expansion of the Internet has seen an unwelcome proliferation of such speech. This takes a number of forms, which are explored below.

The most noticeable online hate speech takes the form of websites (and associated chat rooms and bulletin boards) established by organized political groups. These are typically far right, ultra-nationalist, white supremacist and

OFFENSIVE CONTENT ONLINE

neo-Nazi in orientation. In addition, the USA has seen an extensive online presence of extreme Christian fundamentalists, anti-abortion and anti-government militia groups. Such sites variously contain offensive and hateful representations of Blacks, Jews, Muslims, Arabs, other people of non-European origin, women, homosexuals, and persons with physical and mental disabilities. The precise number of such websites is difficult to gauge, as they often appear, disappear and move location (Craven, 1998: 3–4; Schaffer, 2002: 72). Moreover, as there is no *precise* agreed definition of what might comprise 'hateful content', there is room for variation in whether or not a particular site may or may not be included in different studies. However, it is clear that their number has grown rapidly over recent years. Ken Stern claimed that in 1997 there were some 300 such sites in the USA; by 1999, the Simon Wiesenthal Centre in Los Angeles had documented the existence of 600 'hate sites' on the Internet (Whine, 2000: 235). A study by UK-based Internet security company Surf-Control claims that the number of 'hate and violence' sites increased 300 per cent over a four-year period – from 2,756 in 2000 to 10,926 in April 2004 (The Register, 2004).

The use of the Internet to disseminate messages offers a number of advantages to 'hate groups'. As for other political movements and organizations, the web provides extremists with an extremely efficient and cost-effective means of communication, enabling actors with limited financial and material resources to reach a potentially global audience (Schaffer, 2002: 71). Moreover, the degree of protection it affords speakers (through anonymous postings, use of pseudonyms, etc.) makes it possible to propagate hate speech with a significantly reduced risk of identification and prosecution under anti-hate speech laws (Deirmenjian, 2000: 1021). Further, given the generally unpalatable nature of their utterances, extremist groups find it difficult to secure avenues to air their views through conventional, mainstream media; the Internet neatly bypasses this dependence, granting such groups access to and control over the means of communication. Finally, the Internet enables extremists to tailor their messages to appeal to particular target audiences who might be deemed open to influence (Craven, 1998: 4). Thus, for example, white supremacist organizations allow visitors to download 'white power music', typically heavy metal accompanied by 'violent, hateful and profane lyrics' (Schaffer, 2002: 78). Offering such material is seen as effective way to capture the attention of young people, providing a conduit for disseminating ideologies of violence. In sum, as Don Black, former 'Grand Dragon' of the Ku Klux Klan states: 'as far as recruiting, [the Internet has] been the biggest breakthrough I've seen in the 30 years I've been involved in [white nationalism]' (quoted in Wolf, 2004: 4).

A second form taken by Internet hate speech is the distribution of such content to targets via email messages. There have been a number of such cases documented in the USA. In one instance, Richard Machado, a student at the University of California Irvine, sent an email to 59 mainly Asian students. In his email, signed 'Asian hater', he asserted that 'I personally will make it my life career [sic] to find and kill everyone one [sic] of you personally. OK??????? That's how determined I am ...' (Wolf, 2004: 6). He went on to demand that they leave the university if they did not wish to be killed. The effect on his targets was pronounced: 'many ... were prepared to arm themselves with pepper spray, became suspicious of strangers, and refused to go out alone in the dark' (Deirmenjian, 2000: 1020). In another case, 22-year-old Kingman Quon sent threatening emails to hundreds of Latino employees at universities, corporations and government agencies across the USA. He stated that Latinos were 'too stupid' to gain entry to university or get jobs without the help of 'affirmative action' (positive discrimination) programmes, and said that he intended to 'come down and kill them' (Wolf, 2004: 8). In a third case, 19-year-old Casey Belanger, a student at the University of Maine in New England, posted a message on the University's Gay/Lesbian/Bisexual Internet discussion system (expletives deleted):

> I hope you die screaming in hell ... you'd [sic] better watch your ... back you little ... I'm [sic] gonna shoot you in the back of the ... head ... die screaming [name of student], burn in eternal ... hell ... I hate gay/lesbian/bisexuals
>
> (Kaplan and Moss, 2003: 8).

In all three of the above cases the offenders were successfully prosecuted, as all had made threats of violence against specific individuals (that is to say, their speech contained 'serious expression of intent to commit an imminent act of violence against an identified individual or group').

Legal, policing and political challenges in tackling online hate speech

6.4 The criminalization of hate speech is itself a controversial and divisive topic, and there is no consensus that such speech ought indeed be made legally punishable. We have already encountered the arguments for prohibiting such representations on grounds of both the directly and indirectly harmful consequences they may have for those targeted. However, there are numerous legal and political commentators who, while condemning hate speech, oppose its criminalization. One line of argument against such sanctions points out the difficulty in defining what is to count as 'hateful', 'degrading', and 'discriminatory'. Who is entitled to arbitrate which utterances fall under such labels? Those subjected to criticisms by others may use claims of 'hatefulness' to silence the critics, denying them the right to exercise free speech. Political, journalistic, academic, and artistic censorship will inevitably result if all speech considered 'hateful', 'degrading' or 'discriminatory' by various social constituencies is silenced. Thus, it is argued that banning hate speech, however offensive the majority may find it, comes at too high a price, namely the loss of freedom of opinion, expression and information (McGonagle, 2001: 21). Those who oppose the prohibition of hate speech in general also wish to safeguard the Internet's potential as a means of free expression. Thus, Steinhardt (2000: 249) argues that: 'Although "hate speech" and other vile utterances can be found in cyberspace, censoring speech in this medium would go against the free, open, anarchic and global nature of the Internet, and severely impede its growth'. Consequently, those taking the anti-prohibition stance argue that the 'best antidote to hate speech is more speech' which aims to 'help educate people, promote positive messages, and spread truthful information' (Wolf, 2004: 16).

Even where there is legal provision in place against hate speech, the global nature of the Internet presents significant difficulties to its effective enforcement. What happens, for example, when the target or victim of hate speech is in one country, the group or individuals responsible for that speech are in another, and the online content is hosted on web servers located in a third territory? Questions of jurisdictional responsibility for dealing with hate speech in such situations pose serious challenges. Since the mid-1990s, the European Union has been taking steps to harmonize provisions dealing with illegal and harmful content online, including the improvement of international cooperation on enforcement across member countries (Rorive, 2002: 10). National authorities have responded, albeit with varying degrees of urgency, to these European initiatives. For example, in 1998, the UK government announced that its National Criminal Intelligence Service (NCIS) was now 'in close liaison with other countries to combat Internet abuse', including 'acting against threatening abusive and racist material' (Whine, 2000: 246).

Perhaps the greatest obstacle to the effective regulation and punishment of hate speech online arises from the variation in hate crime laws across national territories worldwide. Given the transnational span of the Internet, extremist groups can effectively bypass hate speech prohibitions in one country by locating websites on servers in other territories where those same restrictions do not apply (Deirmenjian, 2000: 1021). Thus, for example, the extremist British National Party (BNP) now has a website registered in Tonga, enabling them to safely post material that would fall foul of the UK's anti-racism laws were the site hosted in Britain (Whine, 2000: 241). Similarly, the French extremist right-wing organization *Charlemagne Hammer Skinheads* relocated their website to Canada after their France-based service was terminated by their Internet Service Provider (ISP) (ibid.: 241); although 13 individuals belonging to the group were charged with 'promoting racial hatred, uttering death threats, and desecrating a grave' in the UK and France, authorities there could not shut down the website due its location in Canada (Deirmenjian, 2000: 1021). A particularly dramatic illustration of this problem is presented by the case of German anti-hate legislation. Due to its unique historical experience, Germany is perhaps the nation with the most stringent of all anti-hate speech laws, including the prohibition of Nazi symbols (such as the Swastika), Holocaust denial, and defaming the memory of the dead (Timofeeva, 2003: 260–3). However, there is nothing preventing the burgeoning neo-Nazi movement in Germany from posting such material in other territories.

The greatest concentration of hate sites today is to be found in the USA, where free speech enjoys a legal protection matched in few other countries. The First Amendment to the US Constitution prohibits lawmakers from encroaching upon the freedom of expression, even where that speech is racist, sexist, homophobic, or otherwise discriminatory in character. The only exemption to First Amendment protection arises, as already noted, when the speech contains a *serious* and *imminent* threat of violence against *identifiable persons*, or *directly* incites others to commit specific criminal acts against those persons. Anything 'falling short of incitement to imminent violent action' enjoys constitutional protection (Wendel, 2004: 1410). For those advocating the legal restriction of hateful speech, the US Constitution gives a 'virtually unlimited license for hate speech' (Tsesis, 2002: 180). For extremists worldwide propagating such speech, the nature of US constitutional law, when combined with the ease of transnational communication afforded by the Internet, inevitably provides something of a 'safe haven' from prosecution under laws in their own countries.

The growth and popularity of Internet pornography

6.5 The production of sexually explicit imagery dates back to the era of human prehistory. One of the earliest depictions of the human form ever discovered, the so-called 'Venus of Willendorf' (dated at 24,000–22,000 BC) is a figurine of a woman with 'large pendulous breasts ... prominent mons pubis with a distinctly rendered vulva ... and well padded buttocks'; an image, it has been suggested, of 'explicitness and thinly veiled eroticism' (Lane, 2001: 1–2). The later development of both artisanal technology and trade in the ancient Greek and Roman worlds created a thriving commercial use of sexual images, which have been found to adorn a bewildering array of objects, including wine coolers, dinnerware, bronze bowls, vases, domestic walls in the form of paintings and murals, and 'even children's drinking bowls and plates' (ibid.: 3–4). In the early modern era, the development of printing from the mid-fifteenth century onwards was rapidly followed by a proliferation of sexually explicit publications, including books, pamphlets, posters, and cartoons (Kutchinsky, 1992: 41; Lane, 2001: 7). The Victorian era was also characterized by a thriving, if largely clandestine, trade in pornography and erotica (Hyde, 1964; Mackie, 2004: 981). Visual representations began to overtake the more traditional written form with the invention first of photography in the 1840s, then the emergence of motion pictures in the 1890s; this move from verbal to visual depiction helped to broaden the appeal of pornography beyond a literate elite to embrace viewers and consumers from all social strata and walks of life (Kutchinsky, 1992: 41–2; Zimmer and Hunter, 1999). Throughout the twentieth century, the popularity of pornography continued to grow across the Western world, in the form of adult movie theatres and magazines such as *Playboy, Penthouse, Hustler*, and a legion of others too numerous to mention. Perhaps the first great technological innovation *vis-à-vis* pornography during the last century was the introduction of mass market VCRs in the 1970s, which permitted viewers to enjoy pornographic films in the privacy of their homes. This was later followed by the availability of pornographic material via dedicated cable and satellite subscription TV channels. Americans now rent an estimated $5 billion worth of adult videos per annum, and pay a total of $150 million dollars to view such movies on pay-per-view cable services (Lane, 2001: xv); worldwide, an estimated $20 billion is spent every year on adult videos, and $5 billion on cable viewing (IWF, 2004). All of the above serves to illustrate two main points: first, that the appetite for sexually explicit material appears to be a consistent feature of human cultures, and, second, that its development has gone hand-in-hand with the technological development of media and communication. Therefore, it should come as no surprise that the circulation of pornography has been a prominent feature of the Internet since its inception.

Even in the early years of networked computing, the distribution of pornographic images was prevalent. In the late 1970s and early 1980s, programmers (mostly young men in university science, engineering and computing departments) were zealously developing software enabling such images to be transmitted, recomposed and viewed through Usenet systems. By 1996, of the ten most popular Usenet groups, five were sexually oriented, and one (alt.sex.net) attracted some 500,000 readers every day (Lane, 2001: 66–7). However, it was with the massive expansion of the Internet resulting from the surge in home computing in the mid-1990s (see Chapter 1.3) that Internet pornography really took off. Amidst all the anxiety generated by the 'problem' of online pornography, it is easy to overlook the critical role that Internet pornographers played in both the technological and commercial developments of the medium. For many years, Internet pornographers were the only web entrepreneurs who were actually making profits, providing clear evidence that e-commerce was a commercially viable proposition. Moreover, many of the key technologies enabling the delivery of digital content to Internet shoppers (such as secure credit card payment systems) were pioneered by pornographers, and subsequently adopted by those selling more 'conventional' online content such as music, software, and movies, as well as e-shopping sites such as amazon.com (Bennett, 2001:381). There are now estimated to be some 4.2 million pornographic websites (12 per cent of all Internet sites), containing 372 million pornographic pages. There are 68 million search engine requests for pornographic material every day, making up 25 per cent of the total searches. Some 1.5 million downloads of pornographic material are performed every month using peer-to-peer (P2P) file-sharing networks; 72 million people visit pornographic websites each year, 72 per cent of whom are male and 28 per cent female. The commercial sector of Internet pornography is conservatively estimated to be worth $2.5 billion per annum (IFR, 2004).

Criminological issues relating to Internet pornography

6.6 There are of course, many difficult definitional (and implicitly moral) questions surrounding the issue of pornography. For example, what are the boundaries (if any) between 'art', 'erotica' and 'pornography'? Such questions, fascinating and important though they are, will not provide the focus of discussion here. Rather, the crucial criminological issue to be addressed relates to the shifting and contested boundaries between pornography and *obscenity*. It is the latter which is typically subjected to formal legal prohibition and sanction, while interest in the former may attract more informal condemnation as variously unhealthy, 'filthy', 'dirty', immoral, unsavoury or deviant. The question facing those confronted with the prevalence of pornography online tends to centre on determining which kinds of representation cross the threshold into being obscene, and thus appropriate targets for legal action.

The definition of obscenity is itself subject to wide historical and contemporary cross-cultural variations. A representation that in a more liberal legal regime may be considered permissible may fall foul of obscenity laws in another country. This issue is of particular relevance when considering material on the Internet, given the medium's transnational, border-spanning character. In British law (following the Indecent Publications Act of 1959): 'an article shall be deemed obscene if its effect ... is, if taken as whole, such as to tend to deprave and corrupt persons who are likely, having regard to all relevant circumstances, to read, see or hear the matter contained or embodied in it' (Akdeniz, 1996: 236). The 1994 Criminal Justice and Public Order Act updated this legislation to take account of such material in an electronic formation (Akdeniz and Strossen, 2000). Two problems are readily apparent when considering these provisions. First, terms such as 'deprave' and 'corrupt' are highly ambiguous and indeterminate, and subject to a wide array of judgements. Second, the attempt to extend the British definition of obscenity to encompass online content is inherently problematic, given that it may be 'published' in other countries with significantly different legal provisions relating to obscenity.

Under US law, there is a distinction between obscene, indecent and offensive speech (Akdeniz, 1996). The latter two enjoy constitutional protection under the First Amendment (as discussed in the previous section of this chapter). There have been attempts by both social conservatives and radical feminist campaigners to remove the constitutional protection traditionally granted to indecent and offensive pornographic materials. Activists such as Catherine MacKinnon and Andrea Dworkin have argued that all pornography harms women, in that it both objectifies women and has a causal relation to sex crimes against women (MacKinnon, 1996). However, evidence in support of a direct link between pornography and sexual violence is inconclusive at best. For example, Kutchinsky's (1992) comparative four-nation, longitudinal study found no such link between increased availability and consumption of pornography and level of reported rape and sexual assault. Consequently, attempts to remove the First Amendment protection have failed before the courts. Obscenity, however, enjoys no such protection. To count as obscene, material must 'appeal to a "prurient" or "shameful" interest in sex, and it must be "patently offensive", according to local community standards' (Akdeniz and Strossen, 2000: 213). The provision for judgement of obscenity according to 'community standards' has enabled controls at a local level, for example, prohibiting adult movie theatres, strip clubs and sex shops from setting up in residential areas where such enterprises are unwelcome, forcing them to locate their businesses in other physical locales. However, the application of such provisions in the context of the Internet presents significant difficulties, for example, explicit material is typically accessed not in publicly available sites, but in the privacy of people's own homes, and those purveying the content are likely to be situated in locales (or even other countries) where 'community standards' about what is 'patently offensive' may be very different. Thus, for example, how can this provision be applied in the following (hypothetical, though not unlikely) case:[1] an individual residing in a highly conservative community in America's so-called 'Bible Belt' views, say, 'hardcore' sado-masochistic (S&M) images and video provided by an Internet business located in the sexually liberal San Francisco or Amsterdam? Whose standards can or ought to be applied here? Those of the community in which the consumer resides, but who are not in anyway exposed to his/her viewing habits? Those of the community in which the provider or publisher resides? Or those of the community of online users who frequent such sites? In short, the localized (and even national) regulation of supposedly 'obscene' content encounters serious obstacles when dealing with a medium that inherently spans geographical and legal territories.

The issue of 'legal pluralism' (the variation in obscenity laws across different countries) becomes even more exacting when we look beyond Western nations which take a generally permissive view when it comes to sexual representation, and consider those countries which have much stricter definitions of obscenity. In Saudi Arabia, for example, Internet access has been channelled through a single control centre controlled by the government, enabling authorities to block access to pornographic sites, which are held to breach 'public decency' (EFA, 2002). This, however, has led to a flourishing 'underground' industry providing access to pornography sites for Saudis willing and able to pay for explicit content (Procida and Simpson, 2003). A recent case in India further highlights some of the cross-national difficulties that can arise. In late 2004, a 17-year-old Indian male used his mobile phone camera to video himself being given oral sex by his 16-year-old girlfriend. A few days later, the recording was posted for sale by 23-year-old student Ravi Raj Singh on the Indian auction site Baazee.com, a subsidiary of ebay.com. In 2000, India had passed the Information Technology Act, criminalizing the online transmission and sale of pornography. Consequently, not only was the 17-year-old arrested, but also taken into custody was Avnish Bajaj, the chief executive of Bazee.com. Bajaj's arrest sparked an international diplomatic incident, since he is a US citizen, and American authorities attempted to intervene, including the then US National Security Advisor, Condolezza Rice (who was reportedly 'furious' over Bajaj's treatment) (Haines, 2004; Harding, 2004).

A further issue, one which has been of great public and political concern, is the fear that minors will be exposed (either wittingly or unwittingly) to sexually explicit adult-oriented content online. It has been noted that even the most seemingly innocuous web searches often return results containing content deemed unsuitable for children (Zimmer and Hunter, 1999: 3; Thorburgh and Lin, 2004: 43, 47–8). For example, an image search for 'Cindy' (the Barbie-like children's doll) returns pictures of numerous models named 'Cindy' depicted in a range of sexual explicit situations (including full-frontal nudity, masturbation and penetrative sex). Similarly, an image search for 'Pokemon' returns as its first 'hit' a sexually graphic cartoon featuring a naked woman being 'sexually pleasured' by Pokemon figures equipped with huge tumescent penises. Moreover, the practice of mass direct-marketing emails (so-called 'spam') exposes children to a range of offers for highly explicit sexual content when checking their inboxes, often disguised under seemingly innocent headings (such as 'hi there', 'about your request', and so on) (Biegel, 2003: 80). It is the fear that children will be inadvertently exposed to such material which fuelled what has been described as 'The Great Cyberporn Panic of 1996', when mainstream media produced a slew of articles about the danger posed to children by online pornographic content (Zimmer and Hunter, 1999: 11; also Wilkins, 1997: 4). Concern over this issue continues to run high; for example, a 2001 survey of parents of 10–14-year-olds in Ireland found that the 44 per cent believed that children's access to pornography was the greatest downside of the Internet (Amarach Consulting, 2001: 7). However, a further dimension is added to this debate when we consider the extent to which minors engage in the *active* and deliberate search for such content. According to research by the Internet Filter Review (2004), the largest consumers of online pornography are the 12–17-year-old age group. A UK-based survey of 9–19-year-olds found that 10 per cent of this age ground admit to deliberately visiting pornographic sites (Livingstone et al., 2005: 13). Such activities effectively mean that minors are acquiring access to material online that they would be legally prohibited from purchasing in more conventional 'terrestrial' forms (such as pornographic magazines, videos and DVDs).

Concerns about minors' access to sexually explicit content have inspired a number of legislative attempts to curtail children's exposure to pornography, especially in the USA. In 1996, Congress passed the Communications Decency Act (CDA). Among the Act's provisions were measures to criminalize whoever:

by means of a telecommunications device, knowingly ... makes, creates, or solicits, and initiates the transmission of, any comment, request, suggestion, proposal, image, or other communication which is obscene or indecent, knowing that the recipient of the communication is under 18 years of age;

and further criminalizes:

the use of an 'interactive computer service' to 'send' or 'display in a manner available' to a person under 18, 'any comment, request, suggestion, proposal, image, or other communication that, in content, depicts or describes in terms patently offensive as measured by contemporary community standards, sexual or excretory activities or organs, regardless of whether the user of such service placed the call or initiated the communication'.

(Moorefield, 1997: 32)

However, in June 1997 the US Supreme Court ruled that that CDA was unconstitutional, since the banning of any online service that displayed 'indecent' content that may be accessible by under-18s amounted to a denial of access to that same material by adults, hence breaching their First Amendment rights (Zimmer and Hunter, 1999: 12; Akdeniz and Strossen, 2000: 215–16). The CDA having being struck down, Congress tried again the following year, introducing the Child Online Protection Act (COPA) in 1998. This Act was less sweeping than the CDA, and made provision for prohibiting: 'any communication for commercial purposes that is available to any minor [those under 17] and that includes any material that is harmful to minors'.

'Harmfulness' was defined as:

> any communication, picture, image, graphic image file, article, recording, writing, or other matter of any kind that is obscene or that (a) the average person, applying contemporary community standards, would find, taking the material as a whole and with respect to minors is designed to appeal to, or is designed to pander to, the prurient interest; (b) depicts, describes, or represents, in a manner patently offensive with respect to minors, an actual or simulated sexual act or sexual contact, an actual or simulated normal or perverted sexual act, or a lewd exhibition of the genitals or post-pubescent female breasts; and (c) taken as a whole, lacks serious literary, artistic, political, or scientific value for minors.

> (Akdeniz and Strossen, 2000: 137)

It was hoped that this new legislation, focused more precisely upon specific commercially available content directed towards young people, could succeed where the CDA had failed. However, COPA was also deemed unconstitutional by the Supreme Court in June 2004; one of the Judges, Justice Anthony M. Kennedy justified the decision by stating that COPA entailed 'a potential for extraordinary harm and a serious chill upon protected speech' (ALA, 2004: 2). The government did finally score a victory when the Supreme Court upheld a third piece of legislation, the Children's Internet Protection Act (CIPA) in 2003. The Act requires 'public libraries that rely on federal funds for Internet use to install filtering devices on library computers to protect children from ... pornography and obscenity' (Sekulow, 2004: 5). However, the remit of this law is so limited that it leaves the majority of avenues by which children might access adult pornographic material untouched (applying as it does only to public (not private) libraries, and only to those which use federal (rather than state, local, or private charitable) funds for Internet use).

The overall failure of statutory regulation in respect of children's access to sexually explicit content has led to an emphasis on voluntary regulation, especially the use of Internet filtering software (of the kind prescribed in the CIPA) by ISPs and/or parents. There now exist a wide range of commercially available filtering packages, such as *Cyber Patrol, X-Stop, Cyber Sitter, Net Nanny, Child Safe, Cyber Sentinel, Content Protect*, and *Winguardian*. Such software contains databases of adult-oriented sites, and parents can use them to 'lock' web browsers' access to such sites; consequently, parents can allow their children to surf the Internet with the reassurance that youngsters will neither be unintentionally exposed to pornographic material, nor will they be able to access such content should they deliberately go looking for it. However, web filters have come in for considerable criticism as child-protection tools. First, studies of filters in operation have show that they block as little as 75 per cent of the content that they ought (i.e. material and websites of an 'objectionable' nature) (Hunter, 1999: 16). Hence, use of filters may give parents a false sense of security, as they will not shield children from all sexually explicit content. Second, and just as seriously, studies have show that filtering software typically 'over-filters' and thereby blocks access to socially acceptable, socially valuable and non-offensive content (EPIC, 1997). Recently, particular concern has been raised over findings that popular filters block access to many adolescent health information sites, misrecognizing the discussion of sexual health issues (such as safe sex) for pornography (Larkin, 2002: 1946). Third, while filtering software is at least partially effective against sexually explicit Internet websites, it has proven to be completely ineffective in blocking access to explicit content via other means, such as peer-to-peer file-sharing systems such as Gnutella. Many such file-sharing services provide unrestricted and free access to large quantities of pornographic material; a study for the US Congress undertaken in 2001 found, for example, that a search for 'porn' on the BearShare file-sharing system made available 25,000 items, of which more than 10,000 were video files (MSIDCGR, 2001: 4). All of the foregoing limitations suggest that neither technological nor legislative 'fixes' are likely to address parental and political concerns over children's access to online pornography, and that it may be time to reconsider some of the prevalent assumptions about the inherently harmful nature of exposure to such content.

Child pornography

6.7 It would be fair to say that no other cybercrime issues has elicited the degree of anxiety as that over the circulation of sexual images of minors on the Internet. The very idea of such images provokes revulsion among the overwhelming majority in society. It also produces fear: fear that children are inevitably being coerced and abused in the production of such images, and fear that the availability of such material will stimulate or encourage viewers to seek out children for sexual gratification. The child pornography issue has garnered even further attention over recent years due to a number of high-profile cases involving celebrities who have been accused of and/or convicted for possession of indecent pictures of children (for example, rock stars Gary Glitter and Pete Townsend in the UK, and Michael Jackson in the USA). Such material is in fact a far from novel phenomenon. For example, historians have documented the prevalence of both child pornography and child prostitution from the Victorian era onwards (see, for example, Pearsall, 1993; and Brown and Barrett, 2002). However, as we shall later see, the migration of such material onto the Internet presents a whole range of new problems for law making and law enforcement.

Gauging the precise extent of child pornography online is itself a difficult task, as a significant portion of such material is likely to be hidden from direct public visibility, given its illegal nature. An early study, conducted in January 1998, found that 0.07 per cent of 40,000 news groups examined (28 sites) contained 'child erotica' or pornography; in addition, the study found 238 'girl-related child pornography or erotica' webpages (Akdeniz, 2000: 233). A more recent study claims that in the period between 2002 and 2004, the number of child pornography and paedophile websites doubled to 19,246 (Telofono Arcobaleno, 2004: 2). This same study found that over half of reported websites were hosted in the USA, with Americans also figuring as the most prominent visitors to such webpages, comprising over 32 per cent of global users (ibid.: 8–10). The majority of such sites were commercial in character, and it has been estimated that the online trade in child pornography is worth some $3 billion per annum (IFR, 2004). The characteristics of those depicted in pornography varies across countries: for example, in the USA over 50 per cent of child pornography seized represents boys; in Canada, the figure is 75 per cent male; in contrast, child pornography in Japan is dominated by images of female minors (ECPAT, 1997: 2). Overall, of sexually explicit images of children located on the Internet, slightly over 50 per cent are of females. The vast majority of children featured in such online material are Caucasian or Asian, with very few images of black children (Taylor et al., 2001: 96).

Legislative and policing measures to combat online child pornography

6.8 Historically speaking, the problem of child sexual abuse has been grossly neglected. It is only in relatively recent times that the nature and scale of the problem have come to be publicly acknowledged and politically addressed. Consequently, the past few decades have seen concerted legal efforts to address child pornography in general, and Internet pornography in particular. In the UK, the 1978 Protection of Children Act makes it a criminal offence 'to take, distribute, exhibit, or possess even one "indecent" photograph of a child' (ECPAT, 1997: 9; Akdeniz, 2001a: 6). In the USA, federal statutes prohibiting child pornography were introduced in the form of The Protection of Children Against Sexual Exploitation Act (1977) and The Child Protection and Obscenity Enforcement Act (1988). Specific provisions relating to the Internet were introduced by the Communications Decency Act (1996) and the Child Pornography Prevention Act (CPPA) (1996). While the CDA has had some of its provisions declared unconstitutional by the Supreme Court (see discussion in 6.5 above), those components of the Act dealing with *obscene* material (as opposed to merely 'offensive' adult pornography) stand; consequently, online child pornography (which has been ruled obscene) is effectively prohibited by this law. Similarly, while the CPPA has run into difficulties with some of its provisions (such as those relating to so-called 'pseudo-photographs' – discussed in 6.9), the general prohibition of pornographic representations of children stands (Graham, 2000: 467–8). Other countries that have introduced such laws specifically aimed at tackling child pornography, both on- and offline, include the Netherlands, Denmark, Switzerland, Sweden, Norway, Germany, France, Ireland, Austria, Canada, Taiwan, the Philippines, Sri Lanka, South Africa, New Zealand and Australia (ECPAT, 1997: 9–11; Akdeniz, 2001b). At the international level, the European Union has extensively debated the need for some kind of common content regulation where it comes to issues such as obscenity. However, considerable cultural divergence across member states has made formal controls difficult to realize. As Charlesworth (2000: 59) notes, there are 'some Member States, for example the UK, operating rigorous regimes of censorship over depictions of sexual activity, while others, like the Netherlands, prefer a rather more laissez-faire approach to their citizens' proclivities in this area'. Consequently, he suggests that:

Even in those areas of moral judgement where some degree of consensus might reasonably be expected, such as the undesirability of child pornography, the extent of that consensus does not appear to extend to the uniform interpretation of subject matter, uniform definition of offences or uniformity of punishment across the EU.

(Charlesworth, 2000: 59)

Another potential mechanism for establishing a global regime of regulation relating to child pornography is the UN Convention on the Rights of the Child. To date, 192 countries have ratified the Convention, and two more (the USA and Somalia) have signalled their intention to do so (UNICEF, 2005). However, ratification of the convention has done little to globalize standards of legal protection for children from sexual exploitation when it comes to the domestic laws of the signatory nations.

The enforcement of anti-child pornography laws has been vigorously pursued in many countries in recent years, and has been notable for the degree of international cooperation involved. Few if any other forms of cybercrime have received such concerted efforts to overcome barriers between national law enforcement agencies, and to ensure that Internet offenders are brought before the law. In 1995, for example, police from across Europe, the USA, South Africa and the Far East were involved in *Operation Starburst*, an investigation of a paedophile ring using the Internet to distribute child pornography; 37 men were arrested worldwide (Akdeniz, 2001a: 8). Similarly, in 1998, investigators from the British National Crime Squad, US Customs and

Interpol coordinated an operation against *The Wonderland Club*, an organized ring of paedophiles spanning at least 33 countries, which had been using the Internet to distribute child pornography for a number of years. Across Europe and Australia 47 suspects were arrested, along with 32 in the USA (Graham, 2000: 461–5). Even more recently, *Operation Ore* (2003) led to 1,600 arrests in the UK of individuals who had subscribed to a US-based child pornography website (Creighton, 2003: 3); the arrests were made possible by cooperation with US law enforcement authorities who provided credit card details of UK residents who had subscribed to the service.

A number of countries have also broadened attempts to combat child pornography by involving Internet Service Providers (ISPs) and other Internet intermediaries. In some nations, this has taken the form of establishing ISPs' legal liability for third-party content placed on sites that they host or provide access to. Thus, for example, ISPs in both Germany and France have faced criminal charges of providing access to child pornography (Akdeniz, 2001a: 14). Other countries, such as the UK, have favoured self-regulation and cooperation with ISPs. In such cases, child pornography has been targeted by organizations such as Internet Watch Foundation (IWF) which have established 'hotlines' on which the public can report suspicious material online; the IWF then passes the information on to ISPs so that they can remove the webpages, and to the police so that they can investigate with a view to bringing criminal charges against those responsible to posting the offending material (Akdeniz, 2001a: 17–18; Sutter, 2003: 75). In 2003, the IWF received 20,000 such reports via its Internet hotline, 33 per cent of which were 'substantiated as potentially illegal' (IWF, 2004). Such hotlines now exist across Europe, the USA and elsewhere, and are coordinated by associations such as INHOPE (Internet Hotline Providers in Europe) (Williams, 1999: 2). The online adult pornography industry has also involved itself in efforts to eradicate child pornography. The ASACP (Association of Sites Advocating Child Protection), for example, is an alliance of US-based adult pornographic content providers that undertakes measures such as: self-regulation through approved membership and certification of legitimate adult sites; informing member providers about child protection laws; engaging in educational and outreach activities directed toward government and the public; and providing a hotline through which both adult content providers and consumers can report child pornography identified on the Internet (ASACP, 2005).

Legal and policing challenges in tackling child pornography

6.9 There are a number of obstacles facing attempts to curtail online child pornography, especially given that the production, distribution and consumption of such material often span national territories. First, while many countries have made efforts in recent years to combat child pornography, there remain many others without adequate provision. Second, even where provisions are in place, there may be significant differences in definitions as to what actually constitutes child pornography (Akdeniz, 1999; Taylor and Quayle, 2003). The UK's PCA (1978), for example, prohibits 'indecent' images of children, yet what precisely constitutes indecency is left vague and up to the courts to decide. This raises the very real possibility that what in one country may be deemed to fall within the bounds of anti-child pornography laws will in another be deemed legally acceptable. Similarly, different national legal regimes may prohibit different specific pornography-related practices. For example, while the UK prohibits possession of child-related materials, others (such as Japan) only prohibit commercial production, publication and distribution, but not possession. Indeed, in Japan, the production and distribution of child pornography were legal until November 1999, and current law still 'preserves the individual's right to possess child pornography and distribute it, recreationally, online' (Graham, 2000: 471–2). An analogous pattern of national differences arises when we consider the legal punishments laid down for child pornography-related offences. To take an extreme cross-national divergence, in the USA the Child Protection and Sexual Predator Punishment Act of 1998 prescribes 10–20 years imprisonment for a first-time offender, 15–30 years for a second-time offender, and 30 years to life for a third-time offender (Interpol, 2005a); however, under Greek law, the punishment for the same production and distribution offences comprises a fine and not more than *one month* in prison (Interpol, 2005b). These differences in the definition, scope and treatment of child-pornography offences make it particularly difficult to establish an international basis for acting effectively against online pornography involving children. Moreover, even where legal provision is in place, the lack of technical expertise, funding and police responsiveness to Internet crime may seriously hamper efforts to combat child pornography (Jewkes and Andrews, 2005).

A further issue, and one which deserves close attention in its own right, is the problem of divergence as to who exactly counts as a 'child' for the purposes of anti-pornography legislation. Under UK law, following the Sexual Offences Act of 2003, a child is defined as any person less than 18 years of age (this replaced the previous provision of the PCA (1978), in which a child was legally defined as a person under 16). This legal definition of children as under 18 is common to anti-pornography laws in many countries, including the USA, Canada, Ireland, Germany, and a host of others. However, in both Spain and Australia, child pornography covers only those materials involving depiction of under-16-year-olds (Interpol, 2005c; Krone, 2005: 1). Under Austrian law, child pornography is taken to mean material that contains explicit sexual depiction of those less than 14 years of age (Interpol, 2005d). Such differences create a situation in which, for example, UK and US authorities are unable to act against Spanish or Australian websites featuring sexually explicit images of 16- and 17-year olds, as they are permitted by Spanish and Australian law, even though they are illegal in other countries in which they may be viewed online. Problems related to the age of those appearing in pornographic images are further generated by the fact that producers, distributors and consumers of such material may not necessarily be aware of the true age of those shown. An illustrative case of this problem, from the pre-Internet era, is that of porn actress Traci Lords (real name Nora Louise Kuzma). Lords/Kuzma started nude modelling in magazines such as *Penthouse* in 1983, and between 1984 and 1986 appeared in almost 100 hardcore movies, becoming one of the world's most famous porn stars. However, it was revealed in 1986 that at the start of her nude modelling career she had in fact been only 15 years old, and 16 when she started to appear in hardcore pornographic films. She had deceived magazine publishers and film producers about her age by presenting a fake birth certificate and driver's licence. Subsequently, US authorities attempted to prosecute the owners of *X-Citement Video*, the company that produced Lords' first pornographic feature, for manufacturing and distributing child pornography (however, the authorities were undermined by the fact that even US customs had been fooled by Lords' fake passport, which she had used to travel to France to make a pornographic film) (EFF, 2001). The legal status of those featured is also made more difficult to assess since, as Lane (2001: 125) points out, 'images of teens at or near their 18th birthday have been proven to be a highly popular and lucrative subject for online pornography business'; there are now thousands of websites which seek to attract visitors by promising explicit pictures of 'barely legal teens'. While some readers might find the male sexual fascination with teenage women unsavoury and unwholesome, the legal point is that the unwary producer, distributor or consumer might completely inadvertently find him or herself falling foul of anti-child pornography laws (as did Traci Lords' employers, co-workers, and millions of fans across the world). This confusion is only exacerbated by the difference in legal definition of the child in different countries, with some territories permitting sexual representations of those as young as 14. It must, however, be borne in mind that this issue only applies to images of persons who are clearly post-pubescent and sexually matured, and thus could easily be mistaken as individuals who have reached the age at which appearance in pornography is permitted by the laws of their country. The largest proportion of child pornographic material online depicts those who are clearly pre-pubescent, and thus cannot be taken to be anything other than minors.

A final, and controversial issue related to child pornography that must be addressed is that relating to so-called 'pseudo-photographs'. It is widely acknowledged that 'in most cases, child pornography is a permanent record of the sexual abuse of an actual child' (Akdeniz, 2001a: 6). However, this is not the case with 'pseudo-photographs'; these comprise one or more non-obscene images that have been digitally manipulated to produce a pornographic representation involving a minor. These, for example, may take the form of a child's face transposed onto the image of a naked adult performing a sexual act (such transpositions are commonplace in adult pornography found on the web, with the faces of famous entertainers (such as Britney Spears and Anna Kournikova) being digitally mapped onto images of nude models, thereby providing their fans with a pictorial rendition of their fantasies of seeing their favourite public figures in pornographic scenarios). They may also comprise digital images which have been computer-generated 'from scratch', and thus no image of an actual child has been used in creating the representation. Under UK law, following the Criminal Justice and Public Order Act (1994) such pseudo-photographs are prohibited alongside real pornographic images of actual children. However, the situation in the USA is rather different. The CPPA (1996) also introduced such a prohibition, but in 2001 this provision was overthrown by the US Supreme Court (Akdeniz, 2001c; also Mota, 2003). In the USA, the traditional justification for excluding child pornography from First Amendment guarantees of free expression has been the harm committed against a child during the production of such images, i.e. that 'child pornography is a permanent record of the sexual abuse of an actual child', and as such the production of such images entails a direct violation of criminal law against child sexual and physical abuse. However, since no such harm need be committed to an actual child to produce pseudo-photographs, this justification does not apply. Nor is it possible under US federal law to appeal to the harms that might ensue against children, in that pseudo-images may encourage viewers to subsequently commit abusive acts against real children; as already noted in the discussion of hate speech (6.2 above), the harm criterion is justifiable grounds for prohibiting speech only if it is 'directed to inciting or producing imminent lawless action [or] likely to incite or produce such action'. In the absence of any concrete evidence that exposure to pornographic pseudo-photographs of children directly contributes to such actions, it cannot be exempted from First Amendment protection (Oswell, 2003: 5–6). All of the foregoing serves to illustrate the problems encountered when trying to find nationally based legal solutions to what are inherently global and transnational problems: as with some other forms of child pornography-related activities, the divergences over whether or not pseudo-images are to be prohibited creates a situation in which producers, distributors and consumers of the same images are subject to different legal treatment according to the country in which they are located. This inevitably obstructs attempts to generate a unified and effective strategy to remove child pornography from the Internet.

6.10 This chapter explored a range of issues relating to illegal, harmful, hateful and offensive content online. Debates in this area generate particular controversy, as attempts to control online expression inevitably come into conflict with the freedom of speech. The issues considered here are complicated, since what may be deemed 'hateful', 'harmful' or 'offensive' may or may not be illegal, depending upon the kind of expression (political, sexual) and the legal provisions in different national territories. A particular difference is notable between the USA and Western European nations. While the former places a premium on the preservation of individual freedom of expression, the latter tend to place greater emphasis upon social harmony, cultural inclusion and the dignity of minority groups. Consequently, we can see a gap between American understandings of prohibitable representations, be they hateful or obscene, and those prevalent in Europe. This 'legal pluralism' is also apparent within Europe itself, with significant differences on the prohibition of hate speech, the definitions of obscenity and the law concerning child pornography. If we extend our view to the global scene, even greater divergences become clear. While hate speech, obscenity and child pornography are not phenomena in any way unique to the Internet, their appearance online intensifies regulatory prob-lems, as the Internet allows the circulation of such representations to span terri-torial boundaries and cultural contexts, with their different moralities about acceptable and unacceptable speech. The greatest advances towards international harmonization and cooperation have emerged in relation to tackling child pornography, reflecting the greater degree of global moral consensus on this issue. Nevertheless, significant differences remain over issues such what counts as an 'obscene' or 'indecent' image of a child, who counts as a 'child', and whether or not artefacts such as computer-generated images (pseudo-photographs) ought to be included within anti-pornography laws. We can anticipate that issues relating to obscene, offensive and indecent material will continue to be among the most intensively debated and contested issues related to Internet crime.

Study questions

- why does the Internet offer advantages to those wishing to propagate hateful ideas and ideologies?
- ought such speech be banned from the Internet, or are the dangers of politi-cal censorship too great?
- is the popularity of pornography online a social problem?
- should young people have access to sexually explicit representations via the Internet?
- what are the challenges facing moves to tackle child pornography online?

Further reading

Useful overviews about the arguments for prohibiting 'hate speech' are provided in L. Nielsen's article 'Subtle, pervasive, harmful: racist and sexist remarks in public as hate speech' (2002), and in Alexander Tsesis' book, *Destructive Messages: How Hate Speech Paves the Way for Harmful Social Movements* (2002). From a perspective defending the freedom of speech, see T. McGonagle, 'Wrestling (racial) equality from tolerance of hate speech' (2001). For an examination of this issue as related to the Internet, see Barry Steinhardt, 'Hate speech', in Akdeniz et al. (eds), *The Internet, Law and Society* (2000) and chapter 12 of Stuart Biegel's book *Beyond Our Control?* (2003). On the issue of pornography, a valuable worldwide survey is provided by Richard Procida and Rita Simon in their book *Global Perspectives on Social Issues: Pornography* (2003). Specific discussion of pornography online can be found in David Bennett's article 'Pornography-dot-com: eroticising privacy on the Internet' (2001) and in Yaman Akdeniz and Nadine Strossen, 'Sexually oriented expression', in Akdeniz et al. (2000). A fascinating account of the development of cyber-pornography as big business is Frederick Lane's *Obscene Profits: The Entrepreneurs of Pornography in the Cyber Age* (2001). On young people's access to pornography online, see Dick Thornburgh and Herbert Lin, 'Youth, Pornography, and the Internet' (2004). The debate about online child pornography is tackled in Philip Jenkins, *Beyond Tolerance: Child Pornography Online* (2001). Also valuable on this topic is the website http://www.cyber-rights.org which contains up-to-date discussion and analysis of legal developments. Issues on the policing of child pornography are addressed in Yaman Akdeniz, *Sex on the Net: The Dilemma of Policing Cyberspace* (1999) and Yvonne Jewkes and Carol Andrews' 'Policing the filth: The problems of investigating online child pornography in England and Wales' (2005).

Note

1 Lest this example be seen as an improbable occurrence, it is worth noting that in the USA, 53 per cent of men belonging to the highly conservative Christian 'promise keeper' movement (committed to sexual abstinence and virginity before marriage) admitted to having viewed online pornography during the week before questioning (IFR, 2004).

SEVEN

The Victimization of Individuals Online

Cyberstalking and Paedophilia

Overview

Chapter 7 examines the following issues:

- *the nature and development of stalking as a form of criminal offence;*
- *the debate about online stalking or 'cyberstalking' as a growing crime problem;*
- *the issue of online child sexual victimization;*
- *the argument that current concerns about Internet stalking and paedophilia are in fact moral panics, and an unwarranted over-reaction to a marginal crime problem.*

--- key terms ---

Child	Cyberstalking	Paedophilia
Child pornography	Moral panic	Stalking

Introduction

7.1 In Chapter 6, we explored criminological issues related to various kinds of harmful and objectionable speech and representation that appear online. Such speech typically takes the form of representations of individuals and social groups that portray them in ways that can be seen as offensive (such as the racist depiction of minority ethnic groups, the sexualized representation of children, and the degrading representation of women in pornography). This chapter further explores criminological issues related to online communication, but focuses upon somewhat different phenomena. The online behaviours considered here comprise communications which are directed by individuals *at* specific persons, and which are unwelcome by their recipients and may contain abusive, threatening or inappropriate words or images. The first problem examined is that of so-called 'cyberstalking', the persistent and targeted harassment of an individual via electronic communication such as email. The second issue is the use of Internet communications by paedophiles to contact children in order to engage them in sexual abuse. Such behaviours may be purely 'virtual' in character, and restricted to the online environment. However, in some instances, they may serve as an accompaniment to, or preparation for, further physical harassment and victimization in direct inter-personal encounters (such as the cyberstalker who combines email communications with physical intrusion or assault upon his or her target, or the paedophile who uses communications with minors in Internet chat rooms to prepare or 'groom' victims for subsequent physical sexual abuse). Cyberstalking has garnered increasing attention in recent years, as society has become more attuned to problems of inter-personal harassment and victimization more generally. The issue of online paedophilia has evoked even greater concern, allied to worries about related child protection issues such as child pornography and child abduction. In this chapter, the patterns and scope of such online conduct will be discussed and their risks will be assessed. However, we will also examine critical perspectives that interpret the issue of online victimization as symptomatic of a 'moral panic' about the threat of strangers, rather than reflecting any extensive risk of criminal victimization as such.

The emergence of stalking as a crime problem

7.2 Cyberstalking can be understood as an online variant of similar behaviours that take place in other non-virtual contexts and environments. Therefore, it will be necessary to situate cyberstalking in the context of stalking activities more generally. The term 'stalking' first can to prominence in the 1980s to describe 'persistent harassment in which one person repeatedly imposes on another unwanted communications and/or contacts' (Mullen et al., 2001: 9). Stalking is held to be characterized by repeated behaviours including: making phone calls to victims, sending them variously letters, gifts or offensive material, following and watching the victim, trespassing on the victim's property, loitering near and approaching the victim, contacting and approaching the victim's family, friends and co-workers (McGuire and Wraith, 2000: 317; Brewster, 2003: 213). Stalking may be a prelude to serious physical assault and even homicide (Fritz, 1995). The impact of stalking upon its victims can be profoundly debilitating. Fear and anxiety are commonplace reactions; one-third of victims have been found to seek psychological treatment as a consequence, one-fifth have lost time from work, and 7 per cent have been unable to return to work (Tjaden, 1997: 2). Victims are also forced to make adaptations to their lives in order to try to evade their stalker: these can include changing telephone number, installing home security devices, carrying personal safety devices, taking self-defence lessons, changing car, moving home, changing job, changing surname, and even moving abroad (McGuire and Wraith, 2000: 323). Estimates about the social prevalence of stalking vary, but one national US-based survey found that 8 per cent of women and 2 per cent of men reported having been stalked at some time, and 1 per cent of women and 0.4 per cent of men reported having been stalked in the 12 months prior to questioning. If the latter figure is accurate, this means that about 6 million women and 1.4 million men are stalked every year in the USA (Tjaden and Thoennes, 1998: 10). In the UK, the British Crime Survey (2003)

INDIVIDUALS ONLINE

revealed that 8 per cent of women and 6 per cent of men were subjected to stalking during the previous year, a total of 1.2 million women and almost 900,000 men (Walby and Allen, 2004: vi).

In the public mind, stalking has tended to be associated with the obsessive pursuit of celebrities by psychologically disturbed fans. Well-known cases of 'star stalking' have involved the likes of Jody Foster, who was stalked by John Hinckley; he went on to shoot President Ronald Reagan in 1982 in an attempt to impress Foster. Others reportedly subjected to stalking include Catherine Zeta-Jones, Mel Gibson, Gwyneth Paltrow, Halle Berry, Steven Spielberg and Brad Pitt. Indeed, the first tailor-made anti-stalking legislation, passed in California in 1991, was introduced in the wake of the stalking and subsequent murder of actress Rebecca Schaeffer by a fan (Mullen et al., 2000: 10; Spitzberg and Cadiz, 2002: 136). Lowney and Best (1995: 39) found that in US media reports of stalking during 1989 and 1990, 69 per cent of stories focused on celebrity victims. Hollywood movies have also linked stalking to celebrity in films such as *The King of Comedy* (1983) and *The Fan* (1996), thereby reinforcing the connection between fame and victimization among media audiences. Such 'stranger stalkings', undertaken by individuals unknown to the victim, tend to be characterized by 'erotomania'. In such cases, the stalker is convinced that he or she has a special and intimate relationship with the victim, that the victim loves them and wishes to reciprocate their devotion, and the victim's words and actions (even if they seem to clearly signify disinterest and rejection) are interpreted by the stalker as signs that they will be eventually united (McGuire and Wraith, 2000: 320). While the stalker may present a physical threat against the victim (as in the case of Rebecca Schaeffer), it is just as likely that violence will be directed towards those the stalker perceives as the enemies of their 'beloved'; thus for example, in 1992 Günter Parche, an obsessive devotee of tennis player Steffi Graf, stabbed her sporting rival, Monica Seles.

However, during the 1990s, understandings of stalking began to shift away from the focus upon celebrities to encompass a wider perception of the phenomenon. Pivotal in this shift was research and campaigning undertaken by feminist academics and women's rights activists. Studies revealed that stalkings by strangers constituted only a minority of all cases. Much more prevalent were cases where the perpetrator (usually male) was the estranged or former partner of the victim (usually female). Overall, around 75–80 per cent of stalkers are estimated to be male, and around 75–80 per cent of all victims are thought to be female (Spitzberg, 2002). This clearly gendered pattern in stalking offences, combined with the preponderance of incidents involving 'intimates', naturally led many researchers to view stalking as primarily an extension of domestic violence and abuse (see, for example, Wright et al.,

1996; Roberts and Dziegielewski, 1996). Stalking by estranged intimates may be motivated by a desire to punish the former partner for having ended the relationship; alternatively, they may pursue the former partner from 'a desire to express their ongoing love and desire to reconcile the relationship', hoping that their persistence will demonstrate their commitment (McGuire and Wraith, 2000: 318). Whatever the motivation, such behaviour induces responses on the part of the victim ranging from resentment, frustration and anger to anxiety and fear. Moreover, domestic stalking is often linked to violent and abusive patterns of behaviour, with about 80 per cent of women stalked by former partners reporting having been physically assaulted during their relationship, and 31 per cent reporting incidents of sexual assault (Tjaden, 1997: 2). In addition to stranger and domestic variants, typologies of stalking also identify a number of other forms, such as 'acquaintance stalking' (where the victim is harassed by someone known to them, but with whom they do not have any close relationship, such as a colleague or neighbour) and 'nuisance stalking' (involving less invasive but nonetheless significant harassment) (Roberts and Dziegielewski, 1996; Emerson et al., 1998).

The rise of stalking as a crime problem over the past few decades can be understood in two distinctive ways. First, it can be suggested that its increasing prominence is a reflection of a massive increase in harassing behaviours. Mullen et al. (2000: 12) identify a number of social changes that might help explain such an increase. First, they point to greater instability and breakdown of relationships, which creates more situations in which conflict between estranged partners can emerge. Second, they point to the growing prominence of celebrity within our culture, which encourages 'intimacy seeking' on the part of fans who are actively invited to form emotional connections with idealized stars. Third, they point to greater social isolation that makes it more difficult for people to establish intimate relationships, thereby creating the possibility of inappropriate behaviour when seeking to find emotional and physical reciprocity as an answer to loneliness. However, it has also been pointed out that the behaviours associated with stalking are not in any sense new; rather, it has been described as 'a new term for an old crime' (McGuire and Wraith, 2000: 316). Clinically documented cases of erotomania and obsessional pursuit date back at least as far as the eighteenth century (Mullen et al., 2000: 9). Indeed, what today is discussed as stalking was once represented in literature as a idealized form of romantic love. Thus, it may be that such behaviour has not necessarily undergone a dramatic increase, but than the ways in which we culturally think about inter-personal relationships have changed creating a social problem with behaviours that once were tolerated or even admired. Pivotal in such a cultural shift has been the impact of the women's movement, which has drawn attention to the various forms of psychological as well as domestic abuse perpetrated by male partners, and has helped Western societies break with the older patriarchal assumption about women as basically the 'property' of their husbands. Women's rights to govern the path of their relationships, including the right to terminate them on their own terms, have sensitized us to those situations in which such rights are violated by abusive or persistent former partners. Thus the rise of stalking as a criminal category can be seen to owe much to shifting perceptions about just what kinds of behaviour constitute a social problem and public concern.

As already noted, the first legislation specifically aimed at criminalizing stalking emerged in the USA in 1991. By 1992, 26 US states had introduced similar legal provisions, and by 2000 all 50 US states had anti-stalking provisions on the statute books (Kolarik, 1992: 35; Spitzberg and Cadiz, 2002: 128). In Australia, the state of Queensland passed an anti-stalking law in 1993, quickly followed by the other states; New Zealand introduced similar legislation in 1997 (Mullen et al., 2000: 10). Also in 1997, the UK's Protection from Harassment Act (PHA) came into effect. Like other anti-stalking laws, the PHA relies upon the mechanism of 'restraining orders' to prohibit stalkers from further contact with their victims. Under the PHA, breach of an order may be punished with a custodial sentence of up to 5 years (McGuire and Wraith, 2000: 321). However, restraining orders have been criticized from a number of angles. First, they may be undermined by sporadic enforcement by police (Fritz, 1995). Second, they may be ineffective in deterring the stalker, especially where the individual suffers from a delusional disorder or other serious mental health problems that impair judgement (McGuire and Wraith, 2000: 321). As Goode (1995: 10) puts it, 'The serious obsessive stalker is unlikely to know or believe that his or her conduct is against the law and is likely, even if he or she does know, to disregard that law'. Third, the prohibition of 'repeated harassing behaviour' may be over-broad, and potentially criminalize legitimate activity. Thus, Goode wonders about the legal standing of individuals such as investigative journalists, protesters, and summons servers. There are, he concludes, 'any number of persistent visitors and callers who, at worst, are a pest, perhaps even a criminal pest, but should not be called stalkers and made subject to heavy criminal penalties' (ibid.: 7). The potential for the misapplication of such laws is clearly illustrated by an Australian case in which a group of Aboriginal youth were prosecuted for loitering in a shopping centre (ibid.: 7). Such difficulties arise from the fact that stalking can comprise a wide range of different behaviours, and consequently any legal prohibitions must be framed in very broad terms; consequently, they inadvertently run the risk of curtailing freedom of action and expression.

7.3 Cyberstalking has been defined as 'the repeated use of the Internet, email or related digital electronic communication devices to annoy, alarm, or threaten a specific individual' (D'Ovidio and Doyle, 2003: 10). It is generally viewed as an extension of more familiar stalking behaviours that may be undertaken through physical presence, telephone, and mail; however, writers such as Bocij et al. (2002: 3) see it as 'an entirely new form of deviant behaviour'. Perhaps, on a balanced view, cyberstalking ought to be understood as a new variant of an existing pattern of criminal conduct, one that exhibits both continuities and discontinuities from its 'terrestrial' counterpart. Commentators such as Koch (2000) and Best (1999) have suggested variously that cyberstalking is a 'trivial' problem, is one whose incidence is rare, or may even be wholly 'imaginary' (see also discussion in Bocij and McFarlane, 2002). However, others have argued that Internet stalking is both increasingly common and has serious effects and consequences for those who find themselves victimized by an online stalker.

Assessing the scope of cyberstalking incidents is rendered difficult due to the relative paucity of systematic and reliable data deriving from large-scale studies. Further methodological problems arise when we take into account the varying definitions of cyberstalking used by different analysts, which makes it difficult to make cross-comparisons or to aggregate data. For example, Bocij and McFarlane (2002: 26) define as cyberstalking only those forms of harassment that 'a reasonable person, in possession of the same information, would think causes another reasonable person to suffer emotional distress'. Setting aside the problem of who counts as 'reasonable', Bocij and McFarlane's understanding is more restricted than that of D'Ovidio and Doyle (cited above), which includes behaviours that merely 'annoy'. Consequently, when examining such data as is available, we cannot always be certain that different measures of cyberstalking activity are necessarily based upon same or similar conceptions of what counts as part of the behaviour. Nevertheless, we can note assessments and estimates that give some broad indication of how widespread a cyberstalking problem might actually exist. For example, the US-based Internet safety organization CyberAngels receives some 500 complaints daily about cyberstalking victimization, and some 65–100 of these are estimated to be legitimate (Bocij et al., 2002: 3; Bocij and McFarlane, 2002: 31). If accurate, this would amount to somewhere between 24,000 and 36,500 cases in the USA per annum. However, it must be borne in mind that CyberAngels is just one of the organizations that monitors and receives complaints, so there inevitably will be many more such incidents which are reported elsewhere. D'Ovidio and Doyle (2003: 11–12) document one of the few statistical sources about cyberstalking to emerge from criminal justice agencies. The New York Police Department's Computer Investigation and Technology Unit (CITU) receives and investigates public complaints about a wide range of computer-related crime, including fraud, hacking, and child pornography as well as cyberstalking. Of the cases reported to CITU between January 1996 and August 2000, 42.8 per cent involved 'aggravated harassment by means of a computer or the Internet' (ibid.: 12). Interestingly, the offender characteristic in such cases showed both similarities and differences from non-computer-related stalking incidents. Some 80 per cent of cyberstalkers were male, a figure almost identical to that for stalking cases more generally. However, in computer-related cases women made up 52 per cent of victims, considerably less than the 75–80 per cent figure for stalking more broadly conceived. This indicates that patterns of online victimization are more likely to vary from the predominant pattern of male offender–female victim that is found in terrestrial cases. However, these data must be viewed as provisional and indicative rather than conclusive, given a number of obvious limitations. First, we know that cyber-crime incidents (like crimes more generally) are subject to under-reporting and under-recording, and that rates of reporting may vary according to the social characteristics of the victims (their class, gender, age, and so on). Second, there is no way to be sure that figures derived from New York are representative of patterns elsewhere in the USA, let alone in other countries.

It is generally held that the most common form of cyberstalking behaviour comprises harassment via the repeated sending of offensive or threatening emails (Ogilvie, 2000: 2). According to the data collected by the CITU, email abuse was involved in 92 per cent of cases. Other forms of stalking included the use of instant messaging services (apparent in 13 per cent of cases), chat rooms (8 per cent), message boards (4 per cent) and websites (2 per cent) (D'Ovidio and Doyle, 2003: 12). A somewhat different pattern is apparent in the Internet-based survey conducted by Bocij (2003). The most commonly reported form of harassment was that of threats and abuse in Internet chat rooms (47.62 per cent), followed by email (39.88 per cent), and instant messaging (38.69 per cent). The different findings derived from these two sources might be explained by the fact that they relate to different periods (1996–2000 for the CITU, and 2003 for Bocij's study). In the intervening years, both instant messaging and chat rooms have become more common and more widely used, and the shift in modes of harassment might reflect this change in availability. Alternatively, the differences might reflect on national differences in cyberstalking behaviours. The largest group among Bocij's respondents were from the UK (45.5 per cent), followed by the USA (39.9 per cent), with the remainder resident in Canada (7.2 per cent) and Australia (2.4 per cent) (for the remaining 5.4 per cent, no country of residence was presented). Bocij's study may also be unreliable because, as he himself notes, there are some serious sampling problems related to the methodology used, that of so-called 'snowball sampling'. This entails the initial distribution of the questionnaire to a small number of respondents (five in Bocij's case), who are each then requested to forward it to a number of others, and those subsequent recipients are asked to do likewise, and so on. Inevitably, respondents will recruit others known to them (such family, friends and colleagues) who are likely to have common social characteristics (such as class background and occupation), and who are likely to share patterns and preferences when it comes to Internet use (the commonalities between respondents was clearly evident in the fact that 30.5 per cent had a degree-level education and 11.4 per cent had a postgraduate qualification, rates much higher than for the populations of the USA, the UK, Australia and Canada generally). In short, while such studies are suggestive and help to map out further avenues for inquiry, we must await more systematic and scientific research before being able to drawn more definite conclusions about both the dominant forms of cyberstalking behaviour and about the perpetrators and victims of such offences.

One significant way in which cyberstalking appears to vary from stalking more generally is that the former is more likely to remain mediated and at a distance. In other words, it is less likely to entail direct, face-to-face harassment in which perpetrator and victim are physically co-present. It would appear, from those cases of cyberstalking reported and recorded, that they are likely to begin and end online, rather than 'spilling over' into terrestrial contexts. Thus 'much cyberstalking remains at the level of inducing emotional distress, fear and apprehension', rather than resulting in physical harm to the victim (Ogilvie, 2000: 3). However, there is no reason why psychological harm should be treated any less seriously than its physical counterpart, as the emotional suffering inflicted by cyberstalking can be just as profound and acute. Moreover, there are a number of recorded instances in which the virtual and terrestrial converge, resulting in grave consequences to the well-being of the stalker's target. In one such case, a man from Los Angeles sought revenge upon a woman who had spurned his romantic advances by posing as her in online chat rooms. He posted the woman's personal details, including her address, and claimed that she was looking for men with whom she could act out her 'rape fantasies'. Subsequently, the woman suffered the terrifying ordeal of being 'repeatedly awoken in the middle of the night by men banging on her front door, shouting that they were there to rape her' (Maharaj, cited in Ogilvie, 2000: 3). In another case, a young man, again in the USA, tracked down a female former classmate, and stalked her online. The two-year cycle culminated in his driving to her workplace and shooting her as she was getting into her car (Romei, 1999).

A second way in which cyberstalking appears to differ from terrestrial stalking is in the prevalence of non-intimate and non-domestic incidents online. It was noted earlier that assessments of stalking typically show that the largest proportion of cases involve harassment by ex-intimates, and that harassment by strangers is very rare. However, a recent study by McFarlane and Bocij (2003) suggests a much greater diversity of offender–victim relationships in instances of Internet stalking. Only 12 per cent of victims reported being stalked by ex-intimates. Most common were cases in which the victim and offender had only recently met in online communications fora, such as chat rooms (33.3 per cent), followed by total strangers (22 per cent), and acquaintances (16.7 per cent). This finding suggests that online and offline stalkers are not comprised of the same individuals; ex-intimates do not, by and large, extend their stalking to the Internet, while others who would be less likely to engage in offline stalking (strangers, acquaintances) are more likely to do so via the Internet. It has been argued that the feeling of anonymity afforded by Internet communication serves to lower inhibitions against aggressive, threatening and anti-social interaction (Kabay, 1998; Taylor, 1999), thereby encouraging web users to engage in harassment.

The issue of anonymity has much exercised commentators on cyberstalking. It is widely noted that the ability of offenders to hide their identities poses a major challenge for criminal justice agencies investigating cyberstalking incidents (Ogilvie, 2000: 2; Bocij et al., 2002: 4; D'Ovidio and Doyle, 2003: 15–16). There are two online technologies that can enable offenders to retain their anonymity, namely anonymous web browsing services and anonymous remailers. The former are online sites that allow web users to explore the Internet without a record being kept by their Internet Service Providers of the sites they have visited. The latter, anonymous remailers, are again web-based services that remove all identifying data about the origins of an email, making it impossible to identify the account from which the mail was originally sent (Teich et al., 1999). Of the cyberstalking cases investigated by CITU between 1996 and 2000, law enforcement were unable to trace any of the perpetrators who had used anonymous remailers to send harassing messages. However, such cases involving use of remailing services accounted for only 2.1 per cent of all incidents (D'Ovidio and Doyle, 2003: 16). This would suggest that the use of anonymizing technologies is rare in cyberstalking cases, something corroborated by other recent examinations of the problem (Hitchcock, 2003); consequently the problem of anonymous cyberstalking may have been inflated. However, it must be borne in mind that as anonymizing services become more widely available and more familiar to web users, the possibility remains that the use of such technologies in stalking cases will become more frequent.

7.4 Concerns about the online victimization of individuals have been most pronounced where they deal with the sexual victimization of children. Since the 1980s, the US and the UK in particular have seen intense anxiety about the problem of child abuse in general, and sexual abuse in particular. Common media discussion of organized ritual abuse, stranger child abduction, and 'recovered memories' of repressed childhood abuse have contributed incrementally to this heightened sense of children's vulnerability. This sensitivity has been further heightened by a number of widely reported cases in which children have been abducted, abused, then murdered by paedophiles, such as the case of Megan Kanka in the USA and Sarah Payne in the UK. In the late 1990s, the focus upon paedophilia turned increasingly to the online environment. We have already explored in the previous chapter the attention devoted to child pornography. The problem of Internet-oriented abuse is often discussed in tandem with the circulation of obscene images of children; indeed, the two issues are frequently treated as different facets of the same problem (see, for example, Forde and Patterson, 1998; Stanley, 2002). It is claimed that many of those investigated for child pornography offences have also participated in the actual sexual abuse of children. For example, British police estimate that some 35 per cent of those targeted by *Operation Starburst* (discussed in Chapter 6.8) for possession of child pornography had also physically abused children. Similarly, the FBI claim that something approaching 50 per cent of child pornography collectors have themselves committed sexual offences against children (NCIS, 1999). However, a question remains over the possible causal relationship between these forms of behaviour: does interest in, and consumption of, child pornography encourage or lead to child sexual abuse? Or is it that those already disposed to abusive behaviour inevitably also take pleasure in pornographic representations of similar activities? The UK and US figures cited above imply that those who abuse are in fact a *minority* among child pornography enthusiasts, and that the majority of consumers of such images *do not* engage in any actual physical abuse. This suggests that the relationship between child pornography and child sex abuse is more complicated than is often supposed (Stanley, 2002: 9). However, this complexity is seldom explored in public discussion, and the two phenomena are typically treated as synonymous or continuous.

Online child sex abuse can be differentiated between that which remains 'virtual' (restricted to communicative abuses committed via the Internet) and that which serves as a prepatory method for later physical contact and abuse (so-called 'grooming' of potential physical abuse victims). Each will be discussed in turn below.

UK-based research by Rachel O'Connell and her colleagues at the Cyberspace Research Unit (CRU) claims to have uncovered a wide range of 'cybersexploitation' practices taking place in Internet chat rooms. In such cases, adults or older adolescents with a sexual interest in young children use online communication in order to 'identify, deceive, coerce, cajole, form friendships with and also to abuse potential victims' (O'Connell, 2003: 2). This may entail, first, adults engaging children in sexually explicit conversations. Example include asking questions of the child such as 'Have you ever been kissed?' or 'Do you ever touch yourself?' (O'Connell, 2003: 7). Second, such behaviour may entail the 'fantasy enactment' of sexual scenarios through online conversation with a child. Third, it may entail what is described as 'cyber-rape', in which coercion and threats are used to force a child into acting out the sexual scenarios proposed by the abuser. It has been suggested by many commentators that adult abusers exploit the Internet to disguise their identity, posing as children or adolescents in order to win the friendship and trust of their victims (NCIS, 1999; Feather, 1999: 7). Children may thus be blissfully unaware that their Internet 'friend' is in fact an adult whose aim is to deceive them into participation in sexual conversation and interaction. O'Connell et al. claim that surveys of children's online interaction show that 53 per cent of chat room users aged between 8 and 11 reported having had sexual conversations online (O'Connell et al., 2004: 5). However, it is unclear what proportion of such conversations involved an adult interlocutor; indeed, given the ease with which disguise is possible, it may be virtually impossible to determine whether a given conversation is an adult–child interaction, or a case of child-to-child or teen-to-teen 'cyberflirting'. Indeed, only 6 per cent of children aged 9–16 reported that 'online conversations of a sexual nature were unpleasant or offensive' (ibid.: 6). Putting the above points together, it may be suggested that the vast majority of children's online interactions of a sexual nature are nothing more than explorations of a burgeoning curiosity about physical relationships. Such curiosity is unremarkable, especially in the context of a consumer culture that actively encourages children and adolescents to take an interest in sex and sexuality. However, this does not imply that adult–child sexual interactions online are a non-existent problem. In the aforementioned studies conducted by the CRU, researchers registered themselves online under the guise of a child, typically a girl aged between 9 and 12 years of age. Subsequently, a number of self-professed adults engaged this 'child' in conversations of an explicitly sexual kind. The UK's Sexual Offences Act (2003) makes it a criminal act to incite a child to engage in sexual activity, 'such as, for example, persuading children to take their clothes off, causing the child to touch themselves sexually, sending indecent images of themselves, etc.' Thus those online child–adult interactions in which the child may be encouraged to engage in sexual acts is defined as 'non-contact abuse' and punishable by up to 10 years imprisonment (Home Office, 2002a: 24; O'Connell et al., 2004: 6).

The second area of online paedophile activity is linked to the commission of offline 'contact abuse'. Recent years have witnessed a growing concern that paedophiles are using Internet chat room contacts with children in order to establish a relationship of apparent friendship and trust, which can then be exploited to arrange face-to-face meetings in which sexual abuse can take place. O'Connell (2003: 6–8) identifies a number of 'stages' to such 'grooming', starting with friendship formation (getting to know the child), progressing to relationship formation (becoming the child's 'best friend'), leading to the exclusivity stage (where intimacy, trust and secrecy are established). It is only when such a bond has been formed that the paedophile will move on to suggest sexual contact. One US-based survey of 10–17-year-old Internet users found that 19 per cent reported having been approached for sex online (Stanley, 2002: 7). In response to such findings, the UK's Sexual Offences Act (2003) introduced an offence of Internet grooming, 'designed to catch those aged 18 or over who undertake a course of conduct with a child under 16 leading to a meeting where the adult intends to engage in sexual activity with a child' (Home Office, 2002a: 25). Conviction for this offence can result in a custodial sentence of up to 5 years. The precise extent of such 'grooming' activity is difficult to assess, as its identification depends upon a judgement about an individual's ultimate intention to abuse. No physical abuse need actually be attempted in order to secure a conviction, merely a perception that an individual *intended* to use a meeting set up via the Internet to engage in the sexual abuse of a minor. As Bennion (2003: 3) points out:

> The object is to catch adults who try to make friends with children so as later to have sex with them. But how is that to be proved? If the suspect goes on to carry out a sexual assault that can be charged as an offence in itself, but there is then no need for the preliminary offence of grooming. Where no assault later ensues, how can preliminary grooming be established?

While implementation of this law may be beset with evidential dilemmas, what is clear is the conviction among most politicians, child protection organizations and members of the public that Internet grooming is a real and palpable threat that must be tackled through criminal legislation.

Thinking critically about online victimization: stalking and paedophilia as moral panics?

7.5 Despite the wide-ranging consensus that online victimization is a serious and growing threat, a number of academic commentators have been quick to critically analyse its rise to prominence. Such analysts operate within a perspective that views crime problems as 'social constructions'. From this viewpoint, it is quite possible for intense public, political and mass media concern to centre on an issue or behaviour to an extent that is in fact quite unwarranted, objectively speaking. A behaviour that is rare (or even non-existent) may come to be the focus of public anxiety, fear and panic. Thus, Joel Best (1999) examines how stalking was 'discovered' as a crime problem during the course of the 1990s. Behaviour that in previous times may well have evoked little concern or comment suddenly came to be seen as an imminent and widespread threat. The extent of such incidents was inflated by incrementally expanding the behaviours that were captured under the evocative and sinister label of stalking. Thus, for example, D'Ovido and Doyle's (2003) definition of cyberstalking (see Section 7.3) includes within its ambit electronic communications intended to 'annoy' their recipients. In all likelihood, the vast majority of people regularly experience communications which annoy them – for example, being 'pestered' by a demanding colleague, friend, family member, or even the sales and marketing departments of companies that repeatedly send 'spam' mail advertising their goods and services. If studies ask respondents whether they have received repeated electronic communications that annoy them, the large majority are likely to respond affirmatively. This then has the effect of making stalking appear as a problem nearing epidemic proportions. Moreover, analysts of moral panics point out the role played in problem-construction by interest groups who have a stake in 'promoting' public and political awareness of a particular issue. Thus, Best notes how the rise of stalking has been accompanied by the expansion of what he calls a 'victim industry'. This industry includes lawyers who represent those who claim victimization; medical professionals and therapists who study, treat and counsel victims; educators and academics who are drafted in to train people and raise awareness about stalking and how to deal with it; and the mass media for whom a novel 'crime wave' makes for attention-grabbing news coverage. Through the efforts of such actors, the newly minted social problem can become institutionalized and the target of concerted political and law enforcement attention.

The case of paedophilia is, if anything, even more open to analysis as a socially constructed moral panic. Over the past few decades, there have emerged successive 'scares' about different forms of child abuse. For example, in the early 1980s there were a number of cases in the USA and Europe in which workers in child care centres and nurseries were accused of organizing ritual, systematic and ongoing satanic sexual abuse of their young charges, in some cases allegedly involving the drinking of human blood, cannibalism and human sacrifice. Such allegations were subsequently proven groundless, but not before they had generated widespread panic among frightened parents and extremely damaging criminal investigations of those accused (De Young, 2004). In the 1990s, there occurred an outcry about child sex abuse when thousands of adults started coming forward claiming to have recovered previously repressed memories of childhood abuse at the hands of their parents and family members. Many academic psychologists subsequently judged a great proportion of such cases as instances of 'false memory syndrome', in which individuals had been persuaded (or persuaded themselves) that they had undergone abuse that in fact had not occurred (Loftus, 1996). From this viewpoint, the apparent threat presented by paedophiles to children online might be viewed as a new instalment of this pattern of over-reaction to the risk of child victimization. Frank Furedi (2005: viii, 32–4) views the recent public response to online paedophilia as symptomatic of what he calls our contemporary 'culture of fear', one which is beset by 'obsessive preoccupations about safety'. This 'obsessive preoccupation' has centred in particular upon the threat to children at the hands of strangers who intend to variously abuse, abduct and/or murder them. Parents have responded by becoming pathologically suspicious of anyone who might come into contact with their children, attributing to them the worst possible intentions. Children are increasingly counselled that danger is lurking everywhere, and all strangers present a threat to their well-being. This percolation of fear becomes clear when we consider the responses of the children interviewed by Burn and Willett (2003: 10–11) as part of an evaluation of a child-oriented Internet-risk education campaign called Educanet. A group of 11-year-old girls have the following to say about paedophiles and the Internet:

> Becky: Most people are perverts, innit [local expression – 'isn't it']?
> Claire: You know, like on the Internet.
> Daniella: There's millions.

In such a cultural context, children as well as their parents are coming to increasingly view all contact with strangers as a potential overture to sexual abuse or worse (Furedi, 2001). Some child welfare agencies have expressed serious concerns over the effects on children's health and development wrought by over-protective parents who isolate their children to keep them safe from predation (Furedi, 2005: 116). More reasonable assessments might point out that the risk of stranger abuse is statistically almost marginal. After all, it is clear that children are more likely to suffer sexual abuse at the hands of their own family members (NAEYC, 1996: 1). Furedi (2005: 110) points out that in the 10 years between 1983 and 1993, 57 children were murdered by strangers in the UK, an average of 5 per year. In contrast, more than 4000 children are killed or seriously injured every year as a result of road traffic accidents (RAC, 2003). Yet child murder at the hand of paedophiles has attracted far greater media attention, public anxiety, and political action than issues relating to road safety, despite the fact that it is the latter that presents by far the greater threat to children's safety. Consequently, critics such as Furedi call for a balanced reassessment of the risks that children actually face, rather than surrendering to a wave of cultural panic that will inevitably further erode people's ability to establish relationships of openness, trust and social bonds with their fellow citizens. The over-estimation of the dangers of online victimization might simply serve to create a generation of adults who view the Internet as a dangerous no-go territory, rather than embracing it as an invaluable opportunity for fostering social communication, interaction and exchange.

Summary

7.6 This chapter has explored recent high-profile debates about the online victimization of individuals in the forms of cyberstalking and Internet paedophilia. Numerous assessments indicate that these are serious and growing threats to people's online safety, and may well spill over into the terrestrial world with tragic consequences for victims. However, critics have argued that risks of online victimization have been grossly over-estimated and inflated, and that the dangers presented by Internet stalkers and paedophiles are in fact negligible. They also point to the damage that can be caused to individuals, families and communities when the perceived risks of such victimization reach a point where they induce individuals to engage in extreme avoidance behaviour. It may well be that while online victimization cannot simply be dismissed as a 'non-problem', the disproportionate estimation of its likelihood may serve to undermine people's trust and engagement with this new media. The Internet offers, after all, unprecedented new opportunities for building social contacts and relationships that transcend barriers of space and culture, enabling us to resist processes of individualization and isolation that have come to characterize Western societies. This medium's potential as a basis for creating social solidarity may yet be damaged if the fear of 'stranger danger' entices us to withdraw from rather than embrace open communication.

Study questions

- *what are the apparent patterns of stalking behaviour on the Internet?*
- *how might they differ from cases of terrestrial stalking?*
- *what do you understand by 'paedophilia'?*
- *is online paedophilia a serious threat to children's safety?*
- *is there a 'moral panic' about online victimization?*

Further reading

A useful overview of the debate about stalking is provided in McGuire and Wraith's article, *Legal and Psychological Aspects of Stalking* (2000). The wide-ranging cyberstalking research conducted by Paul Bocij and his colleagues is available online at http://www.stalking-research.org.uk/. For a critical look at stalking, Chapter 3 of Paul Best's book, *Random Violence* (1999) is recommended. On the issue of online paedophilia, the work of the Cyberspace Research Unit is available for download at http://www.uclan.ac.uk/host/cru/. A critical reading of this issue is offered by Frank Furedi in his books *Paranoid Parenting* (2001) and *Culture of Fear* (2005).

EIGHT

Cybercrimes and Cyberliberties

Surveillance, Privacy and Crime Control

Overview

Chapter 8 examines the following issues:

- *the development of surveillance as a tool for social and crime control;*
- *the development of Internet surveillance;*
- *the resistance that surveillance efforts have encountered;*
- *the tensions between surveillance and liberty apparent in conflicts over encryption technology.*

---

key terms

Anonymity	Encryption	Surveillance
Dataveillance	Privacy	

Introduction

8.1 It is clear from discussion in the preceding chapters that the Internet carries with it significant new risks of criminal victimization, and thus presents some pressing challenges for legislators and criminal justice agencies. However, attempts to police the Internet for the purposes of crime control also raise serious dilemmas and dangers. Central here is the tension between surveillance and monitoring of online activities, on the one hand, and the need to protect users' privacy and confidentiality, on the other. Law enforcement agents need to able to identify offenders and collect evidence of online crimes. Offenders, however, are able to exploit anonymity and disguise to hide themselves and their activities from prying eyes. Privacy-enhancing technologies (such as anonymous remailers, anonymous web-surfing services, and encryption software) may be used to thwart policing. Consequently, the imperative for criminal justice actors is to reduce the potential abuse of Internet privacy by greater surveillance and monitoring of people's activities, which inevitably invades the privacy and confidentiality of online communications. However, from the perspective of many users, there is great unease at the prospect of their every move and utterance being subject to intrusion and examination. Critics of Internet surveillance point out that we risk losing control over the personal information that circulates on the web – the content of our emails, the sites we visit, our financial and other sensitive information. While authorities argue that there is a legitimate need to access such details in the course of law enforcement, the potential for abuse is all too apparent. For example, political dissidents and others suspected of sympathies opposed to the state may find themselves the subject of electronic surveillance, an issue which has come increasingly to the fore in the wake of September 11 and the 'war on terror'. Moreover, those selfsame privacy-enhancing technologies that offenders may use to evade detection and prosecution are at the same time essential for protecting legitimate users *from* criminal victimization. Thus encryption technologies are now routinely used to secure sensitive information such as credit card details, thereby protecting such data from interception and abuse by unauthorized third parties. As a result, reducing public access to online privacy protection in the name of policing may leave us less, not more, secure from criminal threats (as with attempts to outlaw public access to and use of sophisticated encryption techniques). At the present time, we are witnessing an intense struggle over the balance between online surveillance and privacy; while authorities move towards greater monitoring in order the tackle organized criminals, terrorists, paedophiles, stalkers, and so on, civil libertarians encourage users to evade such invasion of privacy by making greater recourse to privacy-enhancing tools. Efforts to secure society against the threat of cybercrime thus carry with them far-reaching consequences for the future of online freedom itself.

From surveillance to dataveillance: the rise of the electronic web

8.2 The past few decades have seen a massive growth in academic studies of surveillance and its social implications. Indeed, 'surveillance studies' now constitutes an inter-disciplinary specialism in its own right, with attendant journals, conferences and research programmes. This attention to surveillance first emerged in the 1970s, greatly influenced by Michel Foucault's (1977) ground-breaking analysis of 'panopticism', those modern techniques by which individuals and social groups were subjected to perpetual visual monitoring. For Foucault, surveillance was a key instrument with which modern societies disciplined and controlled populations; observation and inspection were used as a basis for judgement and intervention, enabling supposedly deviant or problematic individuals (such as the 'criminal', the 'sick', and the 'insane') to be exposed to a regime of corrective intervention aimed at 'normalizing' them. Foucault and others have observed how, with the emergence of modern society, a whole host of institutional sites appeared, each utilizing surveillance as a basis for training minds and bodies to conform with dominant expectations about proper, decent, healthy and productive behaviour. Such sites included the prison, the hospital, the school, the reformatory, the insane asylum, and the industrial factory. More recently, however, analysts such as Deleuze (1995) have claimed that the use of surveillance for corrective or normalizing interventions (disciplining) is on the wane. Instead, we are now moving into a 'society of control', in which surveillance functions as a means of managing populations through mechanisms of inclusion and exclusion (see also Rose, 2000; Diken and Lausten, 2002). Monitoring now informs judgements about who is to be included in social spaces, and who is to exiled to its margins, refused entry through the locked doors that protect gated communities, apartment blocks, airports, shopping malls, banks, workplaces, and leisure complexes. CCTV operators and private security guards zealously watch over our movements, barring those who are deemed unwelcome, illegitimate, undesirable, or suspicious (Davis, 1990; McCahill, 2001). The massive growth in use of video monitoring in particular (what Lyon (1994) calls the 'electronic eye') has seemingly created a society in which we are always being watched, examined, and judged (Norris and Armstrong, 1999).

Historically, the development of surveillance has taken shape around the visual monitoring of physical persons as they move and act in a variety of terrestrial settings (the street, the workplace, the shop, the transit area, public transport, and so on). However, with the appearance of networked electronic communications, it has become possible for individuals to engage in a variety of behaviours and exchanges in spaces in which they are not physically present; social life now increasingly takes place in what Castells (1996) calls the 'space of flows', those virtual terrains created by webs of electronic communication which do not exist in any place in particular. The Internet represents the most prominent and widely used such virtual space. Surveillance in this arena consequently takes a rather different form from its terrestrial counterpart. Rather than monitoring the physical presence and bodily actions of subjects, Internet surveillance observes and collects the digital footprints that all online activities leave in their wake. All web users, whether they know it or not, leave a 'data trail', the electronic record of their mouse clicks and keystrokes, the websites they have visited, the searches they have run, the materials they have downloaded, the personal information they have entered, the words and images they have sent via email, and so on. From such dataveillance (Gandy, 1993) it is possible to construct a digital double or simulation of an individual and her or his activities, without ever having to engage in physical observation (Poster, 1990; Bogard, 1996). From a web user's online activities it is possible to discover and track, among other things, her or his consumer choices and preferences; sexual orientation, fantasies and fetishes; political opinions and sympathies; professional interests and career aspirations; personal associations, friendships and intimate relationships (King, 2001: 40–1; also Huey and Rosenberg, 2004: 603). The collection and collation of such data are now routinely gathered, bought and sold by businesses. One's digital reconstruction can have a profound impact on access to social goods, resources and opportunities. For example, the aggregation of such data can be used in deciding whether or not we are given credit, loans and other financial services, or whether or not we will be insured against death, injury or accident. Beyond the commercial uses of this data, we can note the ways in which state and other security agencies utilize electronic monitoring to determine whether or not we present a risk to the economic or political order ('organized criminals', 'terrorists') or to society and morality ('paedophiles', 'pornographers', 'stalkers'). Indeed, it has been suggested that the use of electronic databases is becoming ever more central to the entire apparatus of criminal justice, with computerized information processing being used both to construct offenders and mediate punishment (Pattavina, 2004; Aas, 2005). While advocates of both business and law enforcement may be fairly sanguine about such developments, seeing them as necessary and desirable, many other observers express alarm about the ways in which surveillance can or is being used to sort, classify, control and exclude.

The development of Internet surveillance

8.3 As Gillmor (2004: 211) notes, the original architecture of the Internet made no provision for tracking who had visited particular websites, or what they had done there. However, as the web developed into a commercial medium, the collection of user information became quickly institutionalized. In 1996, the manufacturers of Netscape Navigator (the most popular web browser in use at the time) introduced 'cookie' files (also adopted by Internet Explorer and other browsers). Cookies are small files created every time a user visits a website. The files contain a record of the user's activities at the site, and the cookie is then sent to the user's computer where it is stored. When the user next visits the site, the cookie is sent back to the host system, enabling identification of the returning visitor. In this way, websites are able to build up a record of an individual's activities (Denning, 1999: 86). Concerns have long been raised about the invasiveness of cookies as they 'allow a Web site to record the user's comings and going, usually without his knowledge or consent' (Fischer-Hübner, 2000: 178; also Hinduja, 2004: 47). Information collected via cookies is but one dimension of a growing effort to accumulate and exploit user's details for commercial and competitive advantage. Huey and Rosenberg (2004: 601) point out that 'private-sector businesses maintain large data banks of personal information on consumers, some of which are interconnected so that data about individuals and aggregates can be shared'. Such information is a valuable commodity in itself, with many companies specializing in providing personal data to third parties, so that businesses can home in on selected individuals for the purposes of marketing (ranging from emails and letters to telephone selling and doorstop visits). For example, in May 2000 the bankrupt online retailer Toysmart.com placed an advertisement in the *Wall Street Journal* offering its database about 250,000 customers for sale to the highest bidder (Caplan, 2001). Another US-based company, SilverCarrot, specializes in establishing member-only websites whose sole purpose is to collect valuable information that users provide in the form of extensive registration questionnaires. This information is then sold as 'leads' to other companies such as Proctor & Gamble, Dell, T-Mobile, and American Express (SilverCarrot, 2005). The company's CEO, Allan Levy, claims to now possess a database covering 20 million individuals, and a tripling of profits between 2002 and 2003 alone (Oser, 2003). Moreover, detailed personal information is also available for sale to individuals, with no questions asked. One company, Data Hound Detective, offers an online service which for a fee of $29.99 will let the buyer 'check out anyone – learn their criminal record, and all the other goodies they want to keep hidden!'. They boast that 'if you can click a mouse you can find what you need. We set everything up so that you can find the information just like finding a book in a library' (Data Hound Detective, 2005). This commercial market in personal information (our telephone numbers, addresses, marital status, employment records, workplace, criminal convictions, and so on) means that anyone, anywhere can discover such details about us without our knowledge or consent, and use it for whatever purposes they wish.

The collectors, sellers and consumers of such information may suggest that alarm is unnecessary since adequate protection against abuses is provided by data protection and privacy laws. Many countries now have such provisions in place. For example, the UK's Data Protection Acts (1984 and 1998) regulate the unauthorized disclosure of personal information to third parties, while the Criminal Justice and Public Order Act (1994) 'created offences relating to procuring the disclosure of, or revealing or selling or offering to sell, computer-held personal information' (Wasik, 2000: 285–88). Similar provisions exist in Canada (under the Personal Information Protection and Electronic Documents Act, 2001), and across the EU countries under the Data Protection Directive (Charlesworth, 2000; Hunter and Bennett, 2002). However, critics may point out a number of problems with reliance upon such statutory measures in order to protect web users' privacy. First, regulations against selling personal information do not cover situations in which the user has 'consented' to share their information; data acquired via the use of cookies and similar monitoring software is generally held to have been provided with consent, and so is not covered by law. Second, there is an inevitable problem of legal pluralism – nothing prevents websites and information services located in non-regulated or under-regulated territories from collecting and selling on such information. Such differences in legal provisions are clear when comparing Europe with the USA. As Charlesworth (2000: 66) notes:

A key difference between the EU position and that of the United States is the extent to which market forces and self-regulatory regimes are viewed as being likely to provide an acceptable level of personal data privacy without some form of underlying legal framework. In the United States, there is little for either a privacy approach on the European model, or a centralised governmental privacy agency. Indeed, two government reports in the mid-1990s explicitly rejected the adoption of such approaches to data privacy.

Inevitably, leaving user privacy to business self-regulation and consumer choice will lead to greater space for exploitation of personal information where it is commercially advantageous to do so. Third, repositories of information held by data brokers and other companies may not necessarily be secure. Such data stores can and have been hacked using stolen passwords or by exploiting weaknesses in systems' security. In one recent case, the databases of information brokers Lexis-Nexis were breached by unauthorized individuals a total of 59 times, resulting in the theft of sensitive personal data about 310,000 US citizens; in another case, ChoicePoint, a trader in personal information (including individuals' police records, and social security, insurance, credit and employment histories) was discovered to have sold such information to criminals (EPIC, 2005). All of the above may lead us to conclude that we are all increasingly vulnerable to invasions of our privacy and personal information security where it comes to web-based communication.

A second important dimension of Internet monitoring relates to surveillance and data collection by governmental agencies. This is not always strictly separated from the commercial trade in personal data. For example, the aforementioned ChoicePoint count among their main customers the American FBI, CIA and NSA, who rely increasingly upon information brokers for sourcing basic intelligence about US citizens as well as foreign nationals. Internal documents from the FBI show that the Bureau's use of information brokers increased 9,600 per cent between 1992 and 2004 (Hoofnagle, 2004: 2). The US Justice Department spent $8 million with ChoicePoint alone in 2001 (*Wall Street Journal*, 2001). In addition to such commercially sourced information, US security agencies have for many years operated numerous programmes for 'data mining' information about individuals from the Internet and other sources. In 2003, the Pentagon launched its 'Total Information Awareness' project, with a budget of $54 million, in order to integrate information technologies for collecting, collating and cross-matching intelligence data (Stratford, 2003: 13). In response to privacy concerns, the US Congress eventually discontinued support for the programme in 2003. However, a report the following year found data mining to be 'ubiquitous' among government departments, with 52 federal agencies running some 1,999 projects aimed at assembling information about 'terrorists', 'terrorist activities' and 'terror suspects' (TIMJ, 2004: 7–8). Particularly worrying is that fact that, as McCullagh (2004) notes,

'Current federal data mining efforts ... are taking place with near-zero over-sight from Congress or the public', creating situation in which there is little or no accountability for which information is gathered, about whom, why, or what uses it may be put to. Federal protections for individuals, such as the Privacy Act (1974) have been amended under the PATRIOT Act following September 11 2001 (discussed in Chapter 3.3), allowing federal agencies greatly increased access to private and personal information (Coriou, 2002: 5). Moreover, while the Privacy Act regulates government databases, its provisions do not apply to the private sector, thereby creating a situation in which agencies can bypass restrictions by sourcing data from the likes of ChoicePoint. Similar concerns about the erosion of online privacy have been raised in the UK, where the Anti-Terrorism, Crime and Security Act (2001) has considerably eroded data protection regimes while enhancing state agencies' ability to acquire and retain communications data for 'national security' purposes (Chance et al., 2004: 8–9).

A third dimension of the emerging online surveillance apparatus relates to the monitoring of emails and their contents. In 2004, Google Inc. (the supplier of the world's most widely used search engine) announced that it was to launch a free email service called 'Gmail'. This service sparked a widely reported row with civil libertarians and privacy advocates, as the Gmail system was designed to scan the contents of users' mail to search for keywords. The purpose, Google argued, was to be able to target advertising for goods and services to users based upon their individual interests. However, the move was seen by many as a clear breach of users' privacy, as the content of mails could be matched to specific persons using their registration details. The concern was further exacerbated when Google revealed that it planned to retain all mails and data from searches indefinitely, and did not rule out sharing it with third parties including government agencies (Swartz, 2004a: 6). As Google (2005) put it:

we do not disclose your personally identifying information to third parties unless we believe we are required to do so by law or have a good faith belief that such access, preservation or disclosure is reasonably necessary to (a) satisfy any applicable law, regulation, legal process or governmental request, (b) enforce the Gmail Terms of Use, including investigation of potential violations thereof, (c) detect, prevent, or otherwise address fraud, security or technical issues ... (d) respond to user support requests, or (e) protect the rights, property or safety of Google, its users and the public.

This litany of broad-brushstroke exceptions naturally raised concerns that users' email contents would be far from secure, and that long-term information security could not be assured.

While the Gmail incident grabbed international headlines, less widely publicized have been the email monitoring efforts by state security agencies, which have been underway for many years. In the USA, the FBI operates an email content search system originally known as Carnivore (now renamed the less menacing DSC 1000). The Carnivore software can be installed on an ISP's system, enabling the Bureau to 'wiretap' emails (Stratford, 2003: 12). The Combating Terrorism Act (passed just two days after the September 11 attacks) now allows intelligence services to use the system without the need for any judicial approval (Coriou, 2002: 5); nor is it possible for ISPs to contest an order from the FBI (a so-called 'national security letter') before a judge (Swartz, 2004b: 6). The current trend clearly conforms to the wider development of a 'network of policing' in which extra-state actors are co-opted into the ever-expanding surveillance apparatus. ISPs have generally proven hostile to such efforts, as is apparent from responses to the UK Anti-Terrorism Act (2001), which requires ISPs to retain records of user's web and email activity and surrender it to authorities upon request. The introduction of similar laws is mandatory for those countries which have signed-up to the European Cyber-Crime Convention (Huey and Rosenberg, 2004: 597). ISPs' reluctance in the face of these demands may be traced to two eminently pragmatic concerns. First, their inclusion within the state's policing efforts may set them against their customers, who may refuse subscription to services if they know that their information and activities may come to the attention of security agencies. Second, the retention of vast quantities of data relating to every users' every move will require a massive increase in ISPs' data storage capacities, thus entailing considerable extra expense. Despite these reservations on the part of participants, there is little sign that such state-sponsored surveillance measures will be reversed in the foreseeable future.

The monitoring of email communication has also been instituted at an international level. The highly secretive 'ECHELON' project has now been running for over 25 years, and involves a partnership between intelligence agencies in the USA, the UK, Canada, Australia and New Zealand (Campbell, 1988: 10; Denning, 1999: 171). Originally designed to intercept and eavesdrop upon international telephone calls using automated voice recognition systems, ECHELON now embraces the searching of worldwide email (as well as fax) traffic for keywords that will trigger an alert. The governments involved have long denied the system's existence, hiding behind appeals to national security and official secrets. However, in recent years various disclosures have brought to light the alarming extent of ECHELON's abilities. Its network includes 'satellite interception stations, microwave ground stations, spy satellites, radio listening posts, and secret facilities that tap directly into land-based telecommunications networks' (Denning, 1999: 172). Its massive processing capacity is thought to give ECHELON the ability to examine 'almost every telephone call, fax transmission and email message transmitted around the world daily' (Poole, 2000). A Report published by the European Parliament, following an inquiry into the ECHELON system, noted how it was being used for purposes well beyond those most people would associate with national security (e.g. anti-terrorism operations). In particular, the report highlighted the ways in which economic espionage had become incorporated into the system's routine activities, gathering secret and confidential information on US business' foreign competitors (Furnell, 2002: 262). It claimed that the purpose of the system is 'to intercept private and commercial communications, and not military communications' (EP, 2001: 9). Authorities in Japan, France, and Brazil have complained that ECHELON has been used to spy on trade negotiations and business deals, and the intercepted details have been passed on to US-based competitors. It has also been reported that monitoring has been extended to political and other organizations who operate within the law, but whose agenda may be critical of the US and other governments – these include the environmentalist group Greenpeace, the human rights organization Amnesty International, and the development charity Christian Aid (Sykes, 1999: 173). Add to this the lack of any democratic oversight of the system's operations, the situation clearly exists in which abuses of privacy laws may be perpetrated by states against their own and other nations' citizens on an ongoing basis.

The dilemmas of surveillance as crime control: the case of encryption

8.4 The controversy over the encryption of Internet communication in many ways exemplifies the tensions and dilemmas raised by the contradictory imperatives of state surveillance and user privacy. The issue of encryption was briefly discussed in Chapter 3.6. It was noted that encryption (along with allied methods of encoding information such as steganography) can be used to protect electronic communications from inspection by third parties. Documented uses of encryption by those involved in criminal activities include the encoding of email communications, of files stored on computers and computer networks, and of information posted on publicly accessible websites (Denning and Baugh, 2000: 106). Use of such techniques has been encountered by investigations of organized crime, terrorist groups, and Internet paedophile and child pornography rings (Rogerson and Pease, 2004: 3). As early as 1998, the FBI's Computer Analysis Response Team (CART) claimed to have encountered use of encryption in 5–6 per cent of computer crime cases with which they dealt (Denning and Baugh, 2000: 112); it may well be that as criminal enterprises has become more technologically literate, and more aware of information security issues, that the use of encryption has increased significantly in the intervening years and will continue to do so (Reitinger, 2000: 135).

Encryption basically works by reordering data (e.g. in a text file) according to a pattern specified by a 'key'. A key is a string of digital code or 'bits' (ones and zeros). Without access to this key, one does not know how to rearrange the data contents of a file back to its original order so as to make it legible; in its encrypted form, the data will look like just a random and nonsensical mass of characters. It *is* possible to discover the encryption key by 'brute force' – using a computer to run through all the possible combinations of one and zeros until the correct order is hit upon that will allow the data contents to be rearranged in their proper form. However, the ability to do so will depend crucially upon the amount of computing power available and the length of the key – adding a single digit to the key length will double the number of possible combinations that have to be tried. In 1998, two American researchers built a supercomputer (called the EFF DES cracker) that could try out 100 billion keys per second; using this machine, they successfully cracked an encryption code 56 bits in length in less than three days (Denning and Baugh, 2000: 118). However, such cracking can be easily avoided by simply increasing the length of the encryption key used – a key of 128 bits

> is totally unfeasible to break ... by brute force, even if all the computers in the world are put to the task. To break one in a year would require, say, 1 trillion computers (more than 100 computers for every person on the globe), each running 10 billion times faster than the EFF DES Cracker.
>
> (Denning and Baugh, 2000: 118)

Many widely used computer applications now include encryption tools as standard, for example, Microsoft's Office software offers 128-bit encryption for its Word documents, email messages, etc. Similarly Adobe's Acrobat software (used to create PDF files) comes equipped with 128-bit encryption. The Pretty Good Privacy (PGP) software, freely available for download from the Internet, enables users to use 256-bit key encryption. In short, such powerful tools for data protection mean that 'encryption, properly implemented, can be nearly foolproof' (Reitinger, 2000: 135). Both business and individual Internet users, concerned about the possibility that their competitor or their or foreign governments may intercept sensitive communications, are making increasing recourse to using such tools to protect their data from prying eyes.

The concern aroused by encryption on the part of states and law enforcement agencies has resulted in an ongoing battle over the past decade to subject encryption technologies to a variety of forms of statutory regulation. In France, for example, the mid-1990s saw attempts to institute a public ban on so-called 'strong encryption', with the state arguing that only those with something illegal to hide need have access to such security tools. The state also attempted to introduce a so-called 'key deposit' system, where all manufacturers of encryption software would have to provide police with a key allowing data scrambled

CYBERCRIMES AND CYBERLIBERTIES

using their programs to be deciphered by the authorities (Cumiskey, 1998). The proposals were finally withdrawn as a result of pressure from the EU, which wanted to promote the use of communication security technologies as part of its blueprint for developing the information economy within Europe. However, the respite was short-lived, and in the wake of the September 11 attacks, the passing of the Law on Everyday Security in November 2001 introduced mandatory requirements for encryption tool providers to surrender codes enabling the authorities to read encrypted messages (Coriou, 2002: 7). A similar trajectory emerged in the UK, with the government proposing in its Electronic Communications Bill (1998) to allow law enforcement to demand keys from encryption users, with failure to comply carrying a 'presumption of guilt' and resulting in a two-year custodial sentence (FIPR, 1999: 2). The proposal was dropped from the final draft of the Bill following concerted opposition from many quarters. However, the proposals requiring surrender of a decryption key were revived and successfully seen into law in the Regulation of Investigatory Powers Act (RIPA) in 2000. Disclosure can be demanded '(a) in the interests of national security; (b) for the purpose of preventing or detecting crime; or (c) in the interests of the economic well being of the United Kingdom' (RIPA, Section 49(2), cited in Walker 2001). The provisions were subsequently incorporated within the 2001 Anti-Terrorism Act. The response in the USA has been, if anything, even more concerted, with governments since the Clinton Administration in the early 1990s promoting a raft of measures which would have placed draconian limits on the use of encryption and given law enforcement wide-ranging powers for interception and decryption. First came the proposal for the Clipper Chip which would be installed in all telephones and computers, and 'would enable the government to decode any electronic communication' (Sykes, 1999: 160). The move was defeated due to resistance from computer manufacturers and civil liberties organizations. Authorities argued that such interception capabilities would only be used to track the communications of drug dealers and terrorists, and that the privacy of ordinary US citizens would be respected. Yet, as well-known Internet freedom campaigner John Perry Barlow pithily quipped, 'trusting the government with your privacy is like trusting a Peeping Tom to install your window blinds' (cited in Sykes, 1999: 160). The years through the mid and late 1990s saw repeated attempts to introduce legislation which would variously require manufacturers to supply keys, build secret 'back doors' into encryption software, ban foreign sales of encryption capable programs, and ban strong encryption all together. As in other countries, the tide finally turned in favour of law enforcement and against computer privacy activists in the aftermath of September 11 2001. The PATRIOT Act of 2001 instituted no specific additional measures against encryption but, as already noted, greatly increased law enforcement's scope for data collection and interception without the safeguards of judicial review or appeal. As I write this, the

US Senate is in the process of discussing the proposed Domestic Security Enhancement Act (which has been popularly dubbed 'PATRIOT II' or 'Son of PATRIOT'). This Act proposes to further tighten the surveillance of electronic communications, and includes specific enhancements in the area of encryption. In particular, there is a provision which would introduce a five-year prison term for anyone who 'knowingly or willfully' uses encryption technology 'to conceal any incriminating communication or information' related to a felony (Jaeger et al., 2003: 202). While ostensibly aimed at tackling criminal activity, privacy rights organizations such as the Electronic Freedom Foundation (EFF) fear that it will further erode citizens' ability to communicate in privacy without state intrusion (EFF, 2005). Moreover, it can be argued that efforts to restrict or regulate use of encryption (as, for example, through key escrow schemes or building 'back doors' into the software) may ultimately be counter-productive in tackling crime and terrorism. Criminal organizations and actors, aware of the authorities' ability to access data encrypted using commercial software, are liable to make recourse instead to tools for which no back doors or master keys exist (or even privately commission software tailored to their needs). Consequently, the access acquired by law enforcement will prove ineffective in countering encryption used by professional criminals – its only use will be to enable surveillance of legitimate organizations and individuals.

The encryption issue has thrown up clear tensions not only between governments and their citizens, but also within governments themselves. While those agencies concerned with crime and national security have pushed for restrictions on non-governmental use of encryption, those departments dealing with commerce, trade, industry and technology have been *encouraging* business use of those selfsame technologies. The perceived necessity for such use arises from the need to establish greater information security. Public engagement with e-commerce (online purchasing, electronic banking, and so on) has been limited by concerns over the security of sensitive data that might be intercepted and exploited by third parties such as hackers and fraudsters. As a result, building greater protection for customer information, and thus greater confidence in the integrity of Internet business systems, is perceived as key for the continued growth of the e-commerce sector. Thus the UK government's Department of Trade and Industry (DTI) argues that: 'Protecting information has never been more important. Organisations face a wide range of risks to their data, including virus attacks, inappropriate usage, unauthorised access and theft or systems failure' (2004: 1). They go on to note how theft of information has profound implications in terms of commercial losses (business sensitive and proprietary information may fall into the hands of competitors), damage to reputation and trust, and financial costs associated with potential legal action and data recovery (ibid.: 9). It should further be noted that negligence in protecting sensitive data relating to others (e.g. customer information) breaches data protection regulations such as the Data Protection Act, and may be subject to sanctions such as fines. As a result, the DTI recommends that businesses use encryption to protect databases containing sensitive information. Such advocacy of information security measures, including use of data encryption, has also been apparent at the international level. The Organisation for Economic Cooperation and Development (OECD) argues that:

> failure to utilise encryption methods can adversely affect the protection of privacy, intellectual property, business and financial information, public safety and national security and the operation of electronic commerce because data and communications may be inadequately protected from unauthorised access, alteration, and improper use, and therefore, users may not trust information and communication systems, networks and infrastructures.
>
> (OECD, 1997, quoted in Jackson 2000: 169)

The OECD goes on to recommend that national encryption controls must respect the rights to privacy, information security, and the needs and demands of business. Thus we see a basic tension between agendas of different authorities, with some advocating the widespread use of encryption, and others seeking to curtail it in the name of crime control and policing.

A second sector from which resistance to anti-encryption laws has emerged is the computer security industry. This sector, which provides computer security goods and services to commercial organizations, communities and individuals, has grown apace in recent years. Research estimates placed US companies' spending on computer security at $2.8 billion in 1999, $3.4 billion in 2000, projected to rise to $9.9 billion in 2005 (Shinkle, 2001). The global financial outlay on such products and services is placed at $27 billion (Grow, 2004: 84). Overall growth in the sector has remained high (30 per cent in 2003 – *Computer Weekly*, 2003: 1), bucking the slowdown in much of the IT sector following the bursting of the 'dot.com' bubble (Castells, 2002: 105–6). The sector furnishes security services such as threat analysis and risk assessment; secure systems design and implementation; design and provision of security-enhancing software; and training for organizations and their employees in using and implementing security systems and procedures (Halverson, 1996: 9; Wright, 1998: 10; Nugent and Raisinghani, 2002: 7–8; Rassool, 2003: 5–6; Vaidhyanathan, 2003: 176–7). Naturally, computer security firms have a vested interest in the increasing uptake to information security technologies such as encryption, and its legal restriction would prove highly damaging to the ongoing prospects for economic growth in this market. Therefore, it comes as no surprise that information security providers have made common cause with privacy advocates and civil libertarians in lobbying to block bans and excessive controls on public encryption. This alliance has continued to frustrate law enforcement in its hopes to effectively outlaw or severely limited encryption technologies in the name of crime fighting.

Summary

8.5 This chapter has dealt with the dilemmas and tensions that have arisen from expanded efforts to institute greater surveillance and monitoring in response to cybercrime. From the perspective of law enforcement agencies, the ability to use anonymity, disguise, and cryptographic encoding are serious impediments in tackling Internet crime. States have taken this claim seriously by instituting ever greater monitoring and interception of online communications. However, it is clear that such measures have clearly breached the limits of rights to privacy that many citizens of liberal-democratic countries might reasonable expect. The wave of legislative innovation in the wake of September 11 2001 has merely served to amplify state security agencies' ability to monitor citizens, with, in many cases, severely limited accountability and democratic controls. This has resulted in ongoing critique of and resistance to Internet surveillance by activists, and greater use of privacy-enhancing tools by Internet users. The tension between surveillance and privacy enhancement also appears insofar as the same tools that can be exploited *for* criminal activity afford users protection *from* criminal victimization. This is nowhere clearer than in the case of encryption, which can be viewed simultaneously as a serious threat to law enforcement efforts, *and* as an indispensable resource for businesses and individuals to protect themselves from crime. This situation leads to competing agendas between different state agencies, with the imperatives of economic growth and law enforcement clashing where it comes to public access to encryption tools. The outcome of such contestations and negotiations in the coming years will have profound consequences for the social development of the Internet, its availability as an arena for criminal enterprise, and its accessibility as a space in which civic cultures and social relations may develop.

Study questions

- in what ways are our day-to-day uses of the Internet subject to surveillance?
- are such surveillance measures justified by claims that they are necessary for tackling cybercrime?
- can citizens trust states where it comes to their privacy?
- why is the regulation of privacy-enhancing technologies such as encryption such a difficult issue to address? Is it possible to meet the demands and needs of all social constituencies at the same time?
- if it comes to a choice between security and liberty, on which side should we err?

Further reading

On the growth of surveillance in modern societies, David Lyon's *The Electronic Eye: The Rise of Surveillance Society* (1994) is recommended, along with his more recent *Surveillance After September 11* (2003). On the development of informational surveillance, or dataveillance, Oscar Gandy's *The Panoptic Sort: A Political Economy of Personal Information* (1993) and Bogard's *The Simulation of Surveillance: Hypercontrol in Telematic Societies* (1996) provide excellent and provocative reading. On the privacy implications of contemporary surveillance practices, Charles Sykes' *The End of Privacy* (1999) provides a stimulating and accessible, if disturbing, assessment. Valuable and non-technical overviews about the encryption debate can be found in Dorothy Denning's *Information Warfare and Security* (1999) and Bruce Schneier's *Secrets and Lies: Digital Security in Networked World* (2000). Finally, the websites of the Electronic Privacy Information Centre (http://www.epic.org) and the Electronic Freedom Foundation (http://www.eff.org) are invaluable resources for critical analysis of developments in the area of Internet surveillance and privacy.

Glossary

ADVANCES FEE FRAUD   Also known as the Nigerian Letter Scam and the Spanish Prisoner, this fraud typically works by offering the victim large returns in return for assistance in extracting monies which are supposedly held captive in bank accounts in another country. An 'advanced fee' is requested from the victim to assist with the extraction, but he or she never gets to see a share of the (in reality non-existent) millions promised.

ANONYMITY   The ability to engage in social action and communication without having one's identity available to others.

ANTI-GLOBALIZATION MOVEMENT   A broadly based social protest movement that emerged during the 1990s, in resistance to economic globalization and its control by Western governments and corporations.

CHILD   Developmental stage in the early years of life. Who counts as a child, and which distinctive characteristics are associated with being a child (childhood) are subject to great variation across cultures and history.

CHILD PORNOGRAPHY   Representations featuring a child or children depicted in an explicitly sexualized manner and/or engaging in sexual activity. A child may variously be defined for the purposes of child pornography as (1) a pre-pubescent, or (2) an individual who may have physically matured but who is still under the legal age of majority. Given legal differences across countries, any given article may or may not be deemed to be child pornography dependent on how the age of legal majority or sexual maturity is defined.

COPYRIGHT   Those property rights associated with 'original' expressions, be they in visual, spoken, written, audio or other forms. The possession of copyright over an expression entitles the holder to control its copying and distribution.

CRACKING   A generally derogatory term used to describe activities associated with 'hacking' in its second sense, that of unauthorized access to computer systems.

CRIME   Any act that contravenes law and is subject to prosecution and punishment by the state.

CYBERCRIME   Any criminal activity that takes place within or by utilizing networks of electronic communication such as the Internet.

CYBERSPACE   The interactional space or environment created by linking computers together into a communication network.

CYBERSTALKING Stalking that takes place via online communication mechanisms such as email, chat rooms, instant messaging, and discussion lists.

CYBERTERRORISM Terrorist activity that targets computer networks and information systems for attack.

DATAVEILLANCE Surveillance that focuses not upon the visual or other tracking of the physical individual, but of collecting, collating and analysing data about the individual's activity, often in the form of electronic records.

DENIAL OF SERVICE An attack on a networked computer or computers that disrupts normal operations to such an extent that legitimate users can no longer access their services.

DEVIANCE Behaviour that may not necessarily be criminal, but which may transgress collective norms about appropriate or acceptable behaviour. While crimes are subject to formal, legal sanctions, those actions deemed deviant may be subject to informal sanctions such as social stigmatization and denunciation.

DIFFERENTIAL ASSOCIATION A criminological concept developed by Edwin Sutherland, which holds that young people in particular learn how to engage in deviant and criminal activity through association with others who are similarly inclined.

DOWNLOADING The act of copying digital material posted online into the storage medium on one's computer.

E-COMMERCE Market economic activity undertaken via the Internet or similar electronic communication networks.

ENCRYPTION Techniques and tools associated with encoding or scrambling data in such as way as to render it incomprehensible to others not in possession of a 'key' that is needed to decipher the data into its original legible form.

FILE SHARING The practice of allowing others to make copies of files stored on a computer via downloading. The practice is generally associated with the sharing of music, movies, images and software via websites dedicated to such copying.

FIRST AMENDMENT RIGHTS Those rights to unobstructed expression guaranteed by the First Amendment to the Constitution of the United States.

GENDER That aspect of male–female differences which is attributable to social upbringing and cultural codes, rather than to any innate sexual or biological differences between men and women.

GLOBALIZATION The social, economic, political and cultural processes in which local and national spatial limits on interaction are overcome, and thus come to span the globe.

HACKING A term with two distinctive meanings. First, the act of creative problem solving when faced with complex technical problems and, second, illicit and usually illegal activities associated with unauthorized access to, or interference with, computer systems.

HACKTIVISM Political activism and social protest that uses hacking tools and techniques.

HATE SPEECH   Any form of speech or representation that depicts individuals or groups in a derogatory manner with reference to their 'race', ethnicity, gender, religion, sexual orientation, or physical or mental disability in such a manner as to promote or provoke hatred.

HIDDEN CRIME   Criminal acts that tend to go largely unobserved, unremarked, and unrecorded in official assessments and measures of criminal activity.

INDECENCY   Any form of representation, expression or action (especially of a sexual nature) which may be held to be potentially offensive to the sensibilities of some or most of a society's members. In many (though not all) Western democracies, expressions that may be considered indecent are nevertheless tolerated and not subject to strict legal prohibition.

INFORMATION SOCIETY   A stage of socio-economic development in which the importance previously allocated to the production of material goods and resources is superseded by the centrality of knowledge and information in economic activity.

INTANGIBLE GOODS   Goods over which an individual or other legally recognized entity (e.g. a company) has rights of possession, but which do not take a materially tangible form.

INTELLECTUAL PROPERTY   Property that takes the form of ideas, expressions, signs, symbols, designs, logos, and similar intangible forms.

INTERNET   The publicly accessible network of computers that emerged in the 1970s and came to span the globe by the late 1990s.

INTERNET AUCTIONS   Online marketplaces enabling individuals and businesses to post a wide variety of items for sale.

LEGAL PLURALISM   The differences in legal regulations and prohibitions apparent across different states.

MALICIOUS SOFTWARE OR 'MALWARE'   A general term for a variety of computer codes (such as viruses, logic bombs and Trojan horses) which are designed to disrupt or interfere with a computer's normal operation.

MASCULINITY   The dominant cultural norms, ideas, values and expectations associated with being male. These can include norms about sexual orientation and behaviour, aggression and violence, legitimate interests and aspirations, emotional expressivity, dress and body language, and a host of similar social attributes.

MORAL PANIC   An unwarranted or excessive reaction to a perceived problem of crime, deviance or social disorder, often produced by representations in the mass media.

OBSCENITY   A notoriously slippery term used to denote representations, expressions or actions (often of a sexual nature) that are held to be generally offensive and thus unacceptable by society at large. Obscenity is almost invariably subject to legal prohibition and formal, criminal sanctions. Just what constitutes an 'obscenity' is, however, deeply contested, and subject to profound variation across cultural contexts and to change over time.

OFFICIAL STATISTICS   Measures of the scope, scale and nature of criminal offending compiled and published by the state and allied criminal justice agencies.

PAEDOPHILIA   The sexual attraction among adults towards children of either sex.

PHISHING   The fraudulent practice of sending emails to individuals that purport to come from a legitimate Internet retailer or financial service. The aim of phishing is to persuade the victim to voluntarily disclose sensitive information, such as bank account and credit card details, which can then be exploited to defraud the individual concerned.

PIRACY   A popular term for copyright violations – the unauthorized copying, distribution or sale of informational goods over which some party claims to possess proprietary rights.

POLICING   A wide range of activities that serve to monitor and control social behaviour. Policing may be undertaken by official state-sanctioned bodies (such as the police), by private organizations, by communities or individuals.

PORNOGRAPHY   Visual or written representations of a sexually explicit nature, whose primary aim or use is to stimulate sexual excitement.

PRIVACY   The right to be left alone; freedom from observation and interference from others.

PROPERTY RIGHTS   Legally institutionalized rights to own and control goods.

RECORDING OF CRIME   The process through which reported incidents are officially classified and recorded as instances of crimes.

REPORTING OF CRIME   The process through which incidents of criminal victimization are reported to authorities such as the police or to other organizations and bodies who monitor crime levels.

REPRESENTATION OF CRIME   The constructions and depictions of crime and criminals that circulate within mass media, political discourse, and official accounts of the 'crime problem'.

SOCIAL INCLUSION AND SOCIAL EXCULSION   The duality in which some individuals and groups are economically, politically and culturally incorporated within the social order, and others are excluded from full participation within it.

SPOOFING   The fraudulent practice of establishing facsimiles of legitimate websites, to which victims can be directed and where they will unknowingly surrender sensitive information such as bank details, credit card numbers and account passwords.

STALKING   Repeated harassing or threatening behaviour, in which an offender persistently contacts, follows, approaches, threatens or otherwise subjects a victim to unwelcome attentions.

SUBCULTURE   The notion of a 'culture within a culture' – a group which has its own distinctive norms, codes and values, which are used to unite its members and differentiate the group from others in 'mainstream' society or rival groupings.

SURVEILLANCE   The systematic observation and monitoring of people and places as a tool for effecting greater control over behaviour.

SURVEYS OF CRIME AND VICTIMIZATION An alternative to official crime statistics, criminal victimization surveys ask members of the public about their experiences of crime, including many that, for a variety or reasons, may not have been reported to the police or other authorities.

TECHNIQUES OF NEUTRALIZATION A concept developed by criminologists Graham Sykes and David Matza to describe those strategies which youth use to dissociate themselves from dominant moral codes about acceptable behaviour, and which serve to loosen inhibitions and assuage guilt, thereby freeing them to engage in criminal and/or deviant acts.

TERRORISM A notoriously slippery and contested term. In its most conventional sense, it denotes the use of violence or the threat of violence in pursuit of political ends.

TRANSNATIONAL CRIME AND POLICING Criminal activities that span the borders of national territories, and crime prevention and control initiatives designed to tackle or reduce such offences.

TROJAN HORSES Malicious software programs which are infiltrated into computers disguised as benign applications or data.

VIRUSES Pieces of computer code that can 'infect' computer systems causing disruption to their normal operation.

WAR ON TERROR Rhetorical and political response among Western governments in the wake of the September 11 attacks, which adopts a highly aggressive and 'pro-active' stance in identifying, capturing and disabling actual, suspected and potential terrorists, along with those who are perceived to sympathize with or support their goals.

WEBSITE DEFACEMENT The activity of altering the code organizing a website so as to alter the visible screen content.

Bibliography

AACP (Alliance Against Counterfeiting and Piracy) (2002) *Proving the Connection: Links between Intellectual Property Theft and Organised Crime*. London: AACP.

Aas, F. (2005) *Sentencing in the Information Age: From Faust to Macintosh*. London: GlassHouse Press.

ABC Newsonline (2005) 'Seller Charged Over Stolen Goods on eBay', 2 February, at http://www.abc.net.au/news/newsitems/200502/s1294115.htm

ALA (American Library Association) (2004) 'ALA Intellectual Freedom Committee Report to Council', at http://www.ala.org/ala/oif/ifgroups/ifcommittee/ifcinaction/ifcreports/ifcreportac04.pdf

Adey, P. (2004) 'Secured and Sorted Mobilities: Examples from the Airport', *Surveillance and Society*, 1(4): 500–19.

Akdeniz, Y. (1996) 'Computer Pornography: A Comparative Study of the US and UK Obscenity Laws and Child Pornography Laws in Relation to the Internet', *International Review of Law, Computers and Technology*, 10(2): 235–62.

Akdeniz, Y. (1999) *Sex on the Net: The Dilemma of Policing Cyberspace*. London: South Street Press.

Akdeniz, Y. (2000) 'Child Pornography', in Y. Akdeniz, C. Walker and D. Wall (eds), *The Internet, Law and Society*. Harlow: Longman.

Akdeniz, Y. (2001a) 'Governing Pornography and Child Pornography on the Internet: The UK Approach', at http://www.cyber-rights.org/yamancv.htm

Akdeniz, Y. (2001b) 'International Developments Section of Regulation of Child Pornography on the Internet', at http://www.cyber-rights.org/reports/child.htm

Akdeniz, Y. (2001c) 'United States Section of Regulation of Child Pornography on the Internet: Cases and Materials Related to Child Pornography on the Internet', at http://www.cyber-rights.org/reports/uscases.htm

Akdeniz, Y. and Strossen, N. (2000) 'Sexually Oriented Expression', in Y. Akdeniz, C. Walker and D. Wall (eds), *The Internet, Law and Society*. Harlow: Longman.

Akdeniz, Y., Walker, C. and Wall, D. (eds) (2000) *The Internet, Law and Society*. Harlow: Longman.

Amarach Consulting (2001) 'Research of Internet Downside Issues: August 2001', report for the Irish Internet Advisory Board, at http://www.

Ananova (2002) 'Movie Industry Hunts Down Online Pirates' posted 20 July 2002, at http//www.ananova.com/enetrtainment/story/sm_632999.html

APWG (Anti-Phishing Working Group) (2005) 'Phishing Activity Trends Report: January 2005', at http://www.antiphishing.org

ASACP (Association of Sites Advocating Child Protection) (2005) 'Why ASACP?' at http://www.asacp.org/index.php

Bandura, A. (1977) *Social Learning Theory*. Englewood Cliffs, NJ: Prentice-Hall.

Barak, A., Fisher, W., Belfry, S. and Lashambe, D. (1999) 'Sex, Guys, and Cyberspace: Effects of Internet Pornography and Individual Differences on Men's Attitudes Toward Women', *Journal of Psychology and Human Sexuality*, 11(1): 63–91.

BBC News (2001a) 'Code Red Cost Tops $1.2bn', Wednesday 1 August 2001, at http://news.bbc.co.uk/hi/business/1468986.stm

BBC News (2001b) '"Mafiaboy" Hacker Jailed', Thursday 13 September 2001, at http://www.news.bbc.co.uk/1/hi/sci/tech/1541252.stm.

BBC News (2004) 'UK and US to Act on Web Sex Sites', 9 March 2004, at http://news.bbc.co.uk/go/pr/fr/-/hi/uk/3545147.stm

Becker, H. (1963) *Outsiders: Studies in the Sociology of Deviance*. New York: Free Press.

Bennett, D. (2001) 'Pornography-Dot-Com: Eroticising Privacy on the Internet', *The Review of Education/Pedagogy/Cultural Studies*, 23: 381–91.

Bennion, F. (2003) 'The UK Sexual Offences Bill: A Victorian Spinster's View of Sex', *Common Law*, 12(1): 61–6.

Bently, L. and Sherman, B. (2001) *Intellectual Property Law*. Oxford: Oxford University Press.

Bequai, A. (1999) 'Cyber-Crime: the US Experience', *Computers and Security*, 18(1): 16–18.

Beresford, A. (2003) *Securities/Investment Fraud*. Washington, DC: National White Collar Crime Centre.

Bergmann, J. (1969) 'The Original Confidence Man', *American Quarterly*, 21(3): 560–77.

Best, J. (1999) *Random Violence: How We Talk about New Crimes and New Victims*. Berkeley, CA: University of California Press.

Best, J. (2003) 'European Cybercrime Squad Gets Green Light', ZDNet New at http://news.zdnet.co.uk/internet/security/0,39020375,39118074,00.htm

Biegel, S. (2003) *Beyond Our Control? Confronting the Limits of Our Legal System in the Age of Cyberspace*. Cambridge, MA: MIT Press.

Bleich, E. (2003) *Race Politics in Britain and France: Ideas and Policymaking Since 1960*. Cambridge: Cambridge University Press.

Boase, J. and Wellman, B. (2001) 'A Plague of Viruses: Biological, Computer and Marketing', *Current Sociology*, 49(6): 39–55.

Bocij, P. (2003) 'Victims of Cyberstalking: An Exploratory Study of Harassment Perpetrated via the Internet', *First Monday*, 8(10), at http://www.firstmonday.org/issues/issues8_10/bocij/index.html

Bocij, P. and McFarlane, L. (2002) 'Cyberstalking: Genuine Problem or Public Hysteria?', *Prison Service Journal*, 140: 32–5.

Bocij, P., Griffiths, M. and McFarlane, L. (2002) 'Cyberstalking: A New Challenge for Criminal Justice', *The Criminal Lawyer*, 122: 3–5.

Bogard, W. (1996) *The Simulation of Surveillance: Hypercontrol in Telematic Societies*. Cambridge: Cambridge University Press.

Boni, B. (2001) 'Building Bridges, Standing Guard', *Network Security*, 5, May, 18–19.

Bollier, D. (2003) 'Preserving the Commons in the Information Order', in WSIS *World Information: Knowledge of Future Culture*. Vienna: Institut für Neue Kulturtechnologien.

Bowers, S. (1998) 'Information Warfare: The Computer Revolution is Altering How Future Wars Will be Conducted', *Armed Forces Journal International*, August, 38–9.

Bowker, A. (1999) 'Juveniles and Computers: Should We Be Concerned?', *Federal Probation: A Journal of Correctional Philosophy and Practice*, 63(2): 40–43.

Bowling, B. and Foster, J. (2002) 'Policing and the Police', in M. Maguire, R. Morgan and R. Reiner (eds), *The Oxford Handbook of Criminology*, 3rd edition. Oxford: Oxford University Press.

Boyd, J. (2002) 'In Community We Trust: Online Security Communication at eBay', *Journal of Computer-Mediated Communication*, 7(3) at http://ascusc.org.jcmc/vol7/issues3/boyd.html

BPI (British Phonographic Industry) (2002) *Market Information*, 184, 7 June. London: BPI.

Brewster, M. (2003) 'Power and Control Dynamics in Prestalking and Stalking Situations', *Journal of Family Violence*, 18(4): 207–17.

Brown, A. and Barrett, D. (2002) *Knowledge of Evil: Child Prostitution and Child Sexual Abuse in Twentieth Century England*. Cullompton/Portland, OR: Willan.

Brugger, W. (2002) 'The Treatment of Hate Speech in German Constitutional Law', *German Law Journal*, 40(1), online at: http://www.germanlawjournal.com/pdf/Vol 04No01/PDF_Vol_04_No_01_01–44_Public_Brugger.pd

BSA (Business Software Alliance) (2003) 'Eighth Annual BSA Global Software Piracy Study', URL (consulted March 2005): http://www.bsaa.com.au/downloads/BSA_Piracy_Booklet.pdf

BSA (Business Software Alliance) (2005) 'Fact Sheet: The Cyber Frontier and Children', URL (consulted March 2005): http://www.bsa.org/resources/loader.cfm?url=/commonspot/security/getfile.cfm&pageid=1323&hitboxdone=yes

Budd, T., Sharp, C. and Mayhew, P. (2005) *Offending in England and Wales: First Results from the 2003 Crime and Justice Survey*. Home Office Research Study 275. London: Home Office.

Bunz, M. (2003) 'Remember: Mimesis is a Form of Creativity', in *World Information: Knowledge of Future Culture*. Vienna: Institut für Neue Kulturtechnologien.

Burn, A. and Willett, R. (2003) '"What Exactly is a Paedophile?": Children Talking About Internet Risk', at http://www.ccsonline.org.uk/mediacentre/Research_Projects/Burn_Willett.pdf

Buxbaum, P. (2002) 'Cyberterrorism: a Sorry Excuse for Government Intervention', at http://searchcio.techtarget.com/originalContent/0,289142,sid19_gci866647,00.html

Cabinet Office (2002) *Identity Fraud: A Study*. London: Cabinet Office.

Campbell, D. (1998) 'Somebody's Listening', *New Statesman*, 12 August: 10–12.

Capeller, W. (2001) 'Not Such a Neat Net: Some Comments on Virtual Criminality', *Social and Legal Studies*, 10: 229–42.

Caplan, J. (2001) 'Dot-Coms, Databases, and Dollars', 23 January, at http://www.cfo.com/article.cfm/2991452?f=archives

Carter, D. (1997) '"Digital Democracy" or "Information Aristocracy"? Economic Regeneration and the Information Economy', in B. Loader (ed.), *The Governance of Cyberspace: Politics, Technology and Global Restructuring*. London: Routledge.

Carugati, A. (2003) Interview with MPAA President Jack Valenti, *Worldscreen*, at http://worldscreen.com/interviewscurrent.php?filename=203valenti.txt

Castells, M. (1996) *The Rise of the Network Society*. New York: Blackwell.

Castells, M. (1998) *The Information Age: Economy, Society and Culture: vol. 3 End of Millennium*. Malden, MA: Blackwell.

Castells, M. (2002) *The Internet Galaxy: Reflections on the Internet, Business, and Society*. Oxford: Oxford University Press.

CEBR (Centre for Economics and Business Research) (2002) *Counting Counterfeits: Defining a Method to Collect, Analyse and Compare Data on Counterfeiting and Piracy in the Single Market*, final report for the European Commission Directorate-General Single Market. London: CEBR.

CERT/CC (2002) 'CERT Advisory CA-2001-23 Continued Threat of the "Code Red" Worm', 17 January 2002, at http://www.cert.org/asvisories/CA-2001-23.html

Cha, A. (2005) 'Police Find That on eBay Some Items Are a Real Steal', 8 January, at http://www.duluthsuperior.com/mld/duluthsuperior/10597328.htm

Chance, S., Tootell. H. and Morris, E. (2004) 'The Impact of Anti-Terrorism Legislation on Dataveillance', Proceedings of the CollECTeR Workshop on eCommerce, May 7/8, Adelaide South Australia, at http://www.collecter.org/coll2004/proceedings/phance_Morris_Tootell.pdf

Charlesworth, A. (2000) 'The Governance of the Internet in Europe', in Y. Akdeniz, C. Walker and D. Wall (eds), The Internet, Law and Society. Harlow: Longman.

Clough, B. and Mungo, P. (1992) Approaching Zero: Data Crime in the Computer Underworld. London: Faber & Faber.

Cloward, R. and Ohlin, L. (1961) Delinquency and Opportunity: A Theory of Delinquent Gangs. London: Routledge.

Cohen, A. (1955) Delinquent Boys: The Culture of the Gang. New York: Free Press.

Cohen, L. and Felson, M. (1979) 'Social Change and Crime Rate Trends: A Routine Activity Approach', American Sociological Review, 44: 588–608.

Cohen, S. (1972) Folk Devils and Moral Panics. London: MacGibbon.

Cole, K. (2004) 'When eBay Bargains Are a Little Too Hot', 13 May, at http://www.cbsnewyork.com/topstories/local_story_134071152.html

Coleman, C. (2003) 'Securing Cyberspace – New Laws and Developing Strategies', Computer Law and Security Report, 19(2): 131–6.

Coleman, C. and Moynihan, J. (1996) Understanding Crime Data. Buckingham: Open University Press.

Comscore Media Metrix (2003) 'Canada Trumps U.S. in Broadband Use', press release 17 March 2003, at http://www.comscore.com/press/release.asp?id=312

Connell, R. (1987) Gender and Power. Cambridge: Polity Press.

Coriou, L. (2002) 'The Internet on Probation', at http://commonsense.epfl.ch/Resources/Internet/InternetOnProbation.pdf

Coutorie, L. (1995) 'The Future of High-Technology Crime: A Parallel Delphi Study', Journal of Criminal Justice, 23(1): 13–27.

Conway, M. (2002) 'What is Cyberterrorism?', Current History, 101(659): 436–442.

Craven, J. (1998) 'Extremism and the Internet (EMAIN)', The Journal of Information, Law and Technology, at http://www.elj.warwick.ac.uk/jilt/98_1crav/

CSI/FBI (2003) 'CSI/FBI Computer Crime and Security Survey', Computer Security Institute. San Francisco.

Creighton, S. (2003) 'Child Pornography: Images of the Abuse of Children', NSPCC Information Briefings. London: NSPCC.

Critcher, C. (2003) Moral Panics and the Media. Buckingham: Open University Press.

Crozier, B. (1974) A Theory of Conflict. London: Hamish Macmillan.

Cumiskey, A. (1998) 'Go-Ahead for Police to Tap Coded Mail', The Daily Telegraph, 24 September, at http://www.chiark.greenend.org.uk/pipermail/ukcrypto/1998-September/002454.html

Curry, S. (2005) 'Online Auctions: The Bizarre Bazaar', at http://www.scambusters.org/onlineauctions.pdf

Data Hound Detective (2005) 'Sniff Out Information on Anyone: FAQ', at http://www.datahounddetective.com/faq.htm

Davis, M. (1990) City of Quartz: Excavating the Future of Los Angeles. London: Verso.

Deirmenjian, J. (2000) 'Hate Crimes on the Internet', Journal of Forensic Sciences, 45(5): 1020–22.

Delgado, R. (1982) 'Words That Would: A Tort Action for Racial Insults, Epithets, and Name-Calling', Harvard Civil Rights-Civil Liberties Law Review, 17: 133–181.

Delio, M. (2001) 'Why Worm Writer Surrendered', *Wired Magazine*, 14 February 2001, at http://www.wired.com/news/culture/0,1284,41809,00.html

Deleuze, G. (1995) 'Postscript on the Societies of Control', in *Negotiations*. New York: Columbia University Press.

DeMarco, J. (2001) 'It's Not Just Fun and "War Games" – Juveniles and Computer Crime', at http://www.cybercrime.gov/usamay2001_7.htm

Denning, D. (1991) 'Hacker Ethics', *Proceedings of the 13th National Conference on Computing and Values*. New Haven: Research Centre on Computing and Society.

Denning, D. (1999) *Information Warfare and Security*. New York: Addison-Wesley.

Denning, D. (2000a) 'Cyberterrorism', at http://www.cs.georgetown.edu~denning/infosec/cyberterror.html

Denning, D. (2000b) *Cyberterrorism*. Testimony before the Special Oversight Panel on Terrorism Committee on Armed Services U.S. House of Representatives, 23 May 2000.

Denning, D. and Baugh, W. (1997) 'Cases Involving Encryption and Terrorism', at http://www.cs.georhetown.edu/denning/crypto/cases.html

Denning, D. and Baugh, W. (2000) 'Hiding Crimes in Cyberspace', in D. Thomas, and B. Loader (eds), *Cybercrime: Law Enforcement, Security and Surveillance in the Information Age*. London: Routledge.

De Young, M. (2004) *The Day Care Ritual Abuse Moral Panic*. Jefferson, NC: McFarland & Company.

Digital Intelligence Centre (DIG) (2004) 'Digital Intelligence Centre: Archived News', URL (consulted March 2005): http://www.itic.ca/DIC/News/archive.html#2004-06-09

Diken, B. and Lausten C.B. (2002) *Zones of Indistinction – Security, Terror, and Bare Life*. the Department of Sociology, Lancaster University at http://www.comp.lancs.ac.uk/sociology/soc091bd.html

DiMarco, H. (2003) 'The Electronic Cloak: Secret Sexual Deviance in Cyberspace', in Y. Jewkes (ed.), *Dot.cons: Crime, Deviance and Identity on the Internet*. Cullompton: Willan.

Dolan, K. (2004) 'Internet Auction Fraud: The Silent Victims', *Journal of Economic Crime Management*, 2(1).

Donoghue, A. (2004) 'Cyberterror: Clear and Present Danger or Phantom Menace?', at http://insight.zdnet.co.uk/specials/networksecurity/0,39025061,39118365-2,00.htm

D'Ovidio, R. and Doyle, J. (2003) 'A Study on Cyberstalking', *FBI Law Enforcement Bulletin*, 72(3): 10–17.

Dowland, P., Furnell, S., Illingworth, H. and Reynolds, P. (1999) 'Computer Crime and Abuse: A Survey of Public Attitudes and Awareness', *Computers and Security*, 18(8): 715–26.

Drahos, P. with Braithwaite, J. (2002) *Information Feudalism: Who Owns the Knowledge Economy?* London: Earthscan.

DTI (Department of Trade and Industry) (2004) *Information Security: Hard Facts*. London: DTI.

Dunn, M. and Wigert, I. (2004) *International CIIP Handbook: An Inventory and Analysis of Protection Policies in Fourteen Countries*. Zurich: Swiss Federal Institute of Technology.

Dworkin, G. and Taylor, R.D. (1989) *Blackstone's Guide to the Copyright, Designs and Patents Act 1988*. London: Blackstone Press.

EC (European Commission) (1998) *Combating Counterfeiting and Piracy in the Single Market*, Green Paper 2COM(98)569 Final. Brussels: EC.

ECPAT (End Child Prostitution, Child Pornography and Trafficking of Children for Sexual Purposes) (1997) *Child Pornography: An International Perspective*, at http://www.csecworldcongress.org/PDF/en/Stockholm/Background_reading/Theme_papers/Theme%200paper%20Pornography%201996_EN.pdf

EFA (Electronic Frontiers Australia) (2002) 'Internet Censorship: Law and Policy Around The World', at http://www.efa.org.au/Issues/Censor/cens3.html#sau

EFF (Electronic Frontier Foundation) (2001) 'Online Censorship and Free Expression', at http://www.eff.org//Censorship/?f=gottesman_lords_video_case.article

EFF (Electronic Frontier Foundation) (2005) 'EFF Analysis of PATRIOT II', at http://www.eff.org/Censorship/Terrorism_militias/patriot-act-II-analysis.php

Eichenwald, K. (1998) 'Reuters Subsidiary Target of US Inquiry into Theft of Data from Bloomberg', *Computers and Security*, 17, 2, 157.

Embar-Seddon, A. (2003) 'Cyberterrorism: Are We Under Siege?', *American Behavioral Scientist*, 45(6): 1033–43.

Emerson, R., Ferris, K. and Brooks-Gardner, C. (1998) 'On Being Stalked', *Social Problems*, (45)3: 289–314.

English, E. (1996) 'SEC Tackles Internet Investment Fraud', *Network Security*, January 1996: 8.

Enos, L. (2000) 'Yahoo! Sued for Auctioning Counterfeit Goods', 29 March, at http://www.ecommercetimes.com/story/2849.html

EP (European Parliament) (2001) 'Report on the Existence of a Global System for the Interception of Private and Commercial Communications (ECHELON interception system)', Final, A5–0264/2001, 11 July. Brussels: European Parliament.

EPIC (Electronic Privacy Information Center) (1997) *Faulty Filters: How Content Filters Block Access to Kid-Friendly Information on the Internet*. Brussels: EPIC.

EPIC (Electronic Privacy Information Center) (2005) 'ChoicePoint', at http://www.epic.org/privacy/choicepoint/default.html

Epstein, R. (2004) 'Liberty versus Property? Cracks in the Foundations of Copyright Law', John M. Olin Law and Economics Working Paper No. 204, URL (consulted March 2005): http://www.law.uchicago.edu/Lawecon/index.html

Escolar, I. (2003) 'Please Pirate My Songs', in WSIS *World Information: Knowledge of Future Culture*. Vienna: Institut für Neue Kulturtechnologien.

Esen, R. (2002) 'Cyber Crime: A Growing Problem', *Journal of Criminal Law*, 66(3): 269–83.

European Commission (1998) *Combating Counterfeiting and Piracy in the Single Market*, Green Paper 2COM(98)569 Final Brussels: EC.

Everett, C. (2003) 'Credit Card Fraud Funds Terrorism', *Computer Fraud and Security*, 5(1): 1.

Evans, K. (2004) 'Virtual Community', *The Electronic Journal of Social Issues*, 2 (1), special issue on 'The Futures of Community', January 2004, at http://www.whb.co.uk/socialissues/indexvol2.htm

Experian (2002) *Internet Fraud: A Growing Threat to Online Retailers*. London: Experian.

FACT (Federation Against Copyright Theft) (2003a) 'Fact Combats Epidemic Levels of Counterfeit Goods Entering UK Domestic Market From Asia Pacific', news release, 28 February 2003, at http://www.prowse.co.uk/FACT/F280203.htm

FACT (2003b) 'Special Report', September 2003, at http://www.fact-uk.org.uk

Feather, M. (1999) 'Internet and Child Victimisation', paper presented at the Children and Crime: Victims and Offenders Conference, Brisbane, Australia, 17–18 June.

Felson, M. (1998) *Crime and Everyday Life*, 2nd edn. Thousand Oaks, CA: Pine Forge Press.

Finer, C. and Nellis, M. (eds) (1998) *Crime and Social Exclusion*. London: Blackwell.

FIPR (Foundation for Information Policy Research) (1999) 'Unprecedented Safeguards for Unprecedented Capabilities', at http://www.fipr.org/publications/hoover.pdf

Fischer-Hübner, S. (2000) 'Privacy and Security at Risk in the Global Information Society', in D. Thomas and B. Loader (eds), *Cybercrime: Law Enforcement, Security and Surveillance in the Information Age*. London: Routledge.

Fitch, C. (2004) *Crime and Punishment: The Psychology of Hacking in the New Millennium*. Bethesda, MD: SANS Institute.

Fitzgerald, V. (2003) 'Global Financial Information, Compliance Incentives and Terrorist Funding', at http://users.ox.ac.uk/~ntwoods/Fitzgerald.pdf

Flahardy, C. (2004) 'Tiffany & Co. Cracks Down on eBay Counterfeiters', *Corporate Legal Times*, 14(154): 1–2.

Fleming, P. and Stohl, M. (2000) 'Myths and Realities of Cyberterrorism', paper presented at the International Conference on Countering Terrorism Through Enhanced International Cooperation, 22–24 September, 2000, Courmayeur, Italy.

Forde, P. and Patterson, A. (1998) 'Paedophile Internet Activity', *Trends and Issues in Criminal Justice No. 97*. Canberra: Australian Institute of Criminology.

Foucault, M. (1991) *Discipline and Punish*. Harmondsworth: Penguin.

Fream, A. and Skinner, W. (1997) 'Social Learning Theory Analysis of Computer Crime Among College Students', *Journal of Research in Crime and Delinquency*, 34(4): 495–518.

Fried, R. (2001) 'Cyber Scam Artists: A New Kind of .con', at http://www.crime-scene-investigator.net/CyberScam.pdf

Frith, S. and Marshall, L. (2004) *Music and Copyright*. Edinburgh: Edinburgh University Press.

Fritz, J. (1995) 'A Proposal for Mental Health Provisions in State Anti-Stalking Law', *Journal of Psychiatry and Law*, Summer: 295–318.

Furedi, F. (2001) *Paranoid Parenting*. London: Penguin/Alan Lane.

Furedi, F. (2005) *Culture of Fear: Risk Taking and the Morality of Low Expectation*. revised edition. London: Continuum.

Furnell, S. (2002) *Cybercrime: Vandalizing the Information Society*. London: Addison-Wesley.

Fyfe, N. (2001) *Geography of Crime and Policing*. Oxford: Blackwell.

Gandy. O. (1993) *The Panoptic Sort: A Political Economy of Personal Information*. Boulder: Westview Press.

Gerrits, R. (1992) 'Terrorists' Perspectives: Memoirs', in D. Paletz and A. Schmid (eds), *Terrorism and the Media*. Newbury Park, CA: Sage.

Gillmor, D. (2004) *We the Media*. London: O'Reilly.

Goffman, E. (1969) *The Presentation of Self in Everyday Life*. Harmondsworth: Penguin.

Goode, E. and Ben-Yehuda, N. (1994) *Moral Panics: The Social Construction of Deviance*. Oxford: Blackwell.

Goode, M. (1995) 'Stalking: Crime of the '90's?', *Criminal Law Journal*, 19(1): 1–10.

Google (2005) 'Gmail Privacy Policy', at http://gmail.google.com/gmail/help/privacy.html

Gordon, G., Willox, N., Rebovich, D., Regan, T. and Gordon, J. (2004) 'Identity Fraud: A Critical National and Global Threat', *Journal of Economic Crime Management*, 2(1): 3–47.

Gordon, S. and Ford, R. (2003) *Cyberterrorism?* Cupertino: Symantec.

Gottfredson, M. and Hirschi, T. (1990) *A General Theory of Crime*. Palo Alto: Stanford University Press.

Grabosky, P. (2001) 'Virtual Criminality: Old Wine in New Bottles?', *Social and Legal Studies*, 10: 243–9.

Grabosky, P. (2003) 'Cyberterrorism', at http://www.alrc.gov.au/reform/summaries/82.htm

Grabosky, P. and Smith, R. (2001) 'Telecommunication Fraud in the Digital Age: The Convergence of Technologies', in D. Wall (ed.), *Crime and the Internet*. London: Routledge.

Graham, W. (2000) 'Uncovering and Eliminating Child Pornography Rings on the Internet: Issues Regarding and Avenues Facilitating Law Enforcement's Access to "Wonderland"', *Law Review of Michigan State University-Detroit College of Law*, 2: 457–84.

Grazioli, S. and Jarvenpaa, S. (2000) 'Perils of Internet Fraud: An Empirical Investigation of Deception and Trust With Experienced Internet Consumers', *IEEE Transactions on Systems, Man, and Cybernetics*, 30(4): 395–410.

Green, C. (1998) 'Policing Cyberspace', *Focus*, 45(3): 66–68.

Green, J. (2001) 'The Myth of Cyberterrorism: There Are Many Ways Terrorists Can Kill You – Computers Aren't One of Them', *The Washington Quarterly Online*, at http://www.washington monthly.com/features/2001/0211.green.html

Grossman, W. (2001) *From Anarchy to Power: The Net Comes of Age*. New York: New York University Press.

Grow, B. (2004) 'Software', *Business Week*, 21, June: 84.

Hagan, J. and Petersen, R. (eds) (1994) *Inequality and Crime*. Stanford, CA: Stanford University Press.

Haines, L. (2004) 'Ebay India Boss Cuffed in Porn Vid Scandal', *The Register*, 20 December, at http://www.theregister.co.uk/2004/12/20/ebay_india_scandal/

Hamblen, M. (1999) 'Clinton Commits $1.46B to Fight Cyberterrorism', at http://www.cnn.com/TECH/computing/9901/26/clinton.idg

Hamm, M. (2004) 'The USA Patriot Act and the Politics of Fear', in J. Ferrell, K. Hayward, W. Morrison and M. Presdee (eds), *Critical Criminology Unleashed*. London: GlassHouse.

Halverson, G. (1996) 'As Internet Booms, So Do Hacker-Proofing Measures', *Christian Science Monitor*, 88(144): 9.

Harding, L. (2004) 'Delhi Schoolboy Sparks Global Porn Row', *The Guardian*, 21 December.

Harvey, D. (1989) *The Condition of Postmodernity*. Oxford: Blackwell.

Hettinger, E. (1989) 'Justifying Intellectual Property', *Philosophy and Public Affairs*, 18(1): 31–52.

Hinde, S. (2003) 'The Law, Cybercrime, Risk Assessment and Cyber Protection', *Computers and Security*, 22(2): 90–5.

Hinduja, S. (2004) 'Theory and Policy in Online Privacy', *Knowledge, Technology, and Policy*, 17(1): 38–58.

Hirschi, T. (1969) *Causes of Delinquency*. Berkeley, CA: University of California Press.

Hitchcock, J. (2003) 'Cyberstalking and Law Enforcement', *Police Chief Magazine*, 70(12), at http://www.policechiefmagazine.org/magazine/index.cfm?fuseaction=display_arch&article_id=166&issue_id=122003

Hollin, C. (2002) 'Criminological Psychology', in M. Maguire, R. Morgan and R. Reiner (eds), *The Oxford Handbook of Criminology*, 3rd edn. Oxford: Oxford University Press.

Holmes, B. (2003) 'The Emperor's Sword: Art Under WIPO', in WSIS *World Information: Knowledge of Future Culture*. Vienna: Institut für Neue Kulturtechnologien.

Home Office (2002a) 'Home Office Annual Report 2001–2', at http://www.homeoffice.gov.uk/docs

Home Office (2002b) 'Chipping of Goods Initiative', press release 24 May 2002, at http://www.homeoffice.gov.uk/docs/pressnotice3.doc

Home Office (2004) *Protecting the Public: Strengthening Protection Against Sex Offenders and Reforming the Law on Sexual Offences*. London: Home Office.

Hoofnagle, C. (2004) 'Big Brother's Little Helpers: How ChoicePoint and Other Commercial Data Brokers Collect and Package Your Data for Law Enforcement', at http://www.epic.org/privacy/choicepoint/cp_article.pdf

Huey, L. and Rosenberg, R. (2004) 'Watching the Web: Thoughts on Expanding Police Surveillance Opportunities under the Cyber-Crime Convention', *Canadian Journal of Criminology and Criminal Justice*, 46(4): 597–606.

Hughes, R. (1993) *Culture of Complaint: Fraying of America*. Oxford: Oxford University Press.

Hunt, A. (1987) 'Moral Panic and the Moral Language in the Media', *British Journal of Sociology*, 48: 629–648.

Hunter, C. (1999) 'Internet Filter Effectiveness: Testing Over and Underinclusive Blocking Decisions of Four Popular Filters', at http://www.copacommission.org/papers/filter_effect.pdf

Hunter, T. and Bennett, C. (2002) 'Personal Information Protection and Electronic Documents Act ("PIPEDA")', at http://www.davis.ca/publications/2002–02_personal_information_protection_and_electronic_documents_act.pdf

Hyde, H. (1964) *A History of Pornography*. New York: Farrar Straus Giroux.

Hyde, S. (1999) 'A Few Coppers Change', *The Journal of Information, Law and Technology (JILT)*, 2, at http://www.law.warwick.ac.uk/jilt/99–2/hyde.html

ICCC (Internet Crime Complaint Centre) (2004) *IC3 2004 Internet Fraud – Crime Report*, online at http://www.ifccfbi.gov/strategy/2004_IC3 Report.pdf.

IFPI (International Federation of Phonographic Industries) (2003) 'The Recording Industry Commercial Piracy Report 2003', at http://www.ifpi.org/site-content/library/piracy2003.pdf

IFR (Internet Filter Review) (2004) 'Internet Pornography Statistics', at http://internet-filter-review.toptenreviews.com/internet-pornography-statistics.html

IIPA (International Intellectual Property Alliance) (2005) 'Statistics', at http://www.iipa.com/copyrighttrade_issues.html

Interpol (2005a) 'Legislation of Interpol Member States on Sexual Offences against Children – USA', at http://www.interpol.org/public/Children/SexualAbuse/National Laws/csaUSA.asp

Interpol (2005b) 'Legislation of Interpol Member States on Sexual Offences against Children – Greece', at http://www.interpol.org/public/Children/SexualAbuse/NationalLaws/csaGreece.asp

Interpol (2005c) 'Legislation of Interpol Member States on Sexual Offences against Children – Spain', at http://www.interpol.org/public/Children/SexualAbuse/NationalLaws/csaSpain.asp

Interpol (2005d) 'Legislation of Interpol Member States on Sexual Offences against Children – Austria', at http://www.interpol.org/public/Children/SexualAbuse/NationalLaws/csaAustria.asp

IPSOS (2004) 'Online Software Piracy Poll', URL (consulted March 2005): http://www.ipsos-na.com/news/pressrelease.cfm?id=2452

ITU (International Telecommunications Union) (2004) 'Statistics at a Glance', 12 February 2004, at http://www.itu.int/ITUD/ict/statistics/at_glance/Internet02.pdf

IWF (Internet Watch Foundation) (2004) 'Significant Trends 2003', at http://www.iwf.org.uk/media/page.70.216.htm

Jackson, M. (2000) 'Keeping Secrets: International Developments to Protect Undisclosed Business Information and Trade Secrets', in D. Thomas and B. Loader

(eds), *Cybercrime: Law Enforcement, Security and Surveillance in the Information Age.* London: Routledge.

Jaeger, P., Bertot, J. and McClure, C. (2003) 'The Impact of the USA Patriot Act on Collection and Analysis of Personal Information Under the Foreign Intelligence Surveillance Act', *Government Information Quarterly*, 20: 295–314.

Jedwab, J. (2004) 'The Lowdown on Music Downloading in Canada: Youth Regard Internet Downloading of Music, Video and Software as Acceptable: Only Threat of Legal Action is Effective Deterrent', at http://www.acs-aec.ca/Polls/18-10-2004-1.pdf

Jefferson, T. (1997) 'Masculinities and Crime', in M. Maguire, R. Morgan and R. Reiner (eds), *The Oxford Handbook of Criminology*. Oxford: Oxford University Press.

Jenkins, P. (2001) *Beyond Tolerance: Child Pornography Online.* New York: New York University Press.

Jewkes, Y. and Andrews, C. (2005) 'Policing the Filth: The Problems of Investigating Online Child Pornography in England and Wales', *Policing and Society*, 15(1): 42–62.

Joseph, J. (2003) 'Cyberstalking: An International Perspective', in Y. Jewkes (ed.), *Dot.cons: Crime, Deviance and Identity on the Internet.* Cullompton: Willan.

Kabay, M. (1998) 'Anonymity and Pseudonymity in Cyberspace: Deindividuation, Incivility and Lawlessness Versus Freedom and Privacy', paper presented at the Annual Conference of the European Institute for Computer Anti-virus Research, March.

Kaplan, J. and Moss, M. (2003) *Investigating Hate Crimes on the Internet.* Washington, DC: Partners Against Hate.

Kasten, E. (2004) 'Ways of Owning and Sharing Cultural Property', in E. Kasten (ed.), *Properties of Culture – Culture as Property.* Berlin: Dietrich Reimer Verlag.

Kelley, J. (2001) 'Experts Say Terrorists Hiding Message on Web', *USA Today*, 18 June, at http://www.usatoday.com/news/washdc/2001-02-05-ejihad.htm

King, L. (2001) 'Information, Society and the Panopticon', *The Western Journal of Graduate Research*, 10(1): 40–50.

Kini, R., Pamakrishna, H. and Vijayaraman, B. (2003) 'An Exploratory Study of Moral Intensity Regarding Software Piracy of Students in Thailand', *Behaviour and Information Technology*, 22(1): 63–70.

Koch, L. (2000) 'Cyberstalking Hype', at http://www.lzkoch.com/column_05.html

Kolarik, G-L. (1992) 'Stalking Laws Proliferate, But Critics Say Constitutional Flaws Also Abound', *American Bar Association Journal*, November: 35–6.

Kounoupias, N. (2003) 'Copyright Piracy Disruption, Deterrence and Destruction', Disruption, Deterrence and Destruction: Targeting the Traders in Fakes, paper presented at the Anti-Counterfeiting Group (ACG) conference, London, 15 May 2003.

Kovacich, G. (1999) 'Hackers: Freedom Fighters of the 21st Century', *Computers and Security*, 18(7): 573–76.

Krone, T. (2005) 'Child Exploitation', *Australian Institute of Criminology High Tech Crime Brief 2*. Canberra: AIC.

Kutchinsky, B. (1992) 'Pornography, Sex Crime and Public Policy', in S. Gerull and B. Halstead (eds), *Sex Industry and Public Policy.* Canberra: Australian Institute of Criminology.

Lacey, N. (2002) 'Legal Constructions of Crime', in M. Maguire, R. Morgan and R. Reiner (eds), *The Oxford Handbook of Criminology*, 3rd edition. Oxford: Oxford University Press.

Lane, F. (2001) *Obscene Profits: The Entrepreneurs of Pornography in the Cyber Age.* London: Routledge.

Larkin, M. (2002) 'Pornography-Blocking Software May Also Block Health Information Sites', *The Lancet*, 360: 1946.

Lawson, S. (2002) *Information Warfare: An Analysis of the Threat of Cyberterrorism Towards the US Critical Infrastructure*. Bethesda, MD: SANS Institute.

Lawson, W. (2002) 'Too Many Passwords', at http://www.icdri.org/biometrics/Too%Many%20Passwords.pdf

Lea, J. and Young, J. (1984) *What Is to Be Done about Law and Order?* Harmondsworth: Penguin.

Lederer, L. and Delgado, R. (1995) 'Introduction', in L. Lederer and R. Delgado, *The Price We Pay: The Case Against Racist Speech, Hate Propoganda, and Pornography*. New York: Hills and Wang.

Lee, D. (2005) 'eBay is Fence of the Young', at http://newsobserver.com/news/v-printer/story/1899135p-8235660c.html

Lemos, R. (1975) 'Locke's Theory of Property', *Interpretation*, 5: 226–44.

Lenk, K. (1997) 'The Challenge of Cyberspatial Forms of Human Interaction to Teritorrial Governance and Policing' in B. Loader (ed.), *The Governance of Cyberspace: Politics, Technology and Global Restructuring*. London: Routledge.

Letterman, G.G. (2001) *Basics of International Intellectual Property Law*. New York: Transnational Publishers.

Levy, S. (1984) *Hackers: Heroes of the Computer Revolution*. New York: Doubleday.

Lilley, P. (2002) *Hacked, Attacked and Abused: Digital Crime Exposed*. London: Kogan Page.

Litman, J. (2000) 'The Demonization of Piracy', paper presented at the Tenth Conference on Computers, Freedom and Privacy, Toronto, 6 April 2000, at http://www.wayne.edu/litman/papers/demon.pdf

Littlewood, A. (2003) 'Cyberporn and Moral Panic: An Evaluation of Press Reactions to Pornography on the Internet', *Library and Information Research*, 27(86): 8–18.

Livingstone, S., Bober, M. and Helsper, E. (2005) *Internet Literacy Amongst Children and Young People*, findings from the *UK Children Go Online* project, at http://www.children-go-online.net

Loader, B. (ed.) (1997) *The Governance of Cyberspace: Politics, Technology and Global Restructuring*. London: Routledge.

Loader, I. and Sparks, R. (2002) 'Contemporary Landscapes of Crime, Order and Control: Governance, Risk and Globalization', in M. Maguire, R. Morgan and R. Reiner (eds), *The Oxford Handbook of Criminology*, 3rd edn. Oxford: Oxford University Press.

Loeber, R. and Stouthamer-Loeber, M. (1986) 'Family Factors as Correlates and Predictors of Juvenile Conduct Problems and Delinquency', in M. Tonry and N. Morris (eds), *Crime and Justice: An Annual Review of Research*, vol. 7. Chicago: University of Chicago Press.

Loftus, E. (1996) *The Myth of Repressed Memory: False Memories and Allegations of Sexual Abuse*. New York: St. Martin's Press.

Love, C. (2000) 'Love Manifesto', URL (consulted March 2005): http://www.reznor.com/commentary/loves_manifesto1.html

Lowney, K. and Best, J. (1995) 'Stalking Strangers and Lovers: Changing Media Typifications of a New Crime Problem', in J. Best (ed.), *Images of Issues: Typifying Contemporary Social Problems*. New York: Aldine de Gruyter.

Lyon, D. (1994) *The Electronic Eye: The Rise of Surveillance Society*. Oxford: Polity Press.

Lyon, D. (2003) *Surveillance After September 11*. Oxford: Blackwell.

Mackie, G. (2004) 'Publishing Notoriety: Piracy, Pornography and Oscar Wilde', *University of Toronto Quarterly*, 73(4): 980–90.

MacKinnon, C. (1996) *Only Words.* Cambridge MA: Harvard University Press.

Maguire, M. (2002) 'Crime Statistics: The '"Data Explosion" and Its Implications', in M. Maguire, R. Morgan and R. Reiner (eds), *The Oxford Handbook of Criminology*, 3rd edn. Oxford: Oxford University Press.

Martin, B. (1998) *Information Liberation.* London: Freedom Press.

Martin, E. (ed.) (2003) *Oxford Dictionary of Law*, 5th edn. Oxford: Oxford University Press.

Maurer, D. (2000) *The Big Con: The Story of the Confidence Man and the Confidence Trick.* London: Arrow Books.

McCahill, M. (2001) *The Surveillance Web: The Rise of Visual Surveillance in an English City.* Cullompton: Willan Press.

McCandless, D. (2004) 'Anatomy of a Virus', *The Guardian*, Thursday 5 February.

McCormack, T. (1998) 'Multiculturalism, Racism and Hate Speech', *Institute for Social Research Newsletter*, 13(1), online at http://www.math.yorku.ca/ISR/newsletter/multi_racism_hate.htm

McConnell International (2000) *Cyber Crime ... and Punishment? Archaic Laws Threaten Global Information*, at http://www.mcconnellinternational.com

McCourt, T. and Burkart, P. (2003) 'When Creators, Corporations and Consumers Collide: Napster and the Development of On-Line Music Distribution', *Media, Culture and Society*, 25(3): 333–50.

McCullagh, D. (2001) 'Bin Laden: Steganography Master?', *Wired*, 7 February, at http://www.wired.com/news/politics/0,1283,41658,00.html

McCullagh, D. (2004) 'Government Data Mining Lives On', at http://news.com/Government+data-mining+lives+on/2010-1028_3-5223088.html

McFarlane, L. and Bocij, P. (2003) 'An Exploration of Predatory Behaviour in Cyberspace: Towards a Typology of Cyberstalkers', *First Monday*, 8(9), at http://www.firstmonday.org/issues/issue8_9/mcfarlance/index.html

McGuire, B. and Wraith, A. (2000) 'Legal and Psychological Aspects of Stalking: A Review', *The Journal of Forensic Psychiatry*, 11(2): 316–27.

McGonagle, T. (2001) 'Wrestling (Racial) Equality from Tolerance of Hate Speech', *Dublin University Law Journal*, 23: 21–54.

McLeod, K. (2001) *Owning Culture: Authorship, Ownership, and Intellectual Property Law.* New York: Peter Lang.

Menta, R. (2003) 'New From the RIAA: Let's Play Starving Artist', at http://www.p2pnet.net/article/8214

Messerschmidt, J. (1993) *Masculinities and Crime.* Lanham, MD: Rowan and Littlefield.

Milone, M. (2003) 'Hacktivism: Securing the National Infrastructure', *Knowledge, Technology and Policy*, 16(1): 75–103.

Mitnick, K. and Simon, W. (2005) *Art of Intrusion: True Stories of Computer Break-Ins Straight from the Criminals.* Chichester: John Wiley and Sons. Ltd.

Miyawaki, R. (1999) 'The Fight Against Cyberterrorism: A Japanese View', Washington, DC: Centre for Strategic and International Studies.

Moore, L. (ed.) (2000) *Con Men and Cutpurses: Scenes from the Hogarthian Underworld.* London: Allen Lane.

Moorefield, J. (1997) 'Legal Update: Communications Decency Act of 1996', *Boston University Journal of Science and Technology Law*, 13: 32–8.

Mota, S. (2003) 'The U.S. Supreme Court Addresses the Child Pornography Prevention Act and Child Online Protection Act in *Ashcroft v. Free Speech Coalition* and *Ashcroft v. American Civil Liberties Union*', *Federal Communications Law Journal*, 55(1): 85–98.

MPAA (Motion Picture Association of America) (2003a) 'U.S. Entertainment Industry: 2002 MPA Market Statistics', at http://www.mpaa.org

MPAA (2003b) '2003 Piracy Fact Sheets: US Overview', at http://www.mpaa.org

MPAA (2005) 'Anti-Piracy', URL (consulted March 2005): http://www.mpaa.org/anti-piracy/

MSIDCGR (Minority Staff Special Investigations Division Committee on Government Reform) (2001) *Children's Access to Pornography Through Internet File-Sharing Programs*. Washington, DC: U.S. House of Representatives.

Mullen, P., Pathé, M. and Purcell, R. (2001) 'Stalking: New Constructions of Human Behaviour', *Australian and New Zealand Journal of Psychiatry*, 35: 9–16.

Muncie, J. (1999) *Youth and Crime: A Critical Introduction*. London: Sage.

Murray, C. (1984) *Losing Ground*. New York: Basic Books.

NAEYC (National Association for the Education of Young Children) (1996) 'Prevention of Child Abuse in Early Childhood Programs and the Responsibilities of Early Childhood Professionals to Prevent Child Abuse', at http://www.naeyc.org/about/positions/pdf/pschab98.pdf

Nash, J. (1976) *Hustlers and Con Men: An Anecdotal History of the Confidence Man and His Games*. New York: M. Evans.

Naughton, J. (2000) *A Brief History of the Future: The Origins of the Internet*. London: Phoenix.

NCIS (National Criminal Intelligence Service) (1999) 'Project Trawler: Crime on the Information Highways', at http://www.cyber-rights.org/documents/trawler.htm

Newman, G. and Clarke, R. (2003) *Superhighway Robbery: Preventing e-commerce Crime*. Cullompton: Willan Press.

NHTCU National Hi-Tech Crime Unit (2004) 'What is Hi-Tech Crime?', at http://www.nhtcu.org./nqcontent.cfm?a_id=12334&tt=nhtcu

Nielsen, L. (2002) 'Subtle, Pervasing, Harm: Racist and Sexist Remarks in Public as Hate Speech', *Journal of Social Issues*, 58(2): 265–280.

NOP/NHTCU (2002) *Hi-Tech Crime: The Impact on UK Business*. London: NHTCU.

Norris, C. and Armstrong, G. (1999) *The Maximum Surveillance Society: The Rise of CCTV*. Oxford: Berg.

NUA Internet Statistics (2003) 'How Many Online?', available online at http://www.nua.ie/surveys/how_many_online/

Nugent, J. and Raisinghani, M. (2002) 'The Information Technology and Telecommunications Security Imperative: Important Issues and Drivers', *Journal of Electronic Commerce Research*, 3(1): 1–14.

O'Connell, R. (2003) *A Typology of Cybersexploitation and Online Grooming Practices*. Preston: Cyberspace Research Unit.

O'Connell, R., Price, J. and Barrow, C. (2004) *Cyber Stalking, Abusive Cyber Sex and Online Grooming: A Programme of Education for Teenagers*. Preston: Cyberspace Research Unit.

Ogilvie, E. (2000) *Cyberstalking*, Trends and Issues in Criminal Justice, No. 166. Canberra: Australia Institute of Criminology.

Oliverio, A. (1998) *The State of Terror*. Albany, NY: SUNY Press.

Onwuekwe, C. (2004) 'The Commons Concept and Intellectual Property Rights. Regime: Whither Plant Genetic Resources and Traditional Knowledge?', *Pierce Law Review*, 2(1): 65–90.

Oser, K. (2003) 'Data Intelligence', 1 May, at http://directmag.com/datalist/marketing_data_intelligence/

Ostrom, M. (2004) 'Online Auctions Are the Newest Place to Hawk Stolen Goods', at http://www.siliconvalley.com/mld/siliconvalley/3443962.htm?template=contentModules/printstory.jsp

Oswell, D. (2003) 'When Images Matter: Internet Child Pornography, Forms of Observation and an Ethics of the Virtual', at http://www.goldsmiths.ac.uk/csisp/papers/oswell_images_matter.pdf

Paletz, D. and Vinson, C. (1992) 'Introduction', in D., Paletz and A. Schmid (eds), *Terrorism and the Media*. Newbury Park, CA: Sage.

Pattavina, A. (ed.) (2004) *Information Technology and the Criminal Justice System*. London: Sage.

Pearsall, R. (1993) *The Worm in the Bud: The World of Victorian Sexuality*. London: Pimlico.

Philippsohn, S. (2001) 'Trends in Cybercrime – An Overview of Current Financial Crimes on the Internet', *Computers and Security*, 20: 53–69.

Play It Cybersafe (2005) 'Parents' and Teacher's Guide', at http://www.playitcyber-safe.com/pdfs/TG-copyrightCrusader-2005.pdf

Poole, P. (2000) 'ECHELON: America's Secret Global Surveillance Network', at http://fly.hiwaay.net/~pspoole/echelon.html

Poster, M. (1990) *The Mode of Information: Post-structuralism and Social Contexts*. Cambridge: Polity.

Prigg, M. (2004) 'Police Alert Over Stolen Goods on eBay', 23 September, at http://www.thisismoney.co.uk/news/article.html?in_article_id=317003&in_page_id=2

Procida, R. and Simpson, R. (2003) *Global Perspectives on Social Issues: Pornography*. Lanham, MD: Lexington Books.

RAC (Royal Automobile Club) (2003) 'Road Traffic Accident Statistics', at http://www.rac.co.uk/web/personalinjuryclaims/claim_categories/road_traffic_accidents/statistics

Rasch, M. (2003) 'Foreword', in D. Verton, *Black Ice: The Invisible Threat of Cyber-Terrorism*. Emeryville: McGraw-Hill/Osborne.

Rassool, R.P. (2003) 'Antipiracy – Trends and Technology (A Report from the Front)', at http://www.broadcastpapers.com/asset/ IBCWidevineAntipiracy.pdf

Reitinger, P. (2000) 'Encryption, Anonymity and Markets: Law Enfor\ and Technology in a Free Market World', in D. Thomas and B. Loader (eds), *Cybercrime: Law Enforcement, Security and Surveillance in the Information Age*. London: Routledge.

Riem, A. (2001) 'Cybercrimes of the 21st Century', *Computer Fraud and Security*, 4: 7–8.

Roberts, A. and Dziegielewski, S. (1996) 'Assessment Typology and Intervention with the Survivors of Stalking', *Aggression and Violent Behaviour*, 1(4): 359–68.

Rogers, M. (2000) 'A New Hacker Taxonomy', at http://www.cerias.purdue.edu/homes/mkr/hacker.doc

Rogerson, M. and Pease, K. (2004) 'Privacy, Identity and Crime Prevention', at http://www.foresight.gov.uk/previous_projects/Cyber_Trust_and_Crime_Prevention/Reports_and_Publications/Privacy_Identity_and_Crime_Prevention/Michelle_Ken.pdf

Romei, S. (1999) 'Net Firms Led Killer to Victim', *The Australian*, 4–5 December: 19–22.

Rorive, I. (2002) 'Strategies to Tackle Racism and Xenophobia on the Internet – Where Are We in Europe?', *International Journal of Communications Law and Policy*, 7: 1–10.

Rose, N. (2000) 'Government and Control', *British Journal of Criminology*, 40: 321–339.

Rutter, J. (2000) 'From the Sociology of Trust Towards a Sociology "E-Trust"', at http://les1.man.ac.uk/cric/Jason_Rutter/papers/eTrust.pdf

Saytarly, T. (2004) 'Russia: Computer Crime Statistics', 13 March 2004, at http://www.crime-research.org/news/13.03.2004/131

Schaffer, J. (2002) 'Spinning the Web of Hate: Web-Based Hate Propogation by Extremist Organizations', *Journal of Criminal Justice and Popular Culture*, 9(2): 69–88.

Schmid, A. (1993) 'The Response Problem as a Definition Problem', in A. Scmid and R. Crelinsten (eds), *Western Responses to Terrorism*. London: Frank Cass.

Scuka, D. (2005) 'Auctions Booming, But So Are The Crooks', April 2002, at http://www.japaninc.net/article.php?articleID=776

Schneier, B. (2000) *Secrets and Lies: Digital Security in Networked World*. New York: John Wiley and Sons. Ltd.

Schwartz, H. (2003) *The Revolt of the Primitive: An Inquiry into the Roots of Political Correctness*. New Jersey: Transaction Press.

Sekulow, J. (2004) 'Pormography on the Net', *Issues in Science and Technology*, Spring: 5.

Shelley, L. (2003) 'Organized Crime, Terrorism and Cybercrime', in A. Bryden and P. Fluri (eds), *Security Sector Reform: Institutions, Society and Good Governance*. Baden-Baden: Nomos Verlagsgesellschaft.

Shields, R. (ed.) (1996) *Cultures of the Internet: Virtual Spaces, Real Histories, Living Bodies*. London: Sage.

Shinkle, P. (2001) 'Computer Security Firms Spy On Uncertain Future', at http://talisentech.com/postdispatch2.pdf.

Sinrod, E. and Reilly, W. (2000) 'Cyber-Crimes: A Practical Approach to the Application of Federal Computer Crime Laws', *Santa Clara Computer and High Technology Law Journal*, 16(2): 1–53.

Smith, R. (2003) 'Travelling in Cyberspace on a False Passport: Controlling Transnational Identity-Related Crime', paper presented at the British Criminology Conference Selected Proceedings, July 2002, at http://www.britsoccrim.org/bccsp/vol05/smith.htm

Smith, R. and Urbas, G. (2001) *Controlling Fraud on the Internet: A CAPA Perspective*. Canberra: Australian Institute of Criminology.

Smith, R., Holmes, M. and Kaufmann, P. (1999) 'Nigerian Advanced Fee Fraud', Australian Institute of Criminology Trends and Issues in Crime and Criminal Justice Paper No.121. Canberra: AIT.

Snyder, F. (2001) 'Sites of Criminality and Sites of Governance', *Social and Legal Studies*, 10: 251–6.

Snyder, M. (2004) 'Pirates of the 21st Century', at http:www.cyberplayitsafe.com/resources/21st-Century-Pirates.pdf

Sodipo, B. (1997) *Piracy and Counterfeiting: GATT TRIPS and Developing Countries*. London: Kluwer.

Sophos (2004) 'The Latest News on the Sasser Internet Worm Outbreak', 8 May 2004, at http://www.sophos.com/virusinfo/articles/saser.html

Spitzberg, B. (2002) 'The Tactical Topography of Stalking Victimization and Management', *Trauma Violence and Abuse*, 3(4): 261–88.

Spitzberg, B. and Cadiz, M. (2002) 'The Media Construction of Stalking Stereotypes', *Journal of Criminal Justice and Popular Culture*, 9(3): 128–49.

Stanley, J. (2002) 'Child Abuse and the Internet', *Journal of the Health Education Institute of Australia*, 9(1): 5–27.

Steinhardt, B. (2000) 'Hate Speech', in Y. Akdeniz, C. Walker and D. Wall (eds), *The Internet, Law and Society*. Harlow: Longman.

Sterling, B. (1994) *The Hacker Crackdown: Law and Disorder on the Electronic Frontier*. Harmondsworth: Penguin.

Story, A. (2003) 'Burn Berne: Why the Leading International Copyright Convention Must Be Replaced', *Houston Law Review*, 40(3): 763–801.

Stratford, J. (2003) 'Internet Surveillance: Recent U.S. Developments', at http://iassist-data.org/publications/iq/iq27/iqvol273stratford.pdf

Sutherland, E. and Cressey, D. (1974) *Principles of Criminology*, 9th edn. Philadelphia, PA: Lippincott.

Sutter, G. (2003) 'Don't Shoot the Messenger?' The UK and Online Intermediary Liability', *International Review of Law, Computers and Technology*, 17(1): 73–84.

Sutton, M. (1998) *'Handling Stolen Goods and Theft: A Market Reduction Approach*, Home Office Research Study No. 69. London: Home Office.

Sutton, M., Schneider, J. and Hetherington, S. (2001) *Tackling Theft with the Market Reduction Approach*, Home Office Crime Reduction Research Series Paper 8. London: Home Office.

Swartz, N. (2004a) 'Google's New E-mail Service Sparks Privacy Concerns', *The Information Management Journal*, July/August: 6–7.

Swartz, N. (2004b) 'Patriot Act Provision Ruled Unconstitutional', *The Information Management Journal*, November/December: 6.

Sykes, C. (1999) *The End of Privacy*. New York: St. Martin's Press.

Sykes, G. and Matza, D. (1957) 'Techniques of Neutralization: A Theory of Delinquency', *American Sociological Review*, 22: 664–70.

Taylor, M., Quayle, E. and Holland, G. (2001) 'Child Pornography: The Internet and Offending', *Recherche sur les Politiques*, 2(2): 94–100.

Taylor, M. and Quayle, E. (2003) *Child Pornography: An Internet Crime*. New York: Brunner-Routledge.

Taylor, P. (1999) *Hackers: Crime in the Digital Sublime*. London: Routledge.

Taylor, P. (2000) 'Hackers – Cyberpunks or Microserfs?' in D. Thomas and B. Loader (eds), *Cybercrime: Law Enforcement, Security and Surveillance in the Information Age*. London: Routledge.

Taylor, P. (2003) 'Maestros or Misogynists? Gender and the Social Construction of Hacking', in Y. Jewkes (ed.), *Dot.cons: Crime, Deviance and Identity on the Internet*. Cullompton: Willan.

Taylor, P. (2004a) 'Hacktivism – Resistance is Fertile?', in C. Sumner (ed.), *The Blackwell Companion to Criminology*. Oxford: Blackwell.

Taylor, P. (2004b) 'Keyboard Protest: Hacktivist Spiders on the Web', in J. Carter and D. Moreland (eds), *Anti-Capitalist Britain*. Cheltenham: New Clarion Press.

Taylor, P. and Jordan, T. (2005) *Hacktivism and Cyberwars: Rebels With a Cause?* London: Routledge

Teich, A., Frankel, M., Kling, R. and Lee, Y. (1999) 'Anonymous Communication Policies for the Internet: Results and Recommendations of the AAAS Conference', at http://www.indiana.edu/~tisj/readers/full-text/15-2%20teich.pdf

The Mentor (1986) 'The Conscience of a Hacker', *Phrack Inc.*, Volume One, Issue 7, Phile 3 of 10, at http://www.mala.bc.ca/~soules/media112/hacker.htm.

Telofono Arcobaleno (2004) *Monitoring Paedophilia on the Internet: 2004 Annual Report*, at http://www.telefonoarcobaleno.com/report2004eng.pdf

The Register (2004) 'Hate Websites Continue to Flourish', 10 May, at http://www.theregister.co.uk/2004/05/10/hate_websites_flourish/

Thomas, D. and Loader, B. (eds) (2000) *Cybercrime: Law Enforcement, Security and Surveillance in the Information Age*. London: Routledge.

Thomas, D. (2002) 'Notes from the Underground: Hackers as Watchdogs of Industry', *Online Journalism Review*, 4 April 2002, at http://www.ojr.org/ojr/business/p1017969515.php

Thomas, D. and Loader, B. (2000a) 'Introduction – Cybercrime: Law Enforcement, Security and Surveillance in the Information Age', in D. Thomas and B Loader (eds), *Cybercrime: Law Enforcement, Security and Surveillance in the Information Age*. London: Routledge.

Thomson, I. (2004) 'Britain Becoming a Nation of Pirates', at http://www.crn.vnunet.com/news/1157189

Thorburgh, D. and Lin, H. (2004) 'Youth, Pornography and the Internet', *Issues in Science and Technology*, Winter: 43–8.

TIMJ (2004) 'U.S. Government Still Mining Data', *The Information Management Journal*, July/August: 7–8.

Timofeeva, Y. (2003) 'Hate Speech Online: Restricted or Protected? Comparison of Regulations in the United States and Germany', *Journal of Transnational Law and Policy*, 12(2): 253–86.

Tjaden, R. (1997) 'The Crime of Stalking: How Big is the Problem?', *National Institute of Justice Research Review*, November. Washington, DC: National Institute of Justice.

Tjaden, R. and Thoennes, N. (1998) 'Prevalence, Incidence, and Consequences of Violence Against Women: Findings From the National Violence Against Women Survey', *National Institute of Justice: Research in Brief*, November. Washington, DC: National Institute of Justice.

TraCCC (Transnational Crime and Corruption Centre) (2001) *Transnational Crime, Corruption and Information Technology*. Washington, DC: TraCCC.

Travis, A. (2001) 'Internet Banks "in Denial" on Hacking thefts', *The Guardian*, 19 April.

Tsesis, A. (2002) *Destructive Messages: How Hate Speech Paves the Way for Harmful Social Movements*. New York: New York University Press.

Tudor, A. (1989) *Monsters and Mad Scientists: A Cultural History of the Horror Film*. Oxford: Blackwell.

Turkle, S. (1984) *The Second Self: Computers and the Human Spirit*. London: Granada.

Turkle, S. (1995) *Life on the Screen: Identity in the Age of the Internet*. New York: Simon and Schuster.

Twist, J. (2003) 'Cracking the Hacker Underground', BBC News, 14 November 2003, at http://news.bbc.co.uk/go/pr/-/1/hi/technology/3246375.htm

UK Parliament (2002) *Hansard*, 377 (75), at: http://www.publications.parliament.uk/pa/cm200102/cmhansrd/vo020108/text/20108w61.htm

UNICEF (2005) 'Convention on the Rights of the Child', at http://www.unicef.org/crc/crc.htm

U.S. Department of Justice (USDOJ) (2003) '11 Indicted in Interstate Theft and Fencing Ring That Sold $2 Million in Stolen Merchandise Via eBay Internet Auctions', 20 November, at http://www.usdoj.gov/USBO/ilo/pr/2003/pr/12003_2.pdf

U.S. Department of State (1997) *Nigerian Advanced Fee Fraud*. Department of State Publication 10465. Washington, DC: State Department.

U.S. Department of State (2003) 'FBI Chief Says Al-Qaeda Threat Still Strong', at http://usinfo.state.gov/topical/pol/arms/03021102.htm

Vaidhyanathan, S. (2003) *Copyrights and Copywrongs: The Rise of Intellectual Property and How it Threatens Creativity*. New York: New York University Press.

Valenti, J. (2002) 'If You Cannot Protect What You Own, You Don't Own Anything', report presented to the U.S. Senate Committee on Commerce, Science and Transportation, on behalf of the MPAA, 28 February 2002. Available online at http://www.mpaa.org/jack/2002/2002_02_28b.htm

Valenti, J. (2003) 'International Copyright Piracy: Links to Organized Crime and Terrorism', testimony to the Subcommittee on Courts, The Internet, and Intellectual Property, U.S. House of Representatives, 13 March 2003, at http://www.mpaaa.org/jack/2003/2003_03_13B.htm

van der Ploeg, I. (2000) 'Biometrics and Privacy: A Note on the Politics of Theorizing Technology', at https://www.bmg.eur.nl/smw/publications/vdp_01.pdf

Vegh, S. (2002) 'Hacktivists or Cyberterrorists? The Changing Media Discourse on Hacking', *First Monday*, 7, 10, October. Online at http://firstmonday.org/issues/issue7_10/vegh/index.html

Verton, D. (2002) *The Hacker Diaries: Confessions of Teenage Hackers*. Berkeley: McGraw-Hill/Osborne.

Verton, D. (2003) *Black Ice: The Invisible Threat of Cyber-Terrorism*. Emeryville: McGraw-Hill/Osborne.

Voiskounsky, A., Babeva, J. and Smyslova, O. (2000) 'Attitudes towards Computer Hacking in Russia', in D. Thomas and B. Loader (eds), *Cybercrime: Law Enforcement, Security and Surveillance in the Information Age*. London: Routledge.

Walby, S. and Allen, J. (2004) *Domestic Violence, Sexual Assault and Stalking: Findings from the British Crime Survey*, Home Office Research Study 276. London: Home Office.

Wales, E. (2001) 'Global Focus on Cybercrime', *Computer Fraud and Security*, (1): 6–6(1).

Walker, C., Wall, D. and Akdeniz, Y. (2000) 'The Internet, Law and Society', in Y. Akdeniz, C. Walker and D. Wall (eds), *The Internet, Law and Society*. Harlow: Longman.

Walker, C. (2001) 'Encryption and the Regulation of Investigatory Powers Act 2000', paper presented at the 16th BILETA Annual Conference, 9–10 April 2001, Edinburgh, Scotland.

Wall, D. (2001a) 'Cybercrimes and the Internet', in D. Wall (ed.), *Crime and the Internet*. London: Routledge.

Wall, D. (2001b) 'Maintaining Order and Law on the Internet', in D. Wall (ed.), *Crime and the Internet*. London: Routledge.

Wall, D. (ed.) (2001c) *Crime and the Internet*. London: Routledge.

Wall Street Journal (2001) 'Big Brother Isn't Gone: He's Just Been Outsourced', 13 April, at http://www.mamut.com/homepages/Belgium/3/7/america/news-det3.htm

Wasik, M. (2000) 'Hacking, Viruses and Fraud', in Y. Akdeniz, C. Walker and D. Wall (eds), *The Internet, Law and Society*. Harlow: Longman.

Webster, F. (2003) *Theories of the Information Society*, 2nd edn. London: Routledge.

Wendel, W. (2004) 'The Banality of Evil and the First Amendment', *Michigan Law Review*, 102: 1404–22.

Weimann, G. (2004) *www.terror.net*, United States Institute of Peace, Special Report 116. Washington, DC: USIP.

Whine, M. (2000) 'Far Right Extremists on the Internet', in D. Thomas, and B. Loader (eds), *Cybercrime: Law Enforcement, Security and Surveillance in the Information Age*. London: Routledge.

White, J. (1991) *Terrorism: An Introduction*. Pacific Grove, CA: Brooks/Cole.

Wilding, E. (2003) 'Corporate Cybercrime Trends', *Computer Fraud and Security*, 6: 4–6.

Wilkins, J. (1997) 'Protecting our Children from Internet Smut: Moral Duty or Moral Panic?', *The Humanist*, 57(5): 4.

Williams, N. (1999) *The Contribution of Hotlines to Combating Child Pronography on the Internet*. London: Childnet International.

Wilson, W.J. (1996) *When Work Disappears*. Knopf: New York.

WIPO (World Intellectual Property Organization) (2001) *WIPO Intellectual Property Handbook: Policy, Law and Use*, WIPO publication no. 489(E). Geneva: WIPO.

Wolf, C. (2004) 'Regulating Hate Speech *Qua* Speech is Not the Solution to the Epidemic of Hate on the Internet', paper presented at the OSCE Meeting on the Relationship Between Racist, Xenophobic and Anti-Semitic Propoganda on the Internet and Hate Crimes, Paris, 16–17 June.

Woo, H., Kim, Y. and Dominisk, J. (2004) 'Hackers: Militants or Merry Pranksters? A Content Analysis of Defaced Web Pages', *Media Psychology*, 6: 63–82.

Wright, G. (2004) 'PC Users Warned Over New Mydoom Threat', *The Guardian*, 10 February 2004.

Wright, H. (1998) 'Biometrics The Next Phase in Network Security', *NZ Infotech Weekly*, 28 September: 10.

Wright, J., Burgess, A., Laszlo A., McCrary, G. and Douglas, J. (1996) 'A Typology of Interpersonal talking', *Journal of Interpersonal Violence*, 11(4): 487–502.

Yar, M. (2005) 'The Global Epidemic of Movie "Piracy": Crime-Wave or Social Construction?', *Media, Culture and Society*, 27(1): 677–96.

Young, J. (1971) 'The Role of the Police as Amplifiers of Deviancy, Negotiators of Reality and Translators of Fantasy', in S. Cohen (ed.), *Images of Deviance*. Harmondsworth: Penguin.

Young, K. (1998) 'Internet Addiction: The Emergence of a New Clinical Disorder', *CyberPsychology and Behavior*, 1(3): 237–44.

Young, K., Pistner, M. and O'Mara, J. (1999) 'Cyber Disorders: The Mental Health Concern for the New Millennium', *CyberPsychology and Behavior*, 2(5): 475–79.

ZDNet (2005) 'Man Charged with Selling Dinosaur Fossils on eBay', 25 February, at http://news.zdnet.com/2100-1040-22-5590529.html?part=rss&tag=feed&subj=zdnet

Zimmer, E. and Hunter, D. (1999) 'Risk and the Internet: Perception and Reality' at http://www.copacommission.org/papers/webriskanalysis.pdf

Index

survey data 14, 129
systems sabotage 29

Taylor, Paul 25, 26, 46–7
techniques of neutralization 34
technologies 94, 140
  see also software
terrorism 51, 145
  see also cyberterrorism
theft
  computer resources 28
  information 28–9
  intellectual property 63–78
Thomas, D 9
time-space compression 11
Total Information Awareness project 145
training, law enforcement agencies 93
Trojan horses 30
trust 89

UN Convention on the Rights of the
  Child 114
unauthorized access 27–8, 32, 39
USA PATRIOT Act 2001 40,
  51–2, 146, 150–1

Vegh, S. 57
'victim industry' 134

victimization 121–37
  moral panics 133–6
  paedophilia 131–3
  stalking 123–30
violence
  hate speech 100–1
  stalking 125
viruses
  force multiplication 54
  hacking 30–1
  hacktivism 49
  numbers in existence 15
  tools for creating 32

web browsers 7–8, 130
websites
  defacement 29–30, 49
  hate speech 101–2
  spoofing 29–30, 87–8
  terrorist groups 59
women's movement 124–6
The Wonderland Club (paedophile ring) 115
worms 30–1, 32, 49

Yousef, Ramsay 59
youth cybercrime
  hacking 25, 36–9
  piracy 69